GARY JOBSON

AN AMERICAN SAILING STORY

GARY JOBSON

with CYNTHIA GOSS

Nomad Press
A division of Nomad Communications
10 9 8 7 6 5 4 3 2 1

ISBN: 978-1-936313-76-1

Questions regarding the ordering of this book should be addressed to
Independent Publishers Group
814 N. Franklin St.
Chicago, IL 60610
www.ipgbook.com

Nomad Press
2456 Christian St.
White River Junction, VT 05001
www.nomadpress.net

front cover photo: Dan Nerney

For Janice

To a great mother, teacher, nurse, and friend,
thanks for being my lifelong partner.

Contents

Acknowledgments — vii

Chapter 1: Troubling Forecasts — 1

Chapter 2: Winning the America's Cup — 18

Chapter 3: My Turning Point — 44

Chapter 4: Taking a Flyer — 69

Chapter 5: Storms — 88

Chapter 6: Reaching a Wider Audience — 106

Chapter 7: New Frontiers — 129

Chapter 8: Making a Difference — 147

Chapter 9: One Nation, Under Sail — 156

Chapter 10: Greatness and My Heroes — 182

Chapter 11: Calm — 215

Epilogue — 240

I chartered *Courageous* for a weekend in 1998 and sailed past my schooner *Silver Heels*, anchored in Brenton Cove in Newport, Rhode Island. Many of my happiest sailing memories took place on these very different yachts. Standing on the stern is my friend John Kent Cooke, who owned the Washington Redskins at the time. I was in attendance at all three Redskins' Superbowl victories.

ACKNOWLEDGMENTS

Over the past decade, I started reading memoirs of great sailors of the past. The list included Sherman Hoyt, Harold Vanderbilt, Clinton Crane, Gerard Lambert, Olin Stephens, Bill Snaith, and Nathanael Herreshoff. Their words jumped off the pages. In essence each book was a reflection of what it was like to be on the water during dynamic times in American history.

I suppose it is bold to write your own memoirs, but I have been lucky to be in the thick of sailing since the 1950s. Now that I've turned 60 I feel comfortable sharing my stories. During my time on the water the changes in boats, materials, sails, sailors, events, and technology have been dramatic. Many changes are for the better and some for the worst. For example, I miss the cooked meals and bunks with blankets and pillows used in the 1970s. In contrast, foul weather gear is more reliable, boats are faster, and competition is far better today. Looking to the future there will be many more advances in technology.

Thirty years ago, who could have imagined that we would have multihulls racing for the America's Cup at speeds three times faster than the speed of the wind? It has been great fun being along for the ride during this evolution in sailing as a competitor, commentator, and writer. My story takes place during this fascinating age. Over the years I have been part of many different sailing campaigns. In this book I present a cross section of these activities, weaving in my family life, a major battle with cancer, and a career promoting sailing. I hope readers reflect on their own sailing experiences as they read about mine.

Co-author Cynthia Goss and I spent countless hours talking and writing. One of these sessions took place driving to Maine and back from her home in Conneticut. She is a wonderful wordsmith, and throughout the process it was great fun working with Cynthia on this project. Kathy Lambert has been my trusted assistant since 1983, and, as always, she helped with endless details in Annapolis, which I appreciate.

This is the 17th book I have authored. Unlike the others that have taken around 18 months to write, this has been a work in progress for over 7 years. It started when I was ill in 2003. During that difficult period I am grateful to my friend Roger Vaughan for conducting weekly interviews with me. It was theraputic to use sailing stories as a way to overcome my cancer. His interviews are incorporated here. Bill Wagner conducted interviews with my father and Bill Campbell.

I would like to thank the team at Nomad Press. Editor Susan Kahan asked many good questions and brought a fresh perspective to my stories. Graphic designer Farah Rizvi worked many long hours on the layout. This is the third book I have published with Nomad. I would like to thank the publisher, Alex Kahan, for his help bringing this project together.

I would like to thank the sailors and colleagues who are interviewed in the book including Dennis Conner, Jed Drake, Peter Montgomery, Anna Tunnicliffe, Olin Stephens, Ted Hood, Bill Ficker, and Nick Scandone. Throughout the text I mention over 350 people. I appreciate every person's insight.

There is an old expression that a picture is worth a thousand words. Many great photographers are represented here and are acknowledged at the end of the text. I am grateful that they were on hand to record so many special moments in my life. I would also like to thank renowned marine artist John Mecray for the use of his painting of *Tenacious* during the 1979 Fastnet storm.

Some of these stories have appeared in different form in my columns in *Sailing World*, or articles in *Cruising World* and *Yachting*. I have been lucky to work with several superstar editors at these publications including David Reed, Mark Pillsbury, Charlie Barthold, Ken Wooton, George Sass, Diana Muhlfeld, Herb McCormick, Bernadette Bernon, and John Burnham. At ESPN there are many people who have helped make sailing a reality on television. I have used some of the stories from these shows in this book. I would like to thank my colleagues at ESPN including John Wildhack, Jed Drake, Geoff Mason, Jamie Reynolds, Stacie McCollum, Leah LaPlaca, Carol Stiff, and former ESPN employees Jim Noel, Tim Dolman, Kelly Laferriere, Jim Kelly, and Steve Bornstein.

I would also like to thank my fellow board members, and the staff and volunteers at US SAILING for working with me to move our sport of sailing forward.

Gary Jobson
Annapolis, Maryland

.1.

TROUBLING FORECASTS

2003 I counted the days. The first race of the 31st America's Cup Finals was soon, scheduled for February 15. Still home in Maryland—8,000 miles from the racecourse—the deadline loomed. As a reporter for ESPN, I needed to get out to New Zealand—to walk the docks and talk to sailors and get behind the headlines. I would normally be itching to get out to the Cup racecourse and capture the story, but something strange was happening to me. For the first time in my career, I couldn't imagine getting on that plane to the Cup races.

←————— ∎ —————→

It wasn't for lack of interest in the America's Cup, an event that has long been such a big part of my career that it's impossible to separate the story of the event from the story of my life. By now, the two are permanently braided together.

I saw my first 12 Meter at age 12, on a family trip to Newport, Rhode Island. *Weatherly* slipped through the water under tow. Her hull was enormous and her rig towered into the clouds—an overwhelming sight to a kid sailing dinghy-sized boats.

I dreamed of someday becoming a Cup sailor on a Twelve. By the time I was in my late twenties, I had my chance when Ted Turner invited me to be his tactician aboard *Courageous* for the 1977 Cup. Over a summer of racing against two other U.S. boats for the right to defend the Cup, our crew developed into a solid team. We had chemistry like no team I had known before and no team I've known since—and we won the Cup against Australia. Since then, I've been involved with every America's Cup as a sailor or a television journalist. But now, that flight to New Zealand seemed as long as a moon shot. I was not ready to go.

It wasn't for lack of finding a good story, either. After several rounds of racing in the Louis Vuitton Cup—an elimination series when challenging syndicates vie for the right to match-race the Defender of the Cup—the Challenger I predicted to win was named. But the outcome seemed too mythic. If a fiction writer crafted the story, it would seem contrived. Truth, however, was stranger than fiction.

1

The Swiss team *Alinghi*—with New Zealanders Russell Coutts at the helm and Brad Butterworth calling tactics—would be on the starting line of the America's Cup Finals. These Kiwi sailors were racing against the syndicate of their homeland, but the irony was, Coutts and Butterworth were once part of the team that won the Cup for New Zealand in the first place. Their win was history making in this small Pacific nation, a classic David-and-Goliath story. But now, these Kiwi sailors were coming like thieves in the night to wrest the coveted prize from their countrymen.

In 1995, Coutts and Butterworth were part of the New Zealand team that came to the Cup racecourse in San Diego as a unified front. They sailed two boats, *Black Magic 1* and *Black Magic 2*, and this syndicate sailed like their boats, like magic. With a limited budget and strong leadership from the late Sir Peter Blake, they spent where it counted. And what this syndicate lacked in funding they made up for in raw talent and heart: they won the challenger selection and swept the America's Cup 5–0 against the U.S. Defender *Young America*, becoming the second nation since 1851 to take the Cup away from the Americans.

The Kiwi sailors returned home heroes, welcomed to Auckland by an explosion of national pride: a crowd of some 350,000 New Zealanders, from a city of only 1.2 million, created a display as heartwarming as long-ago newsreels of ticker tape raining on the streets of New York.

Team New Zealand easily defended the 2000 America's Cup. But things were different in 2003 when skipper Russell Coutts and five crew members switched to Switzerland's *Alinghi*.

Team New Zealand (TNZ) successfully defended the Cup again in 2000, and in the final race, helmsman Russell Coutts stepped off the boat and handed the helm to a 26-year-old sailor named Dean Barker. With that move, Coutts, a rare sailing talent who was then in his late thirties, signaled his desire to move on to a new role—to migrate from the cockpit of a Cup contender and assume a management role.

But only four months after the Cup was successfully defended in 2000, New Zealanders were shocked to learn that Coutts and Butterworth had signed with Swiss billionaire Ernesto Bertarelli and his *Alinghi* syndicate of Switzerland. Other Kiwi talent soon followed them away from New Zealand, and their tale became a front-page soap opera in this island nation.

The America's Cup Finals on February 15 would be the showdown between the sailors branded turncoats and those painted in the press as true to their homeland—and the soap opera was ripe for its next plot twist. So my hesitation to travel to New Zealand was not for fear of not finding a good story. No, my body was failing and no one could tell me why.

In the past two years, I'd gone through two prostate biopsies, but both were negative. I had lymph nodes popping out of my skin like small pebbles. Then a God-awful cough, that wouldn't quit, appeared. Different doctors were treating different parts of my body. I had antibiotics for the cough, antibiotics for the lymph node inflammation. I was weary to the point that I considered postponing my trip to New Zealand. Maybe a day or two of rest would put me back on track again.

But it wasn't my habit to slow my schedule down because my body couldn't keep up. On the contrary: I relied on my health to keep pace. Sailors may not exert themselves physically like college basketball players; a sailboat race is not a 40-minute court dance of jumping and running and ball handling. Sailboat races are longer—they are mentally taxing and can be physically punishing. Plus, I had a demanding speaking schedule. After an event like the Cup or the Olympics, my life was a whirlwind of speaking engagements. Travelling out to California, to Florida, to Detroit, to the Chesapeake, back to California again: that route of speaking stops kept me moving like a ping-pong ball, bouncing between the waterborne margins of the country.

I could not delay my trip to New Zealand any longer, and so I boarded the plane for the long flight to Auckland. Maybe, I figured, I could rest once I reached New Zealand.

"*Please* tell me you're not contagious . . . You're not, are you?" joked ABC anchorman Paul Page. Four days after landing in New Zealand, Paul, writer Roger Vaughan, and I were in a rented television studio, laying down the track for a one-hour America's Cup preview. I was having coughing fit after coughing fit and so I brought a new piece of equipment into the tiny booth: a wastebasket I could use as a spittoon.

Paul, who was on loan from ABC to ESPN for this job, had a big voice. Roger called it a voice that could dent fenders. Between coughing fits, my tones were more conversational. We were trying to make it work, to balance the voices. But we could already count the hours on our fingers when the show needed to be completed and put on a flight to ESPN headquarters in Connecticut.

"Hey, don't get any of that on me!" Paul joked when I stuck my entire head in the can to puke. The deadlines of TV, precise down to the minute, would not bend for anyone. Gallows humor got us through.

Outside the studio, Cup fever raged. All over Auckland banners displayed the word *Loyal*. The purpose of this public relations campaign was to build support for the home team while expressing displeasure at Coutts and his teammates for abandoning their homeland. The local press bit. They churned out stories that played on the mythic tale of traitors and loyalists getting ready for battle.

But despite *Team New Zealand's* ubiquitous Loyal slogan, *TNZ* had enlisted Clay Oliver of Maryland as principal yacht designer, past match-racing world champ Bertrand Pace of France, and Roger Badham of Australia as weather guru. I wondered, did the syndicate powers consider these individuals disloyal to their countries for signing with *TNZ*?

The fact is, free agency reigned in the America's Cup, and a number of syndicates had team rosters that read like a United Nations roll call. *Alinghi* was a case in point: in addition to Coutts and a Kiwi contingent of Cup veterans dubbed "The Tight Five"—including Butterworth, Dean Phipps, Murray Jones, Warwick Fleury, and Simon Daubney—key players included Bertarelli of Switzerland, four-time Olympic medalist Jochen Schümann of Germany, and U.S. America's Cup winners Josh Belsky and John Barnitt.

I believe the Cup should still be a battle between national teams—but times have changed.

4

The mood of acrimony engendered by the Loyal campaign, however, didn't appear to be circling amongst the sailors themselves. On going up against his formidable teammates, Barker said: "It's going to be quite good, actually . . . just like sailing against former teammates." The Loyal campaign didn't rattle Coutts either; if anything, it gave him more resolve. "I think I'm pretty determined anyway, but it certainly hasn't affected me negatively," he told me.

But anyone who knows Russell Coutts knows that Barker's nonchalance about the prospect of facing Coutts and his teammates on the Cup racecourse glossed over the intensity of this match. Coutts is one of the most formidable talents in sailing—especially Cup sailing. At that point, he had already helmed two America's Cup wins; a third Cup victory would put him in league with the only other men in history to capture a trio of Cup wins, including the legendary Scotsman Charlie Barr, Mike Vanderbilt, Dennis Conner, and the duo of General Charles J. Paine and designer Edward Burgess.

But it's not necessary to consult the history books to know that Coutts is brilliant on the water—intuitive and, as an engineer by training, a sailor with a solid grasp of technology. Sailing is part art, part science, and that is the exact mix Coutts possessed. How could Barker beat him? Then again, how could Barker lose, with an entire nation relying on him to keep the Cup in New Zealand's hands?

Roger, Paul, and I worked in the studio on getting the story right, putting the final touches on the preview show as our deadline loomed.

The words I read were punctuated off-air with coughing fits. I knew Roger and Paul were looking at me and thinking, What is *wrong* with Gary? I was wondering the same thing myself. But they didn't know the half of it.

Once I reached New Zealand, not only was I starting to cough to the point of throwing up, but I'd wake up in the middle of the night, soaked with sweat. I started getting itchy red blotches on my legs, my hands, my arms. My belly was distended, like someone with a beer gut (only thing was, I wasn't a beer drinker). I was getting skinnier and skinnier, so when I looked in the mirror, I didn't look like myself.

But I had a job to do, so I kept pushing, conserving energy for what I absolutely needed to do. I passed on the whole social aspect of the Cup and spent a lot of time crashed back in the apartment that ESPN had rented in Auckland.

Life for me at this Cup was unlike any existence I'd had at a past America's Cup. And once the sailing started, it became clear to the world that this Cup was unlike any Cup that had come before it.

A Conversation with Peter Montgomery

When it comes to sailing, well-known broadcast journalist and good friend Peter Montgomery is recognized as the voice of New Zealand. His narration reflects the excitement of the sport; it's been said he could narrate paint drying on a wall and make it sound thrilling. Here he talks about his country's romance with the oldest trophy in sporting history—from the nation's early attempts to capture the Cup and the litigious Big Boat campaign in 1988, to New Zealand's stunning win in 1995—and the burning question of whether this small Pacific nation has the potential to build the greatest dynasty in America's Cup history.

Gary Jobson (GJ): Did you ever think 30 years ago that New Zealand would one day be a holder of the America's Cup?

Peter Montgomery (PM): When I first went to the America's Cup it was in Newport, Rhode Island. In those days, I thought that New Zealand would get a man on the moon quicker than challenging for the America's Cup. Number one, financially, it was beyond New Zealand. Number two, the technology was way beyond New Zealand. And number three, New Zealand just did not have experienced sailors to sail the big, powerful boats that were being used in the America's Cup. So the short answer, No.

GJ: What did Michael Fay bring to the table in 1986?

PM: Without Michael Fay, the America's Cup would not have come to New Zealand. The original challenge was actually made by a Belgian-born Sydney businessman, Marcel Fachler. There were several New Zealanders who tried to support him, but they just didn't have the financial grunt. And that's what Michael Fay brought. Michael had the financial acumen, he arranged the financing for the first challenge by a New Zealand team in '86-87 off Fremantle. And he also brought an awful lot of management skill.

GJ: When Michael Fay launched the surprise challenge with the 90-foot "Big Boat" instead of a 12 Meter in '88, was the move well supported by the New Zealand public?

PM: The '88 Big Boat challenge was certainly supported by New Zealand, initially. A lot of New Zealanders thought, What a wonderful idea. They got hold of Michael Fay's concept that here was going to be a modern version of the J-Boats. And they liked the audacity of what New Zealand was doing, but they were quickly turned off by the litigation. And sadly that lingers today.

GJ: When New Zealand won the Cup in 1995, what did it mean to the country?

PM: There is only one other occasion in the history of New Zealand that even comes close to the welcome home for *Team New Zealand* and it was not a sporting event. I'm told the victory parades after World War II welcoming home our troops and military personnel were absolutely joyous and overwhelming . . . It certainly was [that way] for the America's Cup. The pleasure and delights that the *Team New Zealand* victory had in 1995 really struck a cord like nothing else.

GJ: What was the mood when Coutts, Butterworth, and company left for Switzerland?

PM: When Russell Coutts and Brad Butterworth announced that they were joining *Alinghi* there was bewilderment, astonishment, shock. What happened? How did this happen? Because *Team New Zealand* was really thought of as the maritime equivalent of the New Zealand rugby All Blacks—and you don't get any bigger than that in New Zealand . . . Of course, Coutts and Butterworth have taken a lot of slings and arrows from people, many whom had no interest in bringing the Cup here but got on the coattails or had some commercial gain while it was here and could see their pot of gold going out the window. Many of them were the biggest voices of condemnation, but really Coutts and Butterworth should have been kept in the picture. And you come to the fundamental issue, Was there a plan of succession [after Sir Peter Blake was tragically murdered by pirates while sailing in Brazil]? And the short story is, things happened that shouldn't have happened.

GJ: Why have Kiwis dominated the Cup for the past 10 years?

PM: New Zealand is certainly punching far above its weight in the America's Cup. So much of that goes back to New Zealand itself. Four and a half million people living on a coastline that is the fourth biggest in the world. Nearly 90 percent of New Zealand's population is right on the water. And so for many young kids it's an environment they're brought up with. Then New Zealand has been involved in so many ways with innovation going back to the late nineteenth century. There were two brilliant designers and boat builders here, Logan and Bailey, and so many others since then . . . And then coming into international competition, right through the '70s, '80s and '90s when finally New Zealand decided to venture out beyond the South Pacific and undertake so many competitions. And now the Royal New Zealand Yacht Squadron is the only club in the world whose burgee has been flying on winners in the America's Cup, Whitbread—or now Volvo Ocean—Round the World Race, the Admiral's Cup, and Olympic Gold medals. I mean, it is just a stunning achievement.

On the morning of the first race of the Finals, the crowds were ready. *Team New Zealand's* departure from its berth was raucous and the crew must have felt as if they were running onto a football field in front of a hometown crowd. All 4.4 million New Zealanders were solidly behind their team. Fifteen minutes after *TNZ's* departure, challenger *Alinghi* slipped away from the dock, receiving only polite applause.

Cup watchers live for the first race of the Finals. The Challenger and the Defender go to the starting line untested against each other. Does one boat have a speed edge? How do they match up downwind? After all the hype and predictions, the opening race is pure suspense: the first opportunity to answer long-awaited questions.

As I watched the boats head off, I flashed back to Newport 1977, when I sailed the Cup as tactician for Ted Turner. I went to that opening race with a mix of excitement and nervousness. These crews were no doubt feeling the same.

But something unprecedented happened in that first race in New Zealand. At the end of the day there were no answers to be found. Even the *TNZ* crew themselves looked stunned, wondering what went so horribly wrong.

The first sign of trouble on the New Zealand boat came soon after the start, when the boat started to take on water on the leeward side as it heeled with the wind. Water poured into the cockpit of the 80-foot sloop from the rough seas, and mid-bowman Matt Mitchell bailed furiously with a blue bucket (which the crew usually used as a toilet), fighting a losing battle. *Team New Zealand* boss Tom Schnackenberg, the team's lead designer, later estimated that 6 tons of water poured into the 25-ton boat.

Then, with a breeze of 19 to 20 knots and gusts to 26 knots, the end of *TNZ's* boom broke with a loud *bang* 10 minutes after the start, keeping the Kiwis from controlling their giant mainsail. The jib blew out a few minutes later when a titanium ring holding it to the bow shattered. At the helm, Barker immediately turned downwind, to take some pressure off the sail, but it still took several sailors to control the flapping beast and wrestle it below decks. They hoisted a new headsail and it blew out as well, because the groove that holds the sail to the forestay was broken. The two-time defending champion of the Cup officially pulled out of the race only 25 minutes after the start.

Alinghi sailed the rest of the six-leg course alone, taking a 1–0 lead in the best-of-nine series. It was a strange sight as *Alinghi* crossed the finish line on the mostly empty Hauraki Gulf, as most of the huge spectator fleet had already headed for port.

"We had a lot of gremlins on the boat today," said Barker after the race. The chaos aboard his boat dampened the festive mood in Auckland. The thousands of people along the waterfront and the spectator fleet estimated at 2,500 boats all felt staggering disappointment.

It was not the first time a defending yacht had retired from an America's Cup race (in 1920, defender *Resolute* damaged its rigging and pulled out, handing the first race to Thomas Lipton's *Shamrock IV*), but the colossal domino-chain of breakdowns was highly unusual in Cup lore—and a bad omen.

*　　　*　　　*

By the time *TNZ* and *Alinghi* were preparing to do battle in the fourth race, 13 days had elapsed since the infamous Race 1. Thirteen days is a long time to have only completed three races. The race committee was waiting for the right weather to run a fair contest. But there were undercurrents in the press and on the docks: Why was the committee waiting so long?

Weather delays are a normal part of sailboat racing. But this race committee under the direction of Principal Race Officer Harold Bennett—a member of the

Royal New Zealand Yacht Squadron, for whom *TNZ* was defending the Cup—was being overly patient.

During those days of waiting for wind, *Alinghi* was ready to race. They sailed by the race committee under a good 10 knots of wind to make a point: There's wind out here, so let's go sailing. *Team New Zealand* sat with a tarp, shielding the crew from the sun and making it clear they were not anxious to race in unsettled winds.

A proactive race committee would have worked harder to get a race underway—and the weather delays were turning our job of covering the Cup into an impossible task. ESPN had paid the organizers of the Cup a sizeable fee to secure the television rights to the event, and we were feeding footage to the rest of the world. But on those days of long weather delays, we had nothing to shoot and our network was left scrambling to fill the time slot.

I Have my Sources

When *Team New Zealand* broke its mast, we were in the middle of a live broadcast. As I watched the rig tumble over the side, two things went through my mind. These will be pretty exciting pictures for *SportsCenter* later that night, I thought. But on the other hand, we still had an hour and 10 minutes of live television to go and there was just the lone *Alinghi*, sailing around the racecourse. What are we going to talk about? We did several instant replays of the dismasting. And during those replays, an unusual thing happened: my special ESPN cell phone started ringing. This phone is only used in emergencies; in the event that our microphone system goes out, I can call the producer and use the cell phone to keep narrating on the air.

"Hello?" I answered, wondering who would be calling me now.

"Gary, Richie Boyd here . . ."

An engineer with Navtec rigging in Connecticut, Richie was also one of the crewmembers on *Courageous*, one of my great friends, and one of the best sailors I've ever raced with.

"Yeah, hi Richie. I'm kind of in the middle of something . . ."

"Gary, I just have to tell you one thing: that is not our rigging on *Team New Zealand*. This is the first time a boat has not used

Bennett communicated frequently with the boats. He wore a microphone and gave interviews to the media—and in his commentary, he always sounded pessimistic. What he should have done is take the average wind direction, put the buoys down, and get the race underway. The sailing instructions allow for a 45-minute time limit for each leg. If the wind dies, the time limit will run out. If the wind shifts, the race committee has the option of changing the course of the next leg to keep the legs square to the wind.

It would have been no problem if *Alinghi* and *TNZ* were sailing by themselves. With their huge commitment to worldwide television and with many thousands of spectators in New Zealand to watch, however, the Royal New Zealand Yacht Squadron could have served their regatta better by working to get the races in—even if the wind was not perfect.

Navtec rigging in the America's Cup Finals since 1970, and *TNZ* is using experimental materials. We advised them not to use them—but they are out there using those materials, and you can see what happened. I just wanted you to know . . ."

Richie continued to add more details but my producer broke in.

"Back on the air in 10 seconds."

"Richie, I gotta go. I'll call you later today."

I have no idea how Richie got my secret cell phone number, but I'm glad he called.

We came back on the air, and my co-anchorman Paul Page launched the first question: "Well, quite a development Gary. You've been studying the situation. What do you make of it?"

And I reported on the air, live, that for the first time since 1970, a contender in the America's Cup Finals was not using Navtec rigging from Connecticut and they were using experimental rigging. I continued on with some technical details, and my producer, Steve Lawrence, quickly shot a question into my headset.

"Jobson, where are you getting this information?"

I hit the talk-back button so I could talk to him without being heard on the air. "Don't worry Stevie, I have my sources."

Alinghi sails past *Team New Zealand* in Race 2 of the 31st America's Cup.
Notice the difference: *Alinghi* is flying a staysail. The extra sail area gave the Swiss
a fraction more speed. The crew at the top of the mast are looking for wind.

And so the weather became its own subplot to the story—and the lead question to the interviews we conducted during the hiatus from racing. What did sailors think of the weather delays? Was it time in Cup history for an independent race committee? On the eve of Race 4, we talked to *TNZ's* Tom Schnackenberg:

ESPN: Is *Team New Zealand* in regular communication with the race committee to decide whether to race or not?

Schnackenberg: Only occasionally. They call when they need to consult people, so in the morning and today for example, I think the race committee chairman called each syndicate. So it's sort of a tri-part decision, although it was made by the race committee chairman.

ESPN: Has the race committee made the proper decisions over the last nine days?

Schnackenberg: I'm quite sure they have. When you look at the circumstances and the decisions rationally, it is quite clear that they have been made correctly.

ESPN: Has *Team New Zealand* benefited by the weather delays?

Schnackenberg: Time will tell, but I think that having a couple of days rest between the last race and the next squall is very beneficial, but from now on, I don't think there is any benefit to be gained by delays and our team is keen to race.

ESPN: Is *TNZ* reluctant to race in the light winds?

Schnackenberg: Well I would say any rational team is hesitant to race where the outcome of the race could be determined by the toss up of a coin. As long as there are fair conditions, they don't have to be fresh [winds]. Life is fine.

ESPN: The America's Cup uses an international jury [umpires] and international measurers. Is it time for an international race committee?

Schnackenberg: It's traditional in the America's Cup [that the host yacht club runs the races] and it's always worked well and there is no real reason to change.

Ernesto Bertarelli was more direct when talking to the *New Zealand Herald* about the weather delays: "This is a zoo," he said. (Ironically, in 2010 Bertarelli created his own zoo with races allegedly cancelled due to weather at the 33rd America's Cup off Valencia.)

I loved this event. I had dedicated my life to promoting it and the sport that surrounded it. But there was a storm brewing in the America's Cup, and the event was spiraling into a series of colossal breakdowns and problematical race management. For our crew providing a feed to the rest of the world, it was disconcerting and expensive to have weather delays—and Bennett understood that perfectly, as we learned one day when we overheard him on the VHF radio: "We are going to postpone this race and I don't give a stuff what ESPN thinks."

Forefront in my mind, of course, was my health: the same kind of storm was brewing in my own body. Once the Finals started, I no longer had the luxury of a taped television performance and the option to reread lines when I erupted into a coughing fit. We were broadcasting live, so I had to employ every trick to control the coughing while on the air: lozenges, Listerine strips, whatever it took. The words "going to commercial" were music to my ears. During those commercials I'd cough wildly and puke in a bucket. The red blotches, the night sweats—they continued to plague me. The fatigue was getting worse. I was also doing radio spots and writing reports for ESPN.com. It was agony to keep pace. Worse, it was confusing. Why was my health disintegrating?

Alinghi had won the first three races, and in Race 4, the plight of this America's Cup spun on another catastrophe. Rain squalls brought strong gusts and the Cup boats navigated through steep, choppy seas. One of them was the nemesis of *TNZ*: as the boat's bow came down off a wave, the mast snapped. Just like that. Watching from afar, the mast looked as if it broke as easily as a toothpick, bringing with it a cascade of sails and the hopes of millions of the fans.

Team New Zealand had a good spare mast, and in the press conference that followed the race, Dean Barker said they would be ready to head back to the race course the next day. "It'll be a pretty late night for everyone and I'm sure there will still be bits and pieces going back on in the morning, but we will be ready to race tomorrow." Some Cup watchers still held out thin hopes for their hometown crew. But the fact remained: *TNZ* now had to win five consecutive races to keep the Cup.

A New Zealand victory wasn't in the cards. On March 2, in the fifth and final race, *TNZ* broke their spinnaker pole and *Alinghi* of Switzerland won the race to capture the America's Cup. For the first time in the event's 152-year history, the Cup would be going to Europe.

As soon as our final reports were completed I got on the first possible plane, flying fast away from New Zealand.

* * *

The minute the airplane wheels touched the runway in Baltimore, the clock was ticking. Leaving New Zealand later than expected due to all the weather delays, I was under enormous time pressure to prepare a show on the Cup and take it on the road. Before the Cup Finals, I had lined up

a speaking tour of 63 cities. People were eager to hear the story of the America's Cup, and I wanted to give them all a great show.

I headed right into an editing studio outside Baltimore with all the raw material, including Cup footage from New Zealand and the news reports I had written. The end result was a good show, probably the best I had ever done.

I love speaking to a crowd, looking out at a sea of eyes and giving them all a vision of the sport with exciting footage, music, funny stories, and the kinds of insights about the sport and its players that sailing fans don't get from news articles. At the beginning of my speaking career, I was not always excited about getting up in front of a crowd. But I learned to be prepared, to have good notes and some good stories. Now, I enjoyed it immensely—whether I was speaking to a crowd of 50 or 500. Once I returned from Auckland I studied the schedule: Chicago, San Francisco, Detroit, Annapolis, New York City, southern California, Cleveland. A lot of people were waiting for a show about the America's Cup that had just concluded in faraway New Zealand—whether they were a group of young Sea Scouts or Manhattanites heading to a night out at the Union League Club. I had not cancelled a speaking engagement in 30 years and I was not about to start now. If I could just get through this next rush of deadlines and get this show on the road, I'd find a window of time to rest afterward.

But once I got on the road, the lectures became increasingly harder and harder to do. Thank goodness I had years of experience. I could modulate my voice and cover up the coughs; I'd take an inhaler 10 minutes before I got introduced and use different kinds of lozenges and Listerine strips. I'd do everything I could not to cough. I am usually a fast walker and can get through airports quickly. Now, I had to make allowances for taking longer, and walked slowly through airports. Once I reached my destination, I rested whenever and wherever I could: a couch in a yacht-club manager's office, a comfortable chair in a secluded spot. It got to the point when once the program ended, I had to get right back in bed. It was hell.

My friend Chuck Inglefield hosted me for a speaking engagement at the Cleveland Yachting Club on April 10. I had just finished and was quickly packing my things up while people were still milling around. A longtime acquaintance, named Lorry Malm, came up to say hello. He was a doctor I met back in the '70s. He reminded me that I had written a letter for his son, a good sailor, when he applied to Stanford. But we didn't talk about old times.

He looked concerned. "You don't look very well," he told me. "Would you allow me to give you an examination tomorrow?"

Early the next morning, he came by the house where I was staying. He looked me over and told me, "You know what, you need to come down to my clinic." So I went down to the clinic and we did all the tests. Four hours of tests: blood work, X-rays, scans. And after four hours we met in his office, that look of concern still on his face. "I don't know what is wrong with you but I can tell you this, you are very ill and you are out of gas." He instructed me to stop what I was doing and get to a hospital. He offered to admit me there, in Cleveland, or I could plan to go home to Baltimore and get myself admitted.

This was a Friday morning, but I had a talk scheduled for Las Vegas Friday night, a talk at Mentor Harbor Yacht Club outside Cleveland on Saturday, and a Sunday talk in Erie, Pennsylvania. I listened to him carefully and reasoned: If I go home today, I'm not going to get anything done until Monday anyway. So I decided to persevere.

Getting out to Las Vegas almost killed me. I could barely walk to my hotel room. I got through my presentation and got myself back to Cleveland. The next day I spoke in Erie and flew back to Baltimore Sunday night, exhausted.

On Monday, more tests started. This time, a biopsy was also performed. After 10 days, I met with Dr. Yudhishtra Markan for results. When I arrived at his office, he looked somber. He slowly walked over to shut the office door, and then he sat down with a stern expression. He took a deep breath and leaned into his desk and gave me the news: You have lymphoma.

Non-Hodgkins lymphoma. That was the reason my health was failing. That was the reason my lymph nodes were popping out of my skin, and the reason why I woke up drenched with sweat, and the reason why I was continually exhausted and running on empty. I had a tumor in my stomach the size of a softball. A high percentage of the people treated for the disease can survive, Dr. Markan told me—for a period of time. It could be five years; it could be fifteen. Unfortunately it is a disease that comes back, in everybody. "Now we hope we have more powerful drugs when it does come back . . ."

I was listening to him, but as he spoke I wondered: What is worse, me sitting here listening to my doctor across a desk, or him telling me? Either way, this was one tough conversation. I actually got a little teary hearing this: the five to fifteen years, the fact that you can't get rid of it, the fact that it returns. In every single case, it returns.

Dr. Markan told me to clear my calendar and to prepare. The treatments, he warned, would be harsh. I had lectures and things to do, but deep down, I knew I had to get my head around this news.

In the days that followed, so many thoughts passed through my mind. For one, this was a little ironic. For 10 years, I had been chairman of the Leukemia & Lymphoma Society sailing regatta series. We had grown that series from one event in Annapolis in 1993 that raised $30,000 to a national circuit of events that had raised some $28 million. (By 2011 the total was nearly $40 million.) How ironic that I was now one of those very people with this illness.

I wanted my own doctor and sailing friend, Glenn Robbins, to be part of my team, to help me digest all the information being put before me—the science and the treatment options. I read a lot about the disease, learning as much as I could. I wanted the most aggressive treatment my body could survive. Only 11 days after my diagnosis I had my first treatment, and Dr. Markan was right. It was harsh.

There was one question I had to ask Glenn. I was not sure I wanted the answer—but I had to know. "If I had not come in for these tests and if I had just kept going, how long would I have lasted?" "About 30 days . . . Then you would have gone out," he said.

By early May, I had my work affairs in order. My assistant Kathy Lambert helped me clear my calendar, and I sent an email to friends and colleagues. I gave them the news and told them that for the next six to eight months I would be receiving chemotherapy to battle back from this disease.

"I am going to be in a quiet period now," I wrote. "Apparently the treatments are hard. Sorry to give you this report. My spirits are good. I hope to be around the waterfront later this summer."

And then psychologically I moved on to face the next chapter of my life. It was as if a curtain went down.

But it was not long after the send button was pushed that responses started flooding in. Emails arrived from all over the world. The switchboard at my company in Annapolis, Jobson Sailing, lit up like a Christmas tree. Kathy fielded all the calls from sailing friends, from acquaintances, from colleagues. Some cheered me on, telling me how they had battled a life-threatening disease and won. Some were messages of sympathy and encouragement. I did not really digest them all—but I do remember the messages that were most encouraging. They did not talk about cancer or recovery. Those people simply reminded me of all the good times we'd had on the water in the past and how there would be more. And that is exactly what I needed to hear. I needed to remember the good times, and to hope there would be more.

.2.

WINNING THE AMERICA'S CUP

1977	Spring signals new beginnings. But as I look back on one April day in 1977—as I walked the winding streets of coastal Marblehead with Ted Turner and headed toward the waterfront—spring signaled something more than a new sailing season. My life was about to change.

◄———————— ■ ————————►

The previous fall, Turner had invited me to sail onboard *Courageous*, the 12 Meter he hoped would defend the America's Cup. At age 26, I had already graduated from SUNY Maritime College, where I made a name for myself racing small boats on the intercollegiate circuit. I had moved on to coach at the Merchant Marine Academy—and success in sailing was born of my methodical approach. I worked hard and planned. I had started keeping notebooks at age 16 where I recorded details about every race I sailed—the weather conditions, wind shifts, my tactics, and finishes. But there was nothing I could have done to plan a berth as Ted Turner's tactician on *Courageous*. For me, it was pure serendipity. For Ted, it was by design.

In 1972, Ted Turner, a hot young racer from Harvard named Robbie Doyle, and I were among 10 invited skippers to race in the Inter-Class Solo Championship in Rhode Island. Each day we raced in a different single-handed boat—all of us having to switch gears from racing high-performance Lasers, to traditional catboats, to a third one-design during the three-day regatta. Robbie and I duked it out for the championship. I led for most of the regatta, but Robbie edged me out by only one point in the final standings. Ted finished sixth, and at the awards ceremony he came up to both of us, put his arms around our shoulders, and said in his characteristic loud voice, "Boys, I hope we'll sail together one day."

"One day" had arrived. Robbie was onboard *Courageous* as mainsail trimmer and sailmaker; I would be calling tactics for Ted.

While Ted helmed *Courageous*, a job that demands 100 percent concentration, I would be his eyes on the racecourse—looking for wind shifts, reporting our speed in relation to the competition, plotting our next move on the course. It was as if two people, helmsman and tactician, had to act as one, so the walks through Marblehead were Ted's idea. And I quickly learned why.

At 38, Ted was already owner of a basketball team and a baseball team, having bought the Atlanta Braves in '76; he had already become a world champion in sailing, in both small dinghies and large ocean-racing boats; he had already set in place the building blocks of his business empire. At a young age, he had collected more accomplishments than most do in a lifetime—and he clearly moved at high velocity.

Robbie Doyle and I shake hands at the 1972 Inter-Class Solo Championship. Robbie won. I was second. On this day Ted Turner suggested we all sail together at a future date.

Life around Ted Turner was a rollercoaster—up, and also down, but always a wild ride. The walks we took down to the waterfront were important moments of quiet conversation. We talked about sailing, tactics on the water, life, world events—whatever came to mind.

On that April day in Marblehead, we walked along the picturesque streets of the coastal town, past tidy historic homes that once housed clipper-ship captains and seafaring New Englanders, until we reached a waterfront park. There, from a knoll overlooking the harbor, the landscape below us opened to an expanse of blue water and the sight of two 12 Meters. *Courageous* and our training partner *Independence* were docked 40 feet below, gleaming in the springtime sun after their winter overhaul. Both masts towered high over the harbor while crews in uniform worked on deck.

Our conversation dropped to silence at that moment, and I stared at the two boats—feeling like a rookie baseball player walking into Yankee Stadium for the first time. "When you were 15, did you ever think you would be sailing a 12 Meter?" Ted asked me. I wanted to sail on a big Twelve as a kid, but it was hard to believe this was happening. I answered, "No, I didn't imagine this would happen."

"Neither did I," Ted drawled in his mild southern accent.

It dawned on me that day: for all Ted Turner had done in his life, nothing in his youth led him to believe he'd someday be an America's Cup skipper. And at that moment, winning the Cup with Ted Turner became my inner goal. But anyone who followed the America's Cup in those days knew the obvious: the odds against *Courageous* defending the Cup were staggering.

We were one of a trio of boats vying to defend. Skippering *Independence* was a laconic New Englander named Ted Hood out of Marblehead, a man of few words and enormous talent who had already helmed *Courageous* to an America's Cup win in 1974. *Enterprise* rounded out the group. Built in City Island to be skippered by West Coast sailmaker and Olympic Gold medalist Lowell North—a figure in the racing world known for his analytical thinking and endless tinkering with sailing technology—*Enterprise* was designed by Olin Stephens, an American yacht designer known for his breakthrough thinking. Then in his late sixties, Stephens and his firm Sparkman & Stephens had already won the America's Cup with one of their designs six times: *Enterprise* represented his latest thinking, and it was billed in the press as "the last word in 12 Meters."

Courageous had already proven to be fast when she won the 1974 Cup against the Australian yacht *Southern Cross*—and *Independence* and *Enterprise* benefited from that track record. Every curve in her hull, the profile of her keel, the shape of her sails: *Courageous* was a floating laboratory, and the features of the boat established data that every successive 12 Meter program could build off of to find a new edge in speed. Especially Ted Hood.

After helming *Courageous* to her '74 win, Hood used the boat's lines as a starting point for his newer *Independence*, and later as a trial horse on the water. Both boats were being campaigned together under the umbrella of the Kings Point Syndicate—and looking back, that was one of the smartest things Ted Hood did. Both *Courageous* and the newer *Independence* sparred against each other as we prepared for the Trials. Even though we were in the same syndicate, there was an uneasy peace between the two boats—for at the end of the day, we were both competing to win the Trials and then the Cup. But in the process, both crews learned from each other and we were all the stronger for it.

After I joined Turner's effort, I spent weekends sailing in Marblehead in the winter of '76 and got a first-hand look at that two-boat testing. That was December—and Hood took advantage of those days while the water off Marblehead was still "soft," before the ice arrived. In those months, *Courageous* was considered old technology, old news. Or was she?

My observations told me that *Courageous* was faster than *Independence*, no matter what. Yet the reports in newsletters sent out to the supporters of our Kings Point Syndicate always reported that *Independence* was faster. Hood's boat was the newest iteration of 12 Meter design—and as usual in the Cup game, the new boat represents new promise.

Turner was not in Marblehead on those winter weekends, so he would read the reports and then call me up and ask for the latest.

"Hey, I hear they are faster. Were you on the boat? What happened?"

I was sailing on both boats and I had a good eye: I could see who was faster and who was slower. So I reported to Ted what was happening.

"Ted, *Courageous* is going faster."

"That's good. Okay. I love you! Bye."

Ted trusted my instincts. Plus, he had a plan. He knew Ted Hood would only use sails from his own sailmaking loft, Hood Sailmakers. Lowell North would use his own North Sails on *Enterprise*. But Ted was planning on the ability to buy sails for *Courageous* from both lofts, taking the best designs from each sailmaker. And that would be his edge.

Ted Turner hoists his replica of the America's Cup during a playful moment in 1980.

Come June, *Independence*, *Courageous*, and *Enterprise* would all be transported to Newport, Rhode Island, the home of the America's Cup, to sail the Defender Selection Trials. There would be three rounds of trials: one each in June, July, and August, followed by the America's Cup in September when the winning defender would match-race the boat that won the challenger selection. The Trials were not a simple mathematical matter of whichever boat won the most races captured the Defender title. They were "observation" trials, and the Selection Committee of the New York Yacht Club (NYYC) would observe each day of racing from a large powerboat and in the end decide which boat was best prepared to defend the America's Cup.

Courageous and her crew had big odds. We would be sailing an older generation 12 Meter. Our afterguard had an average age of 32. And Turner stood out: He was not of the New York Yacht Club fold, not East Coast and not West Coast, but Cincinnati-born and Georgia-based and described in the press as colorful, unpredictable, flamboyant, and a showman. To top it off, Turner and many of the *Courageous* crew had come off a failed and frustrating campaign in the 1974 Cup on a 12 Meter named *Mariner*. Designed by Britton Chance, the boat was supposed to be revolutionary with its flat underbody astern of the keel. Instead, she turned out to be slow, hence the memorable Ted Turner quote when asked about the infamous boat: "Even a turd is pointed at both ends."

After a return to her builder for extensive surgery, *Mariner* still did not have the speed needed to champion the Cup competition, and Ted was fired from the boat before the Trials for the '74 Cup concluded. The boat was still slow—no matter who sailed her.

The *Mariner* crew did not consider the 1974 Cup their final act. When asked if he would do the Cup again, crewmember Richie Boyd said, "Sure—if we could race on *Courageous*." The lightbulb went off, and Turner started to spin his web for his next run at the Cup. There was plenty of motivation among the *Mariner* veterans on our crew to right past history. In 2010, at the America's Cup 12 Meter Reunion, Ted Hood explained how he decided to ask Ted Turner to skipper his stablemate, *Courageous*, "The year after I won the Cup aboard *Courageous*, I was asked to put together a new syndicate. I said okay if we have two boats and two good skippers. We had five different skippers on the list. I picked Turner. Not that he was the best sailor but I figured he'd put together a good team. Which he did."

As our crew prepared to move to Newport and enter the Defender Trials, we had a lot of strikes against us—and none of the seasoned America's Cup hands expected the old *Courageous* to show strongly in the Selection Trials.

The New York Yacht Club America's Cup Selection Committee kept a close watch while we raced in the Trials. The pressure was always on.

But once in Newport, we had a chance to show what we were made of. We were now engaged in a three-way contest among *Courageous*, *Independence*, and *Enterprise*. *Courageous* took four straight wins in those early June trials: two races against *Independence* and two against *Enterprise*. Suddenly there was a whole new tune around Newport: This *Courageous* crew must be pretty good.

What a long way we had come as a crew. When I first got onboard *Courageous* in Marblehead, I was used to sailing small dinghies where I could trim my own sails and make my own decisions. This 12 Meter with 11 crew was more complex: it was larger with more personalities and more moving parts and more power in the giant rig. And I wasn't prepared for the feel of the apparent wind, the combination of the actual wind with the wind the boat makes as it speeds through the water. It was so much stronger—and colder, in those early season sails—than anything I'd felt on the dinghies I was used to sailing.

On *Courageous*, we had our struggles in the beginning. On one leeward-mark rounding in Marblehead, we rounded on the wind and the jib was half up and the spinnaker was half down and dragging in the water and the spinnaker pole was in

A Day with the Selection Committee

The methods of the NYYC Selection Committee were always mysterious to the competitors. We'd be out racing our boats, thinking, *OK, we've got this brand new jib we are going to hoist today and the committee is going to be really impressed . . .* Or when they'd come over to the compound, we'd make sure every line was perfectly coiled, our tools were organized, and our compound was neat and clean—all to show we were ready to defend the Cup.

In 1983, I talked the Selection Committee into allowing the skipper and tactician from each boat to spend a day with them on the water. The idea was, if we could spend a day with the committee, we would all better understand what they were looking for in a defender. The chair of the committee, Bob McCullough, bought into the idea.

I finally had my first chance to observe on the water with the committee. So while the other teams raced skipper Tom Blackaller, who I campaigned with in '83, I rode with the men who would choose the Defender and had a chance to observe and learn their methods of choosing. Before I stepped onboard, I had an image: *Boy, those guys are up there talking about how fast we are turning the boat, how the main's leech is looking, where the jib leads are . . .* I imagined that they noticed even the tiniest of details.

But as the racing unfolded, there was no serious analysis going on. They took penny bets on what the time difference between the boats would be at the windward mark. They talked about what time lunch would be. They told stories of the old days, when they sailed onboard the great 12 Meters. My image of the experienced Cup men and their great analytical process of selection was shattered!

Now, as I write this I have already reached age 60, just about the same age neighborhood as the Selection Committee members were in those days. If the NYYC still held the Cup, I imagine I might be on that committee with many of my contemporaries. And I wonder to this day, how would we have handled it all? And what—exactly—would we be talking about as our American crews circled the buoys on the racecourse?

the water. It's like trying to start a sprint with one running shoe on and the other untied: you are not yet ready to surge forward with speed. I remember thinking after that rounding, This is going to be a *long* summer. Plus, as we sparred against *Independence* back in Marblehead, we'd continually find ourselves in every kind of tactical situation. At first I was miffed at Ted for purposely slowing down to put us into prone positions at the marks, after starts, and in tacking duels. But it gave us a valuable opportunity to learn how to fight our way out of holes.

In public, Ted's image was loud, colorful, and wild, but underneath that veneer I found a strong leader and a strong competitor who understood what it takes to win.

Since the newer *Independence* and *Enterprise* had been built using *Courageous* as a benchmark, we knew from the start it would be hard to gain an edge in boatspeed. Instead, we concentrated on the last angle available to us—sailing hard. Crew member Richie Boyd was part of the team who helped design the deck layout to make the boat easy to sail. We felt that less time spent on mechanical trivia and needless experimentation would give us more time to work on tactics, sail trim, and boathandling. This could give us an edge, if we were to have one at all. Let the other boats experiment, we figured.

Turner also knew how to pick a crew that was hungry to win. Many had returned from the *Mariner* campaign and we'd all had a certain amount of success sailing on our own, with each of us having won a national championship in sailing or its equivalent.

Twelve in all, our crew included Bill Jorch, 33, our navigator and a computer engineer from Grumman on Long Island, whose computer design and programming skills were valuable in those early days of using computers onboard; four-time Olympic medalist in rowing and sailing Conn Findlay out of California, who stood 6 feet, 7 inches (a stature that earned him the nickname Paul Bunyan) and at age 47 handled the physically grueling belowdecks "sewer," mainsail trim at the starts, and jib-winch grinding in the tacking duels; winch grinder Dick Sadler, 23, who grew up on New York's City Island and had battled back from a serious illness in 1976 (we called him Savage); portside tailer Carl "Bunky" Helfrich, 39, who started sailing with Turner as a junior racer in Savannah and continued to race with him all over the world, and who designed all of CNN's facilities around the world for Turner Broadcasting and oversaw the construction of the stadiums for the Atlanta Braves and Atlanta Hawks; bowman John "L.J." Edgecomb, 25, a California sailor and the only veteran onboard from the 1974 *Courageous* campaign; Gould "Stretch" Ryder, 29, a helicopter pilot in Vietnam who now flies for a Long Island company; coach and crew alternate Marty O'Meara, 47, who sailed with us on practice days and was especially valuable to me on tactics as we reviewed his detailed notes each night; Princeton grad Richie Boyd and University of Michigan grad Paul Fuchs, both 25 and the unsung heroes of our campaign because they worked for over a year—long days and long nights, seven days a week—to perfect the rigging and deck layout and maintenance; sailmaker and Harvard grad Robbie Doyle, 28, without whom we would not have won since he managed our small sail inventory (24 new sails in all, compared to 69 on *Independence*); and Ted and me.

By the time we reached Newport for the June Trials, our team chemistry had definitely gelled: we all had an equal desire to follow Ted Turner and win the Cup. I knew it the moment I arrived on Aquidneck Island. I had left my coaching job and drove up to Newport in my small Honda Civic, arriving at night with my life's possessions in the back seat. I got lost winding my way past the Gilded Age mansions that grew out of the thick pea soup fog as I rolled slowly down each street, searching for the *Courageous* dorm. With the help of a local cop, I finally found Conley Hall, the English Tudor mansion designed by Sanford White that would be our summer home and headquarters. As soon as I walked inside I looked at the grand entrance and the high ceilings and the magnificent structure that was, like Ted, larger than life. I dropped my seabags and thought, Now *this* is going to be a good summer.

We all knew how hard we needed to fight to conquer the Cup, but we took a certain pride in our underdog status. Later in the series, our wives—including my wife Janice, whom I married in '74—started playing the theme song from the *Rocky* movies on the stereo each morning before we took off for the docks. It worked us into a sailing frenzy, for, like Rocky Balboa, each of us on the crew knew that given the chance, we could go the distance. The U.S. Coast Guard vessel that escorted us out to the racecourse (ironically named *Point Turner*) followed our lead, playing the song as we left the harbor each day. Even the French contender—Baron Marcel Bich's *France 2*, in Newport to race in the challenger trials—got into the act. As a wry counterpoint to our *Rocky* theme, they headed to the course one morning with a theme song blaring over the harbor of their own: Henry Mancini's theme from the *Pink Panther* movies.

By the time the June Trials ended, the storyline of underdog success stuck. We had logged the strongest record among the trio of defender candidates: wins to losses, 9–1. Our only lost race was an eight-second loss to *Enterprise*. We did not fit the scenario the NYYC Selection Committee had carefully constructed as they planned for this Cup defense. But as they watched from their big powerboat, I

The U.S. Coast Guard vessel *Point Turner* escorted *Courageous* out to the racecourse every day. After the Cup I presented my medal to the crew. It is still on display down below. Years later I joined the board of the U.S. Coast Guard Foundation.

trust we had them scratching their heads. *Courageous* was supposed to be the B-boat playing second fiddle to the varsity teams on *Independence* and *Enterprise*.

What was happening?

Clearly the committee forgot to factor one thing into their carefully crafted plans. They never realized just how hungry our young crew was for victory.

* * *

That summer in Newport our *Courageous* crew learned how easy life can be when you are winning—and how much tougher it is to lose. Our leading edge did not continue into the July Trials, and our win-loss record in July was 7–7. It was a back-to-square-one moment for all the crews hoping to defend the America's Cup—for as the July Trials came to a close, there was no clear favorite among the three boats with defender aspirations.

We had all ended up in just about the same place, all with different approaches to defending the America's Cup. On *Courageous*, we had focused not on finding an edge in boatspeed but on crew work, tactics, sail trim, wind shifts, and boat handling. On the contrary, both *Independence* and *Enterprise* had searched for speed breakthroughs—but their search was in vain.

As even as we all were in the standings at that point in the Trials, two important developments had been established: *Courageous* did indeed have a shot at defending the America's Cup, and *Enterprise*—the boat we had affectionately dubbed the "Starship" and the latest word in 12 Meter design—did not have breakaway speed.

The racing scorecard the NYYC Selection Committee kept was not the only story developing in Newport that summer. Like every America's Cup, there is a lot of dimension to the turn of the events; like a piece of fabric, there were hundreds of story lines woven together to make up the whole cloth. And so it was in Newport that summer—and one of those threads had to do with sails. You may not think a boat's sails would add a dramatic twist to this story, but mix sails, a high-stakes game like the America's Cup, and the high-voltage personality of Ted Turner, and you have dramatic tension that rivals the best of Hollywood.

Ted Turner and I contemplate the next race aboard *Courageous* in 1977.

Because Ted had been counting on buying sails from both Hood Sailmakers—founded by our training partner Ted Hood on *Independence*—and from Lowell North's company North Sails, the news that the *Enterprise* syndicate and North had later decided not to sell sails to us was more than a blow to Ted Turner: it made him spitting mad. So on the day Ted informed me the two of us were going over to the *Enterprise* compound to straighten Lowell North out, I knew this was not a good thing.

When it came to sailing, Ted Turner was not one to curb his emotions. Before the '77 Cup, one exchange with Britton Chance— the yacht designer of the notoriously slow 12 Meter *Mariner* that Ted sailed—resulted in Ted taking a swing at Chance inside the venerable St. Petersburg Yacht Club in Florida, a club like all the other old-guard yacht clubs in the United States that prized itself on fierce battles on the water and blue-blazered civility on land. But that was not Ted's style.

The two of us headed to the *Enterprise* compound, and Ted burst in like a tornado. I followed in his wake, thinking to myself, holy shit, I have never seen anybody as mad as Ted Turner. North gathered fellow afterguard member Malin Burnham and we headed down to the docks, to talk in private on one of the syndicate's powerboats. But no sooner did we get down below when Turner targeted North with a tirade: "You NO GOOD lying son of bitch. You told me you were going to SELL SAILS . . ." Burnham and I sat there, at first in stunned silence. If you had taken a picture, our eyes would have looked as big as golfballs.

"Isn't that right Jobson?" Ted yelled over to me.

"Yeah . . . sure," I answered, not yet comprehending every piece of the story.

The yelling went on for a good half hour. People on the dock passed by and peered into the ports of the small powerboat, drawn by all the commotion. Ted was spitting and spewing and screaming, until finally, he had had enough and stormed off. For the rest of the summer, Ted was not shy about telling others what he thought of Lowell North—including Walter Cronkite, who had come to Newport to interview Ted for a piece on the Cup for *60 Minutes*. "That Lowell North is a no-good lying son of a bitch," Ted said to the camera.

Those of us on the *Courageous* crew figured some insurance of our own was in order to avoid more fireworks when Ted was in shouting distance of Lowell North. We had our biggest crewmember—the fit, strong, 6-foot-7 Olympic medalist Conn Findlay—shadow Ted at all social events. Just in case.

By July our sails were tired, especially our five-ounce light air genoa, an important jib in our inventory. But crew Robbie Doyle, a talented sailmaker at the

Hood loft, was turning out to be our secret weapon. He built us a new mainsail that we used in the last race of July, which we won. Robbie would also build us some new genoas. When he wasn't on the water racing he was putting in long hours at the sail loft, re-cutting sails to perfect their shape.

Although the tide had turned in the July Trials from our June promise, the *Courageous* crew morale was still intact. We had momentum, spirit, and a desire to win—and we were taking steps to overcome our weaknesses.

In July, two defeats in races against *Enterprise* were caused by my tactical blunders. After the second loss, Ted was upset and I was confused. After a long night and some deep soul-searching, it became clear that I had been allowing too many people to take part in my decisions. New York's East River, which ran past my alma mater, was where I got my early education in reading the wind, using all the signs—the smoke stacks, the direction of the waves and ripples on the water, the flags, and other boats—to detect the patterns in the way the wind behaved. Back in college, I had to make all my own decisions on the water. It was clear to me now that I needed to return to my roots.

I had a little additional confidence to draw from after a talk with Bob Bavier, publisher of *Yachting* magazine and a former commodore of the New York Yacht Club. We went behind the *Courageous* toolshed for a private chat. He saw the mistakes we made in July, but he reminded me that many on the Selection Committee liked the way I was sailing that summer and looked forward to seeing me perform as the summer unfolded. That private moment of encouragement sustained me during moments of doubt.

While we worked as a crew to sharpen our game, something else was happening on land. The crowds kept growing—the fans and followers, groupies, and the media. They thronged the docks when we left in the morning and returned to greet us after racing. There were over 500 news professionals in Newport that summer, and every major television network was represented, as were the national magazines: *Time* and *Newsweek*, *60 Minutes* and *Good Morning America*, *The New York Times*, *The Washington Post*, *The Providence Journal*, *The Boston Globe*, *Sports Illustrated*, and the *Associated Press*. They were all covering the Cup. Ted Turner was clearly making sailing interesting to the nonsailing public.

The press and the public got wise to the walks Ted and I took each morning, and again each day after sailing. We were followed by photographers, by people trying to overhear what we were saying. We varied our route each day, jumping over hedges and sneaking through backyards. Most days we could duck the crowds, at least for part of our route.

In the summer of 1977, America was ripe for Ted Turner. The previous year Americans had elected a president from Georgia, and as Jimmy Carter took office along came another Georgian, moving from virtual obscurity and into the public eye—breaking in the sports pages by buying two professional sports teams and challenging the establishment. Mix a personality like Ted Turner with the Cup, when all of America was being tested for the oldest prize in sporting history, and let the show begin. At the end, everyone was cheering for *Courageous* and Ted Turner. And with every race, we gained more fans among the ranks of the New York Yacht Club. *Courageous* had a white hull and a pale green deck, and as we neared the end of the Defender Trials, we'd spy more people with the NYYC wearing *Courageous*-green jerseys.

Our crew would follow Ted Turner into battle, anywhere. And no one except those of us on *Courageous* really understood how much the controversy with Lowell North fired Ted up. He fought best with his back up against the wall. Ted had already suffered the humiliation of *Mariner* in 1974—and he was determined to beat the other U.S. boats and defend the Cup. In the end, the *Enterprise* syndicate's refusal to sell sails to *Courageous* fanned the blaze that destroyed their America's Cup hopes.

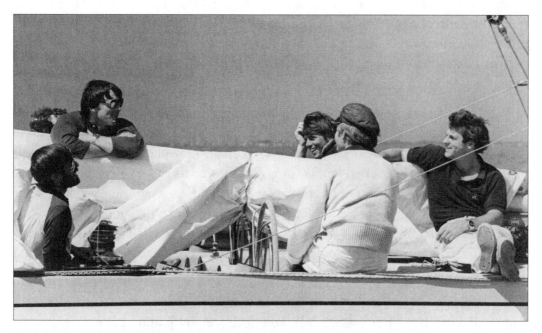

Bill Jorch, Paul Fuchs, Robbie Doyle, me, Ted Turner, and Richie Boyd
share a laugh while towing out to the starting line.

Ted's volatile passions for sailing could work for us, or against us. But in late July, an article by sportswriter William Wallace in *The New York Times* gave me confidence that what we were doing onboard *Courageous* was working. The headline read, "Patience of Jobson May Be the Key to Turner's Success at the Cup Trials."

Wallace, a seasoned sportswriter for *The Times*, talked about the partnership between Ted and me, about the moods of Ted Turner that ran from "infectious enthusiasm to infectious gloom," and about my role to keep him focused on driving *Courageous*. I talked constantly on the boat in an even tone, so Ted couldn't talk—for I knew if we could keep him quiet and concentrated, no one could beat us. I took Wallace's analysis in the paper as a message: Be patient, young man.

Our crew entered the August Trials with renewed determination—and we came out with the strongest record of wins to losses, 10–1. By the middle of August, I was sure we would be chosen to defend the Cup.

In the final days, it was *Enterprise* we matched. *Independence* had already been asked by the committee to step out of the running; their bid for the Cup may have been over, but having them as a training partner was a big key to our strong performance.

Enterprise was stocked with strong sailors and top talent, and as I think back on those trials today I remember that there were caveats. *Enterprise* was more of a heavy-air boat, and that summer we had the good fortune to always match them in light air. Their forestay was designed to be closer to the mast and their jib had less sail area—and they just didn't have the same acceleration as we did coming out of the tacks with their smaller headsail. And I think the *Courageous* crew was simply hot that summer.

So on a late August day, when rain and thunder squalls and intermittent sun rolled over Newport Harbor, Commodore George Hinman, who chaired the Selection Committee, traveled across the harbor to give our crew the official word.

"Gentlemen, it is with great pleasure that I inform you that *Courageous* has been selected to defend the America's Cup."

"Commodore, we did it for you," said Ted, giving the commodore a bear hug.

The volatile weather was a fitting scene to receive the news. There were those who believed that even if Ted Turner won most of the races of the Defender Trials, the NYYC Selection Committee would never choose him. But just like the movement of air masses and the weather systems that showered that day over the harbor, a certain unstoppable dynamic took hold during that summer in Newport.

I stretch out aboard *Courageous* on the way out to Race 1 of the 1977 America's Cup.
It was my good luck routine. Bunky Helfrich steers at right.

Ted Turner and the *Courageous* crew may have been the unexpected choice at the season's start, but we had won the slot. We had become the best boat to fight for a trophy that had been in America's hands since 1851.

*   *   *

On the morning of September 12, Ted Turner and I left Conley Hall to walk down to the docks and step onboard *Courageous*. We had done this walk many times that summer, but this day was different: we were heading down to the water for the first race of the America's Cup.

On the eve of this opening race, Ted told me, "I can't think of anything more we can do. I've never been as prepared for anything as I am for this." His thoughts were shared by all of us on the crew. Yet, we all knew there was plenty of reason to worry.

Race 1 of the America's Cup is the most magic moment in the sport of sailing. No one knows which boat is faster. The mood on the starting line is tense and anticipation is high. After you have raced in an America's Cup Final you understand that nothing really compares. Racing in the Trials is like playing in the playoffs. But racing for the America's Cup is a quantum leap from the Trials. It's the big dance; it's the result that gets recorded in the history books. You just hope in your heart your boat is faster—but you're scared to death your opponent is quicker.

The most exciting moment in the America's Cup is the start of Race 1. There are hundreds of fans on the Coast Guard vessel watching. We all realized what a big deal this was.

The Selection Committee was adamant about keeping it that way. We were forbidden to sail against Alan Bond's crew on *Australia*, the boat that won the challenger selection series that summer in Newport. Ted and "Bondy," as he called him, were great friends from ocean racing against each other. But that was irrelevant. We were not to sail near them: not for a second, not give anything away. No boats broached that rule, for we were all under the iron fist of the Selection Committee. But I knew something, and I told no one.

Just days earlier, we had been sailing against *Independence* and near *Australia* off Castle Hill. *Australia* was to leeward and behind, but she gained several boat lengths on us in just a few minutes. Was she really as *fast* as she seemed that day?

Australia **had already proven to be a strong competitor that summer in Newport. This crew had beaten all of its opponents with surprising ease, and the Aussies couldn't have been more qualified (plus, they knew how to light up a bar).**

Alan Bond already knew what it was like to lose the America's Cup. Just three years earlier, his first Cup yacht, *Southern Cross*, faced *Courageous* in the Cup with Ted Hood at the helm. Bond knew the potential of *Courageous*, and he had some unfinished business. So on September 12, when the sun rose over Newport and all the yachts sat quietly in their berths in the dawn light, the Australians knew that this could be their day: they had a shot at overturning the longest winning streak in sports history. The fact was, Australia had everything to gain and we had everything to lose.

I carried that suspicion of *Australia's* speed with me on the morning of the first race, but I couldn't reveal any worry or any doubt. It was my job to keep Ted cool—and we had all talked about it. Ted is going to be nervous this morning, walk him around Newport, don't let him come down early, keep him late: those were my marching orders. But Ted couldn't wait to get down to the boat that morning. He was nervous—he rushed his breakfast and downed cups of coffee and even puked on the walk down to the boat. So when we arrived earlier than expected, I heard a chorus of complaints from my crewmates: "Hey, you were supposed to keep him walking around for a while!"

Ted was a nervous wreck, pacing the dock. So we left right on schedule, at 0930. As we were towed out to the course, he downplayed what we were about to face: There's not going to be that much interest, this isn't that big of a deal, look, nobody's coming out. People waved goodbye from shore, and it was just us and the Australians, charging out to sea for battle.

There is this one buoy that I love, off Breton Reef: R2. There are four of those red nuns on the way out to the course, but R2 is magic, for when you get to R2 it signals you are making your departure to sea. You pass the shores of Newport, past long green lawns topped by towering mansions, but at R2 the landscape opens up to all blue. From there, it is about six miles to the America's Cup course.

As we passed R2, it was still just us and the Australians, and Ted remarked again, Hey, it's not that big a deal. No one's coming out.

"Ted," I said, "look behind us."

And when he turned away from the sea and looked back toward Newport Harbor, there was a wall of blimps and planes and helicopters and ships and boats on the horizon, for about three miles. The sky and the water were filled with traffic. This, I thought to myself, is a very big deal.

We both got to the starting line, got our sails up, and then engaged in that pre-race dance for position at the start. An American named Andy Rose was calling tactics on *Australia* for helmsman Noel Robbins. It was a bit controversial, having an American in a key afterguard spot on the Australian boat. But controversy aside, I had faced Andy Rose at the Congressional Cup in California, and I knew one thing: he was damn good.

The starting gun fired. We were off for an historic match-up between these two 12 Meters, and looking back today, I realize the next 15 minutes were the greatest moment in my sailing career.

We started on different tacks, but up the course both boats held on port tack for about 10 minutes. It seemed the Australians were gaining when both boats sailed into a breeze that headed us off our upwind course by about 7 degrees, what sailors call a header. Navigator Bill Jorch plotted our position to be 12 degrees from the layline, the imaginary direct line to the next mark of the course. Fearful of being pinned out to the layline by *Australia*, *Courageous* made the first move. We called for a tack and the *Courageous* crew was ready. I heard Conn Findlay mutter, "Let's get 'em!" We spun into the opposite tack and headed on our new course. "Starboard!" Ted hailed to the Australians to signal our right-of-way, their bow rapidly converging with our course. Would the Aussies get the safe leeward position?

We did not want to be forced to tack since the breeze appeared to be freshening straight ahead from the south, and not from the prevailing west. Robbins, *Australia's* skipper, decided to tack under our leeward bow. Ted drove *Courageous* off the wind slightly for speed, and both boats came within inches of establishing the lead. But after one very intense minute of seesaw battle *Courageous* finally drove over *Australia*, forcing her to tack away to the unfavored west. *Courageous* held on for several boat lengths, sailing into a freshening breeze before covering. *Australia* had lost about seven boat lengths and the chase was on. When *Australia* tacked away to the west, it was a decisive moment. And in that very second I felt we had a slight edge in speed, at least when sailing to windward. Plus, we had the confidence to handle them.

At that moment, I turned to Ted, wearing his trademark engineer's cap. Sweat was pouring down underneath his brow. "Well, they aren't slow," I said.

"Yeah," Ted answered in his slight southern drawl, his eyes alight and flashing a Cheshire-cat grin, "but they aren't fast either."

Thanks to the freshening breeze, *Courageous* rounded the first mark with over a one-minute lead. We kept that leading edge over the six-leg course, picking up some time on the final leg when the wind piped up slightly to win the first race of the series by 108 seconds.

The Australians opted for a day off after Race 1. As it turned out, it was too windy to race anyway. The following day brought a light southeasterly breeze. Neither boat won this frustrating race, as the wind died with *Courageous* just 300 yards from the finish line.

Race 2 followed the same pattern as Race 1 except *Australia* gained significantly on the last run. But on *Courageous*, we held our slim lead to win by one minute and three seconds, which factors out to about nine boat lengths. *Australia* gained on the run in the third race as well, and people started speculating: Were the Aussies quicker downwind?

Speed theories aside, we continued to lead *Australia* at every mark. Finishing that fourth and final race was an experience I will never forget. Spectator boats sat 150 yards off the layline for a full mile and a half from the finish line, and the fleet got deeper as we approached the line. The fleet was so big it blanketed our wind, so we changed headsails twice as we approached the finish. I felt as if we were caught in some kind of void among a thousand yachts, a dozen ships, helicopters, planes, and even a blimp. It was hazy as we approached the finish—the only sound the dull roar of the spectator fleet as they all sat with engines idling, watching and waiting. All our training and sailing came down to this moment— and it seemed to take forever to get across the finish line. But when we did, the gun went off and the sounds were deafening: horns, sirens, cannons, whistles, shouts, and the sounds of revving engines filled the air as all of us on *Courageous* shot our fists skyward.

The photo is blurry, but it captures the happy moment Janice and I shared riding back to the dock following *Courageous's* victory in the America's Cup.

And in those moments after we crossed the line, I saw a new side of Conn Findlay. Ted had a game where he would describe each crew with one word. For Conn, it was *steady*. He didn't show elation at our wins, or deep depression at our losses. He was just as Ted described him: steady. But after we won, Conn came over and gave me a huge bear hug. Whomph. And I could see—just for a second—a tear in his eye.

The reception we got as we traveled into the harbor as the new winners of the America's Cup was like no reception I have ever gotten, at any point in my sailing career. In fact, it's likely that few Cup crews have experienced such a victory lap: people were lined up on the rocks and on the shoreline that rimmed the passage into the harbor; fans had crawled out their second-story windows to sit on rooftops and watch us come home; watercraft of all kinds filled the harbor. As we traveled by the crowds, we waved and Ted tipped his cap to the crowd. Waiting on the docks was a swarm of people. My dad was there too, and he seemed simply overwhelmed.

As we neared the dock, we passed the Aussies and our crews exchanged three cheers. Our wives, including Janice, Nancy Jorch, and Janet Doyle somehow made their way aboard the boat for the triumphant ride into the harbor. Once berthed, the fun began: the Australians came over in a small motor launch and were ceremoniously thrown overboard, until one crewmember decided to take some *Courageous* crew with him. From then, it was mayhem: we all went swimming. And when the sailors were done throwing each other overboard, our wives and girlfriends also received a ceremonious swim.

On that frenzied day, the Dom Pérignon flowed—and it seemed as if everyone in Newport and possibly the world cared about *Courageous*.

The press conferences were held after racing in the National Guard Armory on Thames Street, which was about a 10-minute walk from the dock. Ted and I strolled down to the conference, buoyed by the good spirits of the day. The crowd flowed around Ted like a rock star, complete with camera shutters clicking. By this time in the Cup, Ted had such a huge following that people were wearing buttons that read, "Ted Turner for President."

The pack grew large enough to stop traffic on Thames Street—and from the crowd emerged a bottle of Aquavit for Ted. He was not a drinker, but he indulged and carried the bottle to the pressroom—with its folding chairs and a long dais and microphones backdropped by national flags. When we entered there was thunderous applause. It was quite a scene. I sat alongside Ted, knowing he had overindulged in the champagne and the Aquavit. I slipped him notes: Thank

George Hinman and the Selection Committee; thank Commodore McCullough; thank the *Courageous* crew. The Australians sang *Dixie* and questions were asked and answered.

By now the Aquavit had been placed under the table, but Ted slid off his chair to retrieve the bottle, flashing a huge grin when he reappeared. Mission accomplished. And then, with perfect timing, Robbie Doyle and Stretch Ryder put an end to the show.

They simply walked up in the middle of the conference and carried Ted away. All of us on the *Courageous* crew instantly fell into rank and marched our leader out. We may have finished our job of winning the Cup, but we were still a team.

Following on the heels of the 32nd America's Cup, our winning crew aboard *Courageous* in 1977 reunited for our 30th anniversary in August 2007. We have a reunion every five years. This is a three-day weekend in Newport, Rhode Island. In my long sailing career I've never been with a tighter group of people.

I suppose every sport will have comparisons of athletes from different eras. In 1977 a film was made by Dick Enersen and he labeled our campaign "The Best Defense." Just last year Ted Hood remarked in a speech he gave at the New York Yacht Club that he thought that the *Courageous* crew was the best America's Cup team he had ever seen. It was a nice compliment. But bringing us back down to earth was a clever slogan that Robbie Doyle's wife, Janet, came up with, "The older they get . . . the better they were." The phrase was printed on a set of T-shirts for our team and families. We wore the shirts with pride.

When we went sailing on *Courageous* during the reunion, I was nervous that everyone would jump into the tactician's spot. After all, the crew had all gone on to successful careers and many were now boat owners. Each was used to being in charge. Lucky for me, the entire crew gravitated to their old positions. Returning to the cockpit of *Courageous* felt very familiar. It was a happy feeling.

On the first day most of our children (now in their twenties) were sailing aboard *Intrepid*. It was a friendly outing until *Intrepid* came across our bow and tacked right on our wind. With that, a tacking duel ensued. As fortune would have it, we found a very nice wind shift to turn the tables and take the lead. It might have been our last hurrah. But we took it.

The synergy of the *Courageous* crew started with a clear vision and strong leadership. All of us had such a strong passion to participate that the individual gave way to the team. It is a lesson that can apply to crews on all boats. Each member of the crew offered some thoughts on this during the reunion.

Ted Turner (Skipper): "I think the '77 Cup race was a high point of our lives. We had such a great time together. We were the underdogs going into that summer. We were going to have to perform at an absolutely superlative level. It was a crew of 100 percent winners."

Bill Jorch (Navigator): "What I remember most clearly is that the crew never got down. We had a positive attitude. I always felt I wanted to give my absolute best because I didn't want to let Ted down."

Robbie Doyle (Main Trimmer): "You learned a lot about leadership the way Ted directed people. He gave everybody a little compartment to do their thing."

Bunky Helfrich (Sail Trimmer): "We were able to form a bond that will never be surpassed. We were all amateurs. We sanded the bottom of the boat and did all the work ourselves. There was never any individual blame. If somebody messed up there was always somebody there to pick up the slack. It is one of the finest things that happened to me."

Richie Boyd (Sail Trimmer): "Everybody was critically important in both sailing and maintaining the boat. We worked together, we slept together, ate together. All the pieces fit."

Paul Fuchs (Grinder): "You could see the way Ted was thinking. Everything worked. There wasn't yelling. Everybody knew what they had to do. Things went smoothly. We were a family."

Dick Sadler (Grinder): "I never felt any overwhelming pressure or strains because I knew everyone else was going to be able to handle their job."

Stretch Ryder (Pit): "With Ted he had this aura around him. His 'can do' attitude was inspirational. He just let us do our jobs. You could rely on the guy behind you and the guy in front of you. Conn Findlay was a stabilizing factor. He never got flustered."

Conn Findlay (Sewer): "I think one time we had a problem. It involved the front end of the boat. After it was all over, Ted came forward and asked, 'Do you know what you did wrong?' And the answer was, 'yes.' End of conversation."

LJ Edgecomb (Bow): "We jelled as a team because people found their roles and jobs. We had to figure out how to keep the boat in one piece. If you do the little things you can win the big things. We kept checking and double checking."

Marty O'Meara (Crew Boss): "The crew was extremely dedicated and very knowledgeable. If you had to sum it up in one word, which became a key word in the Turner campaigns, it would be tenacious."

Jeff Neuberth (Project Manager): "It was a tight unit. Ted always had the theory that the sum of the whole is greater than the parts. It was a no-rock-star deal, everybody pulled together."

In addition to sailing, our group had dinner at the famous Clarke Cooke House, visited the Herreshoff Marine Museum and the International Yacht Restoration School, and enjoyed John Biddle's lecture—which he performed live. At age 82, John had long retired from giving film lectures around the country. For our reunion John spliced together 24 minutes of brilliantly shot clips and added his dry humor. At the end we gave John a sustained standing ovation. John passed away a year later, in September 2008.

Within days of John Biddle's death all of us on the crew were saddened when our teammate Bunky Helfrich passed away as well. He had been battling leukemia for two years. With 48 hours notice nine of our crew made it to Hilton Head, South Carolina, in time to carry the casket at his funeral. Bunky's wife Andrea and son Teddy were grateful for our presence at such a difficult time. Ted spoke eloquently at the service about his long friendship with Bunky, reminiscing about racing together as 10-year-olds. The day reinforced the strong bond we still have.

Bunky Helfrich, 1937–2008.

.3.
MY TURNING POINT

 Where I grew up on the New Jersey Shore, sailing was simply a part of life and how I spent my summers at home on Barnegat Bay. There are those who consider New England and Long Island Sound the sailing centers of the East Coast, but on the New Jersey Shore, people think differently.

←——————— ▬ ———————→

Barnegat Bay was formed by a unique geologic feature of the East Coast, a chain of barrier islands that extends from Down East Maine to Florida. For 56 miles from Bay Head and Manasquan Inlet south to Brigantine, just above Atlantic City, one such string of islands forms the outer rim of the Bay and protects those waters from the Atlantic Ocean. Inside that barrier is a pool of mainly shallow water that was a perfect place to sail as a kid.

My mother Helyn, me, and my brother Jamie sit on Sneakboxes that have been left on the lawn for safekeeping during Hurricane *Hazel* in 1954 at our bungalow in Beachwood, New Jersey.

There are only a few natural passages between the Bay and the ocean, mainly twisted inlets and shifting sands that for years have driven the U.S. Coast Guard crazy trying to place buoys to keep boats from running aground. It is an area that is rich with natural life. A wildlife refuge at the southern end of the Bay is the winter home of a species of small northern goose called brant that migrate from summers in the Arctic to the eelgrass of the Bay in winter.

Under the weight of asphalt roads and too many buildings, it's easy to misunderstand how fragile these barrier islands really are. Easy, that is, until Mother Nature strikes back. Hurricanes have devastated the islands since before there were written records—and those weather events that threatened the area stick in my mind as some of my earliest memories.

In 1954, Hurricanes *Carol* and *Hazel* rolled up the Eastern Seaboard. *Hazel* was the worst of the '54 hurricane season; the system had already killed several hundred people in Haiti and wreaked havoc when it made landfall in the Carolinas before it reached the Jersey Shore. But at the time I was only four and all I remember is the commotion such a storm system caused in our coastal community. Members from the yacht club rolled their small boats up the hill to our house, transporting them on wooden dollies so they could park on our front lawn—farther from the water and farther from harm's way.

The ecology of the mainland rimming the Bay is also fragile, now taken over by overdevelopment that began years before my family decided to call the area home. When my parents moved there, this coast of salt marsh and pine barrens was already popular as a summer haven. If you had some money, you built a large summer house in Bay Head or Seaside Park or Mantoloking. If you were like my father's family, you were content with the summer cottages along the mainland shore, where life centered around the sailing club.

That migration of summer people to the area, many of whom came down to the shore to race sailboats, has an illustrious history. Once the railroad opened Barnegat Bay to visitors from New York and Philadelphia, names like Rockefeller, Vanderbilt, Gould, Astor, Kipp, Rhinelander, and Wanamaker were heard more and more in the villages. By 1871, there were enough sailboats informally racing on Barnegat Bay to prompt the town of Toms River to organize the Toms River Challenge Cup and to create the Toms River Yacht Club to host the racing. Captains and crews took great pleasure in outsailing each other. Wagering was prevalent, and passions ran high during these races. A suitable trophy was made: a 3.5-pound ornate silver mug, made by Tiffany for the enormous sum of $175. This remains the second-oldest American sailing trophy in continuous competition, second only to the America's Cup.

Barnegat Bay was the area where my father's family always vacationed, so when my father retuned home from serving in the Marines in the Second World War and was building his career as a newspaper editor, he and my mother moved from northern New Jersey and settled in Toms River. My father loved to sail, so the area seemed like a fitting place to call home.

We lived right on the Toms River, on a small hill just up from the Beachwood Yacht Club. I started going to sailing class at the yacht club when I was six, which is a pretty young age to start in a junior program. But even before then, life centered around the shoreline, and the water is what I remember most: seeing the boats out racing, eating peanut butter and jelly sandwiches while watching the ducks. I used to get in a lot of trouble for going down to the water when I was small—and there was good reason. One day I fell off the dock and into the water. Fortunately, my father was there to fish me out. When I was five, we moved off the mainland to a house on Money Island.

After we moved to the island, we became a family of five: my mother and father, me, my younger brother Jamie, and my younger sister Ginger.

Legend has it that there is buried treasure at Money Island. We did not find any treasure, but we did have adventures afloat.

My father had a sailboat, the *African Queen*. It wasn't like the old riverboat that Katharine Hepburn and Humphrey Bogart traveled downriver on in the movies, but it was an Atlantic City Catboat. It was wide with a huge sail and had a lot character. (My parents had a penchant for Hollywood names. Gary Cooper, James Cagney, Ginger Rogers: like our boat, we all had namesakes in the movies.)

Later we had a 28-foot sloop, named *Helyn J.* after my mother. It was an adventure to sail our sloop on overnight cruises and visit a neighboring yacht club or anchor in a nearby cove. But it wasn't always idyllic, as I learned one Friday night when my father, my brother, and I were berthed at the dock of the Shore Acres Yacht Club. The club bar was in full swing—and so were the mosquitoes. When we went back to the boat that night, it felt like it was raining. We weren't pelted by rain but by mosquitoes, a particularly vicious breed on the New Jersey Shore.

Even before our days on the *African Queen* and the *Helyn J.*, both my parents' families were tied to sailing. My mother didn't sail, but she came from a seafaring family in Delaware, with ship captains among her ancestors. On my father's side, a great-aunt named Frances Wemple was the most well known of our nautical family members on the Bay. She sailed a Sneakbox, a small boat developed in the 1920s for the shallow waters of Barnegat Bay. Gaff-rigged, 15 to 17 feet long, with swept-back centerboards, the Sneakboxes reigned supreme for a long time. Aunt Frances' Sneakbox had a sail dyed scarlet—and it must have struck terror in the hearts of her opponents, for she won everything. I don't remember Aunt Frances, but I do remember her trophies, boxes of them, from the 1920s and '30s.

Back then, the club where Aunt Frances sailed was the Polyhue Yacht Club, because each family with a boat had a different color sail. Families would take the train down from Jersey City or Newark or over from Philadelphia and race their Sneakboxes. But the club eventually went out of business, and in 1933, with hard times affecting the local residents as well as the rest of the country, the Polyhue Yacht Club was dissolved.

Butch Broome and I sail a Toms River Pram in 1958.

An Auspicious Beginning

At age six, I got to sail my first sailboat regatta. That fateful first race was onboard a Sneakbox in a regatta called Hotaling Trophy, which is a big event on the Toms River. Now the Sneakboxes tend to be leaky, so as the junior member of the crew sailing with two other kids in their late teens, I was given three jobs. First, don't ask any dumb questions. Second: "Here is a bucket, here is a sponge; the boat leaks so you are going to keep it dry." And third: "Here is the course chart; when we get to a buoy you are going to tell us what buoy we go to next."

Now on the Toms River, they didn't set nifty windward-leeward courses with special buoys like they do in the modern era of racing. The course was around a series of channel markers and buoys set up around the Toms River and Barnegat Bay. You randomly sailed from one buoy to the next, so you were never quite sure where you were heading without your trusty course chart.

So off we went. There were 40 boats, and I'll never forget my first mark, in my first race. We rounded in the lead—and I had done my jobs. I had not said a peep upwind and the boat was bone dry. Everything was going great. But then the skipper asked me: "What's the next mark of the course?" So I reached into my pocket to get the course chart out, and instantly had this sinking feeling. My pocket was empty. Somehow, the paper chart that had been folded up in my pocket had fallen overboard. We went to the wrong mark and lost the race.

Needless to say, I never got to sail with those guys again. They were mad! However, that first race taught me a valuable lesson that extended itself throughout my career: you always have to know where you are going. I also learned that you really need a goal. So that early experience taught me the value of having a direction and a goal—and it taught me something else: what you learn in a sailboat race is far more important than how you do. It is a philosophy that has always served me well.

My father Tom and I in 1962 in front of my new Penguin named *Pea Nut*.
He loved sailing and encouraged me to pursue the sport.

I enjoy a single-handed afternoon sail on the Toms River in 1963.

The members disbanded, but their sailing continued. They kept on sailing and entertaining, now at their homes and on the beach. By the close of the '30s, the old yacht club building was being restored and in 1947, the club was reborn as the Beachwood Yacht Club—which is where I spent my summers as a youth.

The clubhouse was nothing special, compared to the "rich" clubs in the area. It had no heat and it wasn't insulated, but in the early 1960s, when my father was commodore, a small group of people dedicated themselves to creating good activities for junior sailors. Most of those club members had lived through the Great Depression and World War II, and helped create the baby boom. So they made sure we all had things to do. There were social events almost every night. So while we did not have a grand clubhouse or an illustrious club history that reached back into the 1800s, we did have a lot of hot, scrappy sailors and a summertime junior sailing program with 150 kids in it.

I did not take to sailing right away. I distinctly remember being afraid of the "low side," or the leeward side closest to the water when the wind heels the boat over. I crewed for older skippers for several years, but at age 11, I got my own boat: a great dinghy called a Penguin. You could build them yourself. They were cheap and competitive and there were hundreds of fleets all around the country.

Having my own boat changed the whole sailing dynamic for me. I progressively got more and more involved in sailing and was lucky to grow up on a body of water where the competition is well organized.

It's extraordinary that so many yacht clubs occupy the precious waterfront property of Barnegat Bay. It would be virtually impossible to start a club from scratch in today's regulatory, high-cost world. But happily, for thousands of members, 13 unique clubs grace the shores of this 40-mile-long stretch of water.

By nature, yacht clubs are tribal. The clubs of the Bay are an eclectic collection of architectural gems, each with its own personality. Members feel comfortable at their own clubs and—not surprisingly—friendly rivalries develop.

This inter-club racing was taking place years before the clubs of the Bay were organized into an official circuit. In 1914, Seaside Park Yacht Club Commodore Herman Muller called a meeting with members of three other clubs to explore organizing an association to both foster and unify racing on Barnegat Bay. Subsequently, the Barnegat Bay Yacht Racing Association (BBYRA) was formed.

The association began organizing a weekly yacht racing circuit, which survives to this day. The junior sailors of my day had sailing lessons or practiced racing every day. On weekends, BBYRA held competitions on Saturday, with the race committee always out in full regalia of white ducks, blue blazers, and yachting caps. On Sunday you raced at your own club. So as I grew older, the standard routine for me was participating in the Bay races on Saturday at whichever club was hosting the regatta. In the morning, most of the kids would race in Penguins and Sneakboxes. In the afternoon, the breeze would come up and the adults would compete. If you were a good enough young sailor, you might crew for them.

Along with other sports, the kids who lived near Beachwood got involved in the typical kid mischief, including me. There was a bad influence down the street named Tommy. One summer, we ran around putting firecrackers in mailboxes. And when the firecracker went off in somebody's mailbox, what happened is the lid opened and smoke came out. And that was that. Well, one day we got hold of an M80. Now an M80 has about twice the power punch of a cherry bomb. And we tried the M80 inside a mailbox, but instead of the door opening up and smoke coming out, the whole mailbox just launched into smithereens, went up about 30 feet, blew apart, and was just simply gone. That scared us to death and we ran

My father's beloved *African Queen* filled with water during Hurricane *Hazel* in 1954. He is preparing to pump the boat out from the rowboat at left.

away, but just our luck, an old lady looking out her window saw us running away. She called the police and the cops came to our house. When they came, I admitted to the crime and took my punishment. Tommy lied about it, about the fact that he was even there. So he was in trouble for a lot more: blowing up a mailbox with an M80, then lying about it.

That was a traumatic experience, and I did my penance. Putting that M80 in the mailbox cost me two weeks of working in the yard. But that wasn't the end of it, and the incident has lived with me for a very long time. In 2007, when my dad was on his deathbed, we reminisced about all the events of the years gone by and he returned to that dreaded day: "Hey, remember that time you put the firecracker in the mailbox . . . So don't put one in a mailbox. It causes a lot of angst."

By my early teens, competitive sailing had begun to take up a significant part of my time. As a teen, I never felt like I was part of the "in" crowd. I always felt I was a little bit on the outs. Maybe that is the insecurity of being a teenager. At the same time, I wasn't doing well in school sports. I tried everything. But sailing is what I gravitated to. The summer I turned 13, I started doing better and better in sailing and I started to like it more. And an interesting thing happened: I started sailing 12 months a year, crewing for people in Penguins, or on a high-performance dinghy called an International 14, or on other small boats. I became the kid who was always available to go sailing.

It was unique in those days, to sail year-round. We'd go out on the Schuylkill River in Philadelphia in January and freeze our asses off. But after putting together a few seasons like that, I accrued a lot of time on boats with some very good sailors.

One was my friend Billy Campbell. As a junior sailor, Bill was a superstar of the BBYRA circuit, and his father, Cliff, was one of the greats: a talented racer who won the Mallory Cup, the National U.S. Men's Championship. I hung around with the Campbell family a lot. In 1965 I started crewing on an E Scow with Tom Chapman. He was one of the fastest sailors on the Bay and helped me with a number of techniques on steering that are with me to this day. I also sailed with Sam Merrick, a lobbyist in Washington, D.C. He invited me to race with him on his E Scow on the Bay, and I sailed with him throughout my high school years. He was very methodical on the boat but had a natural touch at the helm, and his style was quiet and determined. He set goals but was pragmatic at the same time, and he helped me develop my skill as a tactician.

When I first started sailing with Sam, I was the $10 extra on the crew, kind of the fourth guy. But then it became apparent that I was doing well in my Penguin,

After teaching sailing all summer, I used all $400 that I earned to buy this 1940 Packard. This picture was taken in my family's driveway in Money Island.

Commodore Clifford A. Warren presents me with the Powell Trophy as Outstanding Junior Sailor on Barnegat Bay in 1966. It was a defining moment in my young career.

so he would ask me questions. Where do you think we should go? What do we do next? At first, I was just reporting on our performance, telling him how we were doing compared to other boats. And then I started focusing on the wind: where it was shifting to, where it was going to come from next. I learned to be ready with advice, for at any moment Sam could ask a question. The trick was to keep observing other competitors and to figure out how to pass them. It was like playing chess. Sam let me develop this new role as his trusted advisor, and the experience would prove invaluable as I graduated into the ranks of big-boat racing in the America's Cup.

I also sailed with Runyon Colie, Jr.—or "Runnie," as he was known. He was one of Sam's arch rivals on the Bay with a strong winning record. He won the Collegiate National Championships three times while studying at MIT in the late '30s, the International Penguin Championships eight times when the Penguin was the hottest class around, and, at age 47, the E Scow Nationals. He was always winning—so hanging around with him gave me good guidance.

I asked him about winning all those college nationals: What is your secret to winning? There was no magic, he told me. He simply told me to go around the buoys more than anybody else, and to keep trying. I took his advice to heart. I sailed around the buoys more than anyone and just kept plugging away.

So that is how the summers flowed all through my childhood and adolescent years. Sailing was something you automatically did when school ended, just like you played touch football or ice hockey during the winter. But looking back now, there was one year when everything seemed to come together. The summer of 1967, that was my turning point.

* * *

At the end of the 1966 racing season, the BBYRA named me Outstanding Junior Sailor of the Year. The recognition inspired me to spend even more time on the water. The award also gained the attention of the Toms River Yacht Club's junior sailing committee. They had an opening for an assistant instructor for the 1967 season and offered me the job. The members of the committee at the time were Jack Summerill, who chaired the committee, Drew Seibert, Jack Fellows, and Pete McLain—all prominent men in the community, accomplished professionals, and enthusiastic sailors.

But I had a secret fear. I was scared to death of speaking in public. If I had to get up and give a report in class, I was shaking in my boots. To overcome the problem I went looking for help.

I first asked my father, Are you ever nervous giving speeches? He told me the key to speaking was preparation. So I started writing detailed notes about how to sail and sought advice from the great Barnegat Bay sailors I had crewed for.

As a kid, I had a good rapport with adults. I was just at ease talking with them and could always find common ground. I started reading *Time* magazine when I was 12. At 15, I started reading *The New York Times* every day, a habit I still continue to this day. Those adults I looked up to were always available to answer my questions.

I used to hang out with my closest friend John Martin, whose mother Eleanor was a high school guidance counselor. She told me that enthusiasm was her secret to public speaking.

I noticed the speaking styles of others, like local sailor Jack Fellows, who told good short stories that always had a point. Using the combination of detailed preparation, enthusiastic delivery, and short stories, I was able to overcome my nervousness. Once I got into the job I was astounded to learn that kids actually listened. I could help them sail better—and my career promoting sailing was born.

In addition to teaching, I had my own racing, including winter frostbiting. In the Penguin, John Martin had been my regular crew, but after he went off to boarding school I had to transition to a new crew. I sailed with several different friends. John and I used to yell a lot. One time he told me if I shouted at him again he would punch me in the mouth. I didn't listen and continued barking. I'll

Bob Johnson and I capsized at a frostbite regatta on the Toms River in 1964. We were still laughing.

Long-time friend John Martin and I sailing at the 1966 International Penguin Championship off Little Egg Harbor, New Jersey.

never forget him spinning around and giving me a good shot. I never yelled at him again. With new crew now taking John's place, I learned to behave better.

Doing as much sailing as I was doing, getting my driver's license was a welcome rite of passage, which also happened in that summer of '67 when I turned 17. No longer would I have to rely on my dad to take me to regattas, or to organize a ride with an older skipper with a car. As soon as I had that license in hand I asked my dad, could I get a car? "You bet," he said. "All you have to do is pay for the car, pay for the insurance, and pay for the gas and you can have a car." How, I wondered, will I be able to do that?

But I was entrepreneurial and always had some kind of job: working in a drugstore, doing deliveries, taking on a newspaper route, cutting lawns, teaching sailing. So I revved up my savings and started hunting for cars. There were lots of them for sale, but one in the advertisements struck me as just right: a 1940 Packard, a 120 businessman's coupe with a big grill, running boards, and a straight 6 with a shift on the column. It cost $400, which was a lot for my earning potential back then (let's just say a $10 day was a good day). The Packard was a character car and I loved it. It shook when you started it up: turn the key on, push the starter button, and then came the rumbling noise. That was my first car and that was how I got around to regattas with my crew. It was quite a scene.

One of those events was a spring regatta on Long Island Sound, in Sea Cliff, New York. I fouled out twice in the five-race regatta, and a competitor, Graham Hall, suggested I go for a good average instead of taking so many risks. That strategy earned me the BBYRA Intermediate Penguin Championship later that summer. The philosophy would serve me well through collegiate racing and beyond.

There was a lot of competition around the Bay. The best junior sailors included my friend Billy Campbell, Tad LaFountain, Debbie Freeman, Jane Bance, Henry Bossett, and Robin Brown. In June 1967, my parents gave me a new Penguin: #8629, built by Beaton. There were several Penguin builders, but Beaton was making fast boats back then, even if they were expensive. My new boat cost $860, and I bought my own sail for $110.

The Penguin was the most competitive dinghy class in America at the time. In 1966 Cliff Campbell won the International Penguin Championship. He set a high standard for all of us to follow. In the eliminations for the Sears Cup—a national championship for triplehanded junior racers that you had to qualify for—Kathy Weber and I crewed for Billy Campbell in a Barnegat 17 that summer. Tad La-Fountain of the Bay Head Yacht Club clobbered us and nine other boats on the

Roadblock or Inspiration?

There was a time when Mrs. Thain, my second-grade teacher, was the bane of my existence. She had short cropped gray hair and no tolerance for second graders and considered me a dreamer and a drifter, which I guess I was because my report cards got progressively worse that year. I ended up failing second grade. As a repeat second grader, I can still remember the taunts of the other kids: getting hit in the head with lunchboxes and being called "Dummy!" That affected me, but in the long run it impacted me in a good way. I had to work hard at excelling, to escape that phase of being picked on. After that, I always did well in school. I had been young for my grade, but after being left behind, I was one of the older kids in my class. There are probably a lot of kids these days who are not ready to go to the next level, and maybe we should do more of this practice today. On the one hand, I have the scars of being taunted—because let's face it, kids are cruel. On the other, I developed a strong desire to excel at a very early age. So I don't know whether to remember Mrs. Thain as the mean second-grade teacher who left me behind, or the one who inspired me to work very hard.

downwind legs and became the Bay champion. It was a good lesson in humility. Billy and I decided to work on our downwind sailing and went out and practiced for the next couple weeks.

In addition to racing my own boat, I continued to crew for Sam Merrick, racing on his E Scow with John Spark and Bert Bricker. They were two of the best crew on the Bay. John had an incredible work ethic, which I admired and tried to copy, and Bert was a free spirit in the mold of John Lennon. Sam kept encouraging me to call tactics and trusting my advice. We ended up third for the season and won the Eastern E Scow Championship. It was the highlight of my sailing career at that point, to win a regatta with Sam against so many great sailors.

And then in 1967, the America's Cup captured my attention. I read everything I could about U.S. skipper Bus Mosbacher and his tactician George O'Day, a team of two who worked like one. O'Day's strengths were meticulous organization, an even temper, and a sense of humor. Their example encouraged me to keep track of my racing record, and I started keeping notebooks where I recorded every

REGATTA	No. of days	Water	Date	No. of boats	Finishes	Place
NEW YEARS	3	Dec. 31 Jan 1,2	68		1- 22,8,25 2- 19,57,21 3- 22,21,21,27	19
SETUAKA	1	Jan. 28	13		8,4,56,7	5
Schuylkill	3	FEB 12	11	7 7 races		8
		FEB 27	8	6 5 races		
		MAR. 12	12	4 4 races		
SEA CLIFF	2	MAR 18 19	23		4,6,2,3	2
SEA CLIFF	1	APR. 1	25		13/DSQ 2, 5,13, 4/DSQ	15
CENTERPORT	1	APR. 8	29		24, 22,15	22
SHEEPSHEAD BAY	1	APR. 22	15		2,4,3,4	2
SPRING SERIES	5	APR. 30 MAY 7 APR.	17		2,5,4,5 ——RAIN——	4
		MAY 14	18		4,5,8	4
DOWNER REGATTA	2	MAY 20	13		6-2-9-8-8	7
Spring Series	1	MAY 28	16		3-3-9	3
Regionals CAPE MAY	1	June 3	13		4,4,5,5,4	5

BBYRA REGATTA CHAMPIONSHIP

REGATTA	No. of days	Water	Date	No. of boats	Finishes	Place
BAY HEAD	1	Jun. 24	16		2 Cancelation	2
IrIYC	1	July 1	19		11 cancelation	11
MYC	1	July 8	32		4	4
IRYC	1	July 15	17		2	2
MRYC	1	Jul 22	22		4	4
S.A.YC.	1	Aug. 19	20		2	2
L.Y.C.		Aug. 26			Cancelled	-
S.P.Y.C.		Sept. 2	22		3	3

FINAL FINISH ①

SUNDAY SERIES

REGATTA	No. of days	Water	Date	No. of boats	Finishes	Place
BYC	1	Jun 25	5		2,2	2
BYC	1	July 2	9		2,2	1
BYC	1	July 9	9		4	4
BYC	1	Aug 6	+8		5,2	3
BYC	1	Aug. 20	8		6,2	4
BYC	1	Aug. 27	8		DSQ, 2	9
BYC						

FINAL ③

REGATTA	No. of days	date	Finishes	No. of boats	Place
A. C.	2	SEPT 20-Oct	12,20,21,13,3	37	16
SAILING CLUB	1	SEPT 22	1-2	6	1
PACKANACK	1	OCT. 14	8	14	8
Gobbler Bowl	1	Nov. 26	2-2-4	12	3
Family Day	1	July 4	3, 1, 2	4	1
Spring/Fall Series	1	SEPT 24	3,4, 5, 2	14	2
Fall Series	1	OCT. 8	2,3,21	15	1
Fall Series	1	OCT. 15	6, DNF, DNS, 14	18	8
Fall S.	1	OCT. 22	7,7,5	11	
Fall S.	1	Oct 29	4,3,5,8	16	5
		Final ⑥			
Bay Head	1	NOV. 26	2-2-4	12	3
Bay Head	1	Dec. 10	5-5-2-1	8	3
				④ Final	

SAILING FOR FUN — RACE

Easter	APR. 15 MAR APR. 15	with Debbie Freeman	
SAILING CLUB	MAY 5	with Kathryn Weber	
E BOAT	MAY 27	with MERRIES	
E boat	June 17	D 2	
			No. boats
crewing Fnl.	NOV. 14 '75	2-2-3-3-2	4 2

CREWING

REGATTA	CLASS	DATE	FINISH	NO. OF BOATS
LARCHMONT	INTERCLUB	MAR 4	6/35	35
TRYC-IMYC	AUXILIARY	Jun. 18	2	29
BAY HEAD	E SCOW	JUN. 24	2	19
Island Hights	E SCOW	July 1	3	15
TRYC-IMYC	AUXILIARY	JULY 2	2	35
MAN. Y.C.	E SCOW	July 8	4	16
TRYC IMYC	AUX.	July 16	1	20
IMYC	E SCOW	July 15	DSQ	14
MRYC	E SCOW	July 22	DSQ 2	17
				11
INVITATIONALS	ES SCOW	July 30	5 6,5,1	25
EASTERNS	E- SCOW	AUG. 3-5	① 7,2	22
L.E.H.Y.C.	E-SCOW	AUG. 12-13	2,3	21
S.A.YC.	E-SCOW	AUG. 19	2	16
L. YC.	E-SCOW	AUG. 26	1	14
TRYC-IMYC	AUX.	AUG. 27	DNF	
S.P.YC.	SCOW	SEP. 2	10 ⑤ F3 MAR	14
L.B.J. R.	AUX.		⑥	
NAT'S	SCOW	7th	4,11,7,8	43

I started keeping track of my days on the water along with regatta results at the age of 16.

detail about my racing and my finishes. Young athletes of a certain era may have wanted to be like the great Michael Jordan, to "be like Mike." I wanted to be like Mosbacher and O'Day. They were as big to me as Hall of Fame football player Joe Namath was to many others.

Dick Curry, a hot local Penguin sailor I had raced with, told Graham Hall, the SUNY Maritime College sailing coach, about my improving racing results. I was quite flattered to receive a letter from Graham about the possibility of attending Maritime. They had an active sailing team that featured two All-American sailors, Rick Meyerose and Art Messinger. I aspired to be like them, and Maritime became my first choice.

On the advice of Spark and Bricker I decided to try out for a high school sport. They felt it was important to participate in a variety of activities. Bill Campbell was a great baseball and basketball player. Tad LaFountain played soccer and tennis. I needed my own second sport. But which one?

I had tried cross-country as a freshman and found it boring. Even though I was intrigued by football, it conflicted with sailing; plus I was way too skinny. I got cut from the basketball team every time I tried out. John suggested wrestling. On paper I wasn't a good fit because I was tall and thin and had no experience. I interviewed with the wrestling coach John Nemetz, who was aware of my sailing activities, and he gave me a shot. I should note that Toms River High School was a wrestling powerhouse. It seemed as if half of the team members were district champions. I showed up for every practice, worked hard, and made the team.

Scholastic wrestling is a very clean sport because you are matched up against someone your own weight, there is a referee watching every match, and the sport is very tactical. I found it to be like sailing. The key to learning moves is repetition. Wrestling to me was exactly like match-racing, when two boats race against each other. The coaches were an amazing help and, most importantly, they cared.

The culture in Toms River puts a premium on junior athletics. It is no accident that the Toms River Little League won the World Series in 1998. That year, the area produced four of the top five finishers in the Optimist Dinghy Atlantic Coast Championship, the Optimist being one of the most prolific one-person dinghies for junior sailors and a class that keeps producing some of the world's top racers.

In my first year of wrestling I became a JV starter by the end of the season. I must have been overhyped trying to get an advantage during a match. Soon after, the coach stopped an entire practice to demonstrate to the whole team of over a hundred wrestlers why my method wasn't working. He said, "If you want to get an arm you just take it in one smooth move."

I was the tall, skinny wrestler in the front row at Toms River High School in 1967.

Even though the demonstration was embarrassing, the concept went off like a lightbulb in my head. I thought of parallels in sailing: when you need speed, just put the bow down. Making your actions deliberate and smooth was a realization that dramatically changed my wrestling and sailing careers.

In my senior year, I began wrestling with the varsity team and had several wins. But I will never forget the agony of being pinned in front of a sell-out hometown crowd against our archrival, Middletown High School. My opponent was a state champion. That loss helped me handle some big sailing defeats later. You simply get off the mat and try again.

In wrestling I found the drills, pressure, tactics, coaching, and physical training to be analogous to sailing. Thanks to my two seasons on the wrestling team, the help of the many mentors I was lucky to get to know, and the loyal support of my sailing crews, the seeds were sewn. All those lessons and experiences of 1967 had built a foundation, and after that summer, I was ready to take on the sailing world.

But at age 17, I didn't see everything coming together so neatly. I knew sailing had become my priority but I hadn't processed just how that happened until years later. Having reached 50, I reflected back and the landscape of my youth became clearer. I could see the peaks and valleys and the turning points in my career—most notably those lessons of 1967.

I tell you this not simply to tell you my story: I hope the tale inspires young sailors to define their goals, and I hope it inspires people in a position to serve as mentors to young people.

I remember watching a college regatta as an adult, noticing how smoothly the coed teams maneuvered their dinghies. Every time they athletically rolled the boat in a roll tack, the move was crisp. Their boat speed was always maxed, their dock landings were perfect, and, best of all, their attitude was focused. I wondered: Does talent like that develop naturally? Or does it only emerge when the circumstances are just right?

I am standing on the left with Willie de Camp, Sam Merrick, and John Spark.
We won the E Scow Eastern Championship in 1967.

Almost any young sailor can become a successful sailor regardless of natural talent, but there are many sailors who have that extra juice to become champions. But without help, few will go far. I have had mentors in my life, and I now know that a mentor can make all the difference.

You don't have to be a superstar to be an effective mentor. Far from it. Your first job is simply setting a good example. I've found that you can give your protégé a reason to work hard by getting them to set goals. A brief talk followed by an encouraging letter initiates the process. Then occasional checkups reinforce the message. When the young sailor starts asking questions, you'll know that forward progress has begun. That's when you can suggest your sailor keep records, so lessons learned will be remembered.

Once the first seeds are sown, the next steps come from the young sailor. But you can encourage your protégé to ask for help, to read about technique, and to experiment on the water in disciplined practice sessions. High but attainable short-term goals measure progress. I define "short term" as under two months. Offer case studies as examples of how successful sailors have achieved long-term goals.

I believe that when setting goals, learning should be the priority—not winning.

Many young sailors give up during times of adversity. They take errors hard. You can help by pointing out specific problems. During a regatta, ask one simple question at a time and allow a sailor to answer for himself what could be done better on the racecourse next time, for too much input creates confusion.

As a mentor, always be calm, as if you expect improvement. It's okay to be a cheerleader, but flatten out the inevitable rollercoaster ride by not getting too excited over a win or too depressed during defeat. Remember, winning is the elimination of errors. Teach a sailor to thrive on working out of bad positions: after a slow start, after making a penalty turn, on the wrong side of a windshift. It takes practice to stay focused in these situations.

There is a fine but dangerous line between helpful coaching and pushing too hard, for if expectations are too high at an early age, young sailors can reject sailing. It's healthy to encourage a young sailor to play other sports; lessons learned in other sports are often analogous to sailing—just as I found when I started to wrestle. It's you or the other guy out on the mat. You either win or you lose, and there is no halfway. Team sports provide good lessons too, as the discipline needed to play these sports is helpful when sailing as part of a crew.

Once the seed of desire starts growing, young sailors need help organizing their regatta schedule. Recommend they test their skills on different waters and that they sail both small boats and larger boats to broaden their experience. Long-term variety keeps interest high and builds new skills, while singlehanded sailing always sharpens skills. In fact, to prepare for big-boat racing, I often sail my singlehanded Laser to get in tune with the wind and the water.

Forward progress may be slow, or even nonexistent at times. But let your protégé know there are times when the only important thing is to keep plugging away. If you detect burnout or rejection, it's okay to take a break from sailing or to change boats, crews, or venues.

I am proud to have mentored some top sailors, like Terry Hutchinson, a collegiate All-American from Annapolis who matured into a strong talent in the America's Cup arena, and All-American Buzz Reynolds.

There are also times when sailors in the public eye don't realize the impact they have on others. I was reminded of that during the 1992 America's Cup in

After landing on the aircraft carrier *Abraham Lincoln*, our ESPN crew Jamie Reynolds, me, Jed Drake, and Jeff Zachary had a great two days shooting our version of the film *Top Gun*.

San Diego, during a middle-of-the-night shoot for ESPN, on the aircraft carrier *Abraham Lincoln*. It was that time period of about two weeks between the end of the Challenger Trials and the beginning of the America's Cup Finals. Even though we were between racing series, we still had a half-hour weekly show to produce for ESPN—so what do you cover? Our producer Jed Drake came up with a good idea, to compare an America's Cup skipper with a Top Gun naval aviator. Are their attributes the same?

We arranged for me and a camera crew to go out on the *Abraham Lincoln*. Now this was pretty exciting, because I actually got to do a takeoff and landing on the carrier. So here I am, sitting in this jet, getting ready for takeoff, and—as I'm sure you can imagine—my heart is pumping hard. Next to me in the pilot's seat is a 28-year-old lieutenant. We are about to take off, and he turns to me and says in his headset: "Is this your first time?" I admit, "Yeah, it's my first time." And he nods his head and says, "Hey, mine too!" My heart skipped a beat—and then he laughed and told me, "Nah. I've done 238 launches so don't worry about a thing." And off we went.

I could see quickly that there are plenty of skills that these pilots and Cup skippers share: good hand-eye coordination, working well on a team with lots of people behind it, using technology artfully. And of course aviation and sailing have a lot in common—with hydrodynamics for boats and aerodynamics for planes.

We spent the night out on the carrier, which was great fun. The second day we were up late at night to watch the night operations. I stood out on the platform with the Landing Safety Officer, known as the LSO, and as the jets came in their wingtips passed only about 15 feet from where we were standing. Pretty exciting stuff.

After four of the jets came in, we had a pause in the action, and the LSO said to me: "Hey, I remember you, you're Gary Jobson . . . Now you don't remember this, but you came to my high school and talked about the Naval Academy, and I was so inspired by your talk that I ended up applying to the Academy and I got an appointment and here I am today, flying these jets. I never would have done this had it not been for your inspirational talk—and I feel badly because I never got around to saying thank you. So tonight, let me offer you my sincere thanks." While it was nice to receive this young man's thanks, the larger outcome of the night was an important realization about the powerful effect we can all have on each others' lives.

I realized how important it is to be inspirational in life.

The Barnegat Bay Yacht Racing Association Champions in 1967. My friend Tad LaFountain,
is in the first row, far right. Cliff Campbell is next to him. I am in the second row.

*   *   *

So in that summer of 1967, I turned a new corner of my life and learned the important lessons that would prepare me for my sailing career—thanks to a number of inspiring adults who helped me reach that point. I can tell you from experience that when you actively mentor a young person by opening doors and providing thoughtful encouragement, there are no limits to what that person can achieve. In the end, both of you end up winning.

.4.
TAKING A FLYER

 The America's Cup in 1977 changed my life. On one hand, winning the Cup was simply a victory at yet another regatta—and by that point in my sailing career, I had victories to my name at many regattas. But it was the *America's Cup*, and winning with Ted Turner that elevated my status in the sailing world. As one friend joked, I became an instant expert. I knew just as much about racing sailboats before the Cup compared to after our win, but that was the perception—and it launched me into a different category as a sailor.

In reality, however, the Cup win was like gold dust: it added some shine and shimmer, but what could you do professionally with a victory at the America's Cup? There were no instant jobs awaiting former America's Cup tacticians, no executive recruiters chasing professional sailors, no speaking circuits waiting to plug in an "instant expert" like me.

So when it came time to go back to work after the Cup, I returned to my roots and accepted a job as head sailing coach at the U.S. Naval Academy in Annapolis. After graduating from Maritime College in 1973—where I was a three-time All-American and twice named College Sailor of the Year—I coached at the Merchant Marine Academy in Kings Point, New York. The 1977 Cup was an interlude, albeit a grand and exciting one. But after our victory in Newport, I came back down to Earth and returned to college coaching.

Collegiate racing, organized by the Inter-Collegiate Sailing Association (ICSA), is the training ground of some of the best sailors in the United States. It began in the late 1890s on an informal basis, and organized racing started in 1928. As I write today, over 200 schools have sailing programs and the circuit is not unlike a garden: mix the right soil and light with the right plants and you can grow super-size talents. A collegiate sailor, "will typically be in 500 races per year—so with that many starts, their boathandling, tactics, understanding of the rules, and mark roundings become exceptional," said Coach Pat Healy, who was coach at the Naval Academy when I returned in 2001 to visit and practice with the team. Most college sailors enter with 80 percent of the skills they need, but it is the repetition that takes them to the next level.

College sailing also teaches versatility. Every weekend you race a different boat, on different waters—some of which are tricky venues to sail in. What is best of all, competitors rotate boats for every race, and you learn to make the most of a slow boat when it is your turn to sail it.

Look at the roster of U.S. sailors who have represented the country in the Olympic Games and you will see proof of the collegiate training ground in every quadrennium. Each U.S. Sailing Team that competes at the Games has a strong concentration of collegiate veterans, and the 2008 team that headed to China was no different, including sailors from college powerhouses like Yale, Old Dominion, Georgetown, and Tulane. But there are caveats. The style of boats used in collegiate racing favor sailors sized for small dinghies, as opposed to the different-sized crews needed to man the diverse lineup of Olympic-class dinghies and keelboats. And the training methods are different: today's Olympians train like professional athletes, with targeted training regimes and a strategic lineup of key regattas and physical conditioning to get their bodies to the weight and shape they need them to be in for their particular class, while college racers hone their skill simply by lots and lots of sailing,

When I began my collegiate sailing career at Maritime College in September 1969, I arrived with a lot of confidence in my ability and broke onto the scene hot as a freshman. Looking back, I was even a little cocky. Back on Barnegat Bay, Runnie Colie had given me that key advice about mastering my skills: just sail around the buoys more than anyone else. That is exactly what I did at Maritime, under the guidance of a great coach, Graham Hall. Between September 1969 and September 1971, I spent 492 days on the water.

By graduation, I had raced 2,000 races. As a point of comparison, I have only raced 3,000 races since my graduation in '73.

After I arrived at school and settled in, I felt this college located in the shadow of the Throgs Neck Bridge was where I belonged. My dorm overlooked the water that edged the campus, and my view was impressive—a seascape of the East River, backdropped by the Manhattan skyline. I had my most prized passions in that room: my lava lamp and my stereo. Music was important, and each night at 10 pm, I tuned into WNEW to hear the smooth voice of Alison Steele, "The Nightbird," roll out her daily mix of music and philosophy. The room did have

Wayne Andrews and I won A Division at the College Nationals in 1972.
This picture was taken on Mission Bay, near San Diego.

a certain aroma, though; the sailing gear of that day did not have the breathable fabrics we have today, so even after a few days of trying to dry my wet sailing gear, my room still smelled.

The school's fleet of boats was right outside my dorm, and I sailed every afternoon and every weekend—spending time working on boat handling by sailing continuous figure eights, practicing my timed runs to the starting line, and tacking and jibing endlessly. Even to this day I find crisp roll tacks, the athletic "rolling" of a boat from one tack and onto the other, one of the highlights of life and, for me, the essence of being on the water. Figure eights around a set pair of buoys gave me practice jibing, tacking, doing windward roundings and leeward roundings, and accelerating. Those simple drills gave me an edge.

Plus, I was getting a first-rate education. The school had only 600 students when I attended, so it was small and the faculty paid attention to you. There were two ways to go at Maritime: Deck or Engine. Under the Engine category came naval architecture and engineering; the deck officers focused on meteorology, navigation, oceanography, and running the deck. I went the Deck route. Back then there was no GPS, and Loran-C barely worked, so you had to use a sextant and become proficient at celestial navigation. I got a lot of practice in the summer. As deck officers in training, we did a summer cruise that lasted about six weeks. My most impressionable was my first year, as a freshman. We went transatlantic to Europe on the *Empire State IV*, a 490-foot troop transport vessel, stopping in Copenhagen and outside Paris and Rome. We ran the ship and navigated, and I enjoyed it immensely.

Graham Hall was a great coach. He was organized. His basic focus was fundamentals: keep your speed up, tack on the headers, time your run to the start. There was no magic to Graham's formula: just keep plugging away.

But in my freshman year, as much as the collegiate scene was a good launch pad for my sailing, I had a hang up. Billy Campbell, who was now sailing at the Naval Academy, was always a step ahead of me.

He was a great friend and we had grown up together and sailed against each other many times, but I never beat him—not on the Toms River, not on Barnegat Bay, not in a single race. Billy was beyond belief. During my first year at Maritime, the Freshman Championships were coming up and I confided in Coach Hall I was nervous because Bill Campbell would be competing.

We would race Interclub Dinghies—a soft-chine boat of 11 feet, 5 inches that is the most perfect boat in the world to roll tack. I had a lot of time in that little boat.

SUNY Maritime College Class of 1973 lined up for a picture during Indoctrination Week, September 1969.

"Well, I'll tell you why you are going to beat him," said Coach Hall, when I confided in him about the regatta. "You are going to start better. He doesn't know how to do timed runs, and you are going to do this better. Plus, he has never sailed these boats before, and the East River has a lot of current . . ."

The start in sailboat racing is critical, and you have to time your route so you hit the starting line—the imaginary line that stretches between the Race Committee boat and a buoy, called the pin end—at the exact right moment. It is a difficult task to master. You have to contend with current, windshifts, the traffic of other boats, and the intense pressure of knowing that the five minutes before the starting gun can make or break your entire race. But Graham Hall had trained me with a secret

Attitude Counts

This regatta was going to be intense. Only two boats from the Middle Atlantic District would qualify for the Intercollegiate Singlehanded Championship. The elimination series was held on my home waters off SUNY Maritime College—so I had a homecourt advantage since I knew the vagaries of the East River currents. But for this regatta we had a nifty new boat called the Laser. At 6 foot 2 and 178 pounds, I was the right size for this boat, but I was unfamiliar with the Laser, and so were my competitors. So as I sailed out to the starting line, I knew I was in for intense competition complicated by the currents of the East River and a brand-new boat.

I lined up for the start in a brisk April breeze, but when the gun went off my foot just missed the hiking strap in the cockpit and over the side I went. I capsized—and that water was cold! By the time I got the boat back upright, I was freezing and in last place. What a disaster. I came back to the dock to rotate boats, changed into dry clothes, then headed back out for the second race. I decided to use a starting technique that had served me well: I'd sail to the line on port tack while most of the other boats would be charging to the line on starboard tack, the right-of-way tack, and I'd hunt for a hole in the line, fit my boat into that space, tack, and gain a good position at the start. But as weapon, a way of timing my run to the line that has never failed me since—in everything from small dinghies to big Maxi boats manned by an army of crew.

So I did that against Bill Campbell: placed my boat on the starting line at one minute to the start, sailed 26 seconds away, and with 34 seconds to the start I spun my boat—a maneuver I had timed down to 8 seconds—and then sailed the last 26 seconds to the line.

I ended up beating Billy Campbell in the championship. After all these years, it was the first time I ever beat him. That race broke the ice. After that, we had a great rivalry. I think the two of us were first or second in almost every college regatta we both competed in.

I made my port-tack approach, I somehow lost control of the hiking stick, the boat spun, and I slammed right into a starboard-tack boat. After the start, I did my penalty turns. By the time I unraveled the mess, I was once again in last place. Two races done, fourteen races to go, and I was in dead last.

I returned to the dock to rotate boats, and I was mad, completely distraught. Coach Hall pulled me aside and said, "Look, you have two problems. The first problem is, all you're thinking about is the final result and qualifying for the Championship. Instead, you should be thinking about one thing at a time. So I want you to go out there and the first thing is, just keep your feet under the hiking strap. And if you can do that, just don't hit anybody. And second, you need a better attitude. You're already in last and you've blown the regatta. You may as well forget about qualifying and just go out, have some fun, and keep the boat upright. And if you can do that, then when you come in for the next rotation, we'll talk more about strategy."

So I went back out with a renewed attitude, not worrying about qualifying because I was already in last place. And the darndest thing happened. I won the race. And I won the race after that, and the one after that, and the one after that. In fact, I won every race in the rest of the regatta. So I learned a very good lesson, that attitude counts. Concentrate on one thing at a time, never worry about the final result, and things will often go your way.

SUNY Maritime College Sailing Team at the Nationals in 1972 in San Diego. Our coach Graham Hall, who had a major influence on my career, stands on the left. My crew, Wayne Andrews, sits on the bar. Bob Martus, standing, was named to the All-American team twice.

The fact is, you only improve if you sail against strong competition. And in the early '70s, there was no shortage of great sailors in the collegiate ranks. Many of them have since gone on to make names for themselves in the sailing world: Bruce Nelson (University of Michigan), Augie Diaz (Tulane), Bill Campbell (Navy), Steve Cucchiaro (MIT), Derrick Fries (Michigan State), Jeff McDermaid (UC Irvine), Doug Rastello (USC), and Manton Scott (Tufts), who was tragically killed in 1973. The competition lifted everyone's game.

At Maritime, not only was I mastering the mechanics of sailing boats, but the mental side of the game was coming into clearer focus. By my sophomore year,

I knew my formula for success on the water: goal setting, practice, and good coaching. I set my goals in my second year at Maritime and wrote down these simple precepts:

- Set high goals
- Aggressive attacks
- Take it as it comes, but keep plugging
- All out—never halfway
- Never give in

During my first two years of college sailing, I frequently found myself in the protest room, where rules infractions on the racecourse are decided by a jury, not unlike a court of law. It took me a while to realize that no matter how "right" I felt, 50 percent of the time the protest went against me. Happily, the "720 rule" came into use during my college career. We all learned that if you were in a rules situation on the course, it was better to spin your boat 720 degrees during that race, as opposed to taking the situation to the jury and lose in the room. I learned to avoid confrontation and my results soared.

Besides the strides I was making in my sailing, there were a lot of other good things that happened at Maritime. For one, I met my future wife Janice Murphy there.

I couldn't help but notice her, a young pretty blonde with a brilliant smile. Her brother-in-law was an engineer on the Maritime ship, so she had reason to come to campus. One night, I couldn't believe my luck. She was at one of our mixers. But my hopes were dashed when I learned she was the date of one of my crew. I still couldn't get her out of my mind, and I'd bump into her at other mixers. There was one I remember a few years later (I can still smell the beer kegs). I chatted her up quickly, then went to get her a beer. But by the time I got back, she was already talking to another guy. Boy was she popular.

I kept trying, and eventually we started spending time together. She was from a different world, having grown up in a row house in Brooklyn as the youngest of six. She wasn't a sailor, so I showed her my world. I took her sailing on a Shields, a large, heavy, stable boat—just the two of us. And she took to the water. So I kept easing her into my high-performance sailing world, and each time we went out on the water we sailed a smaller, more athletic boat!

I was quick to get serious. By the time we got to that point in our relationship, I was 22 and she was only 19. Still, we started talking about getting engaged. I wanted to get her a ring in the worst way, but I had no money. Zero. But I remembered a guy in Greenwich Village who would make you a ring for $1 out of paper—and so I took him some duct tape and asked if he could do the same with tape. He did, and when I popped the question to Janice, she was thrilled (despite the ring).

By this time, she was a nursing student in Manhattan, and she was really directed: a good student and very organized. But her father was not in favor of the match, which was a hard thing to take as a young man asking for his daughter's hand in marriage. But I told him, "Well, we are going to get married anyway." And so on a hot August night in 1974, we walked under crossed swords to take our vows at a ceremony at Kings Point, where I went to coach after graduation.

During the years I went to Maritime, it was a great time to be living in New York City. While I was there, the Mets won the World Series, the Knicks won the NBA Championship in my freshman and senior years, and the New York Jets won the Super Bowl. For the Knicks, this was the era of Bill Bradley, Dave DeBusschere, Walt Frazier, and Willis Reed. And a team like that gave me a lot of inspiration. Ironically, in the late 1980s, I had an opportunity to sail with Walt Frazier, and I got to return the favor; he wrote in his book, "Gary, you are my inspiration to be on the water."

In May 1970, the Mid-Atlantic College Championship—a major regatta that drew 16 teams—was held at Maritime. I was a freshman and was sailing A-Division Varsity for the first time. Only the top two teams from this regatta would go on to the college nationals—so there is intense pressure to be number one or two. But I got plenty of inspiration on the eve of the regatta, when I went into Manhattan and to Madison Square Garden to see if I could get a seat at the NBA Championship.

This was during the Vietnam era, and the Garden had a policy that if you went to a certain entrance and there were extra tickets, they would let sailors and soldiers in uniform into the game. So I stood at the door in my dress khakis. There were only three or four military types and enough tickets for all of us. "We don't have any seats tonight, but there is some standing room so you guys can get a standing room pass," the attendant told us. I was in to watch the Knicks play the seventh game of the NBA championship against the Los Angeles Lakers.

The Knicks had been up 3–1 but lost two games in a row, mainly because their star center, Willis Reed, was hurt. The Lakers had Wilt Chamberlain.

As I walked into the arena, they were announcing the Knicks—and the team did a very clever thing. During the shoot around, as they now call it, Willis Reed didn't come out. He was injured so nobody thought he'd play. The national anthem was played and the team was introduced. But then, the search lights veered

78

In 1970, I ran into the locker room after the Knicks defeated the L.A. Lakers in Game 7 of the NBA Finals. I got the entire team's autographs as well as that of actor Dustin Hoffman. It was a bold move that would not be tolerated today by security.

away from the team on the bench, and landed on one lone figure in the dark, jogging out onto the court, Willis Reed himself! I thought the place was going to go nuts. I get tears in my eyes just thinking about that moment today.

Willis Reed lost the tap to Chamberlain, but somehow Bradley got the ball and they came down and Willis Reed sank the first bucket. And Madison Square Garden—the entire place, thousands of fans—went berserk. As it turned out, Reed injured himself and he got pulled out of the game right away, and he never played again. But the inspiration he provided the team was unbelievable.

I stood in the first quarter, then I spied a seat behind the bench and I went and sat there the rest of the game. Walt Frazier had 37 points that night, and I sat next to the actor Dustin Hoffman—both of us being where we probably weren't supposed to be, watching the whole spectacle. The Knicks won, and in those final moments the team ran out onto the court. I got so carried away with it all, I just ran out with them—and right into the locker room. You could get away with things like that in those days.

I was pretty inspired, and the next day I went out and raced in the Mid-Atlantic Championship. I was as high as a kite, and here I was, a freshman sailing A-Division Varsity for the first time. The powerhouse teams were there: the Naval Academy, Kings Point, and 13 others. I outsailed everybody, that weekend.

Those were great years, sailing every day in the shadow of the giant Throgs Neck Bridge. Those years made me the sailor I am today. I've since taken on more challenges, and experience has moved me up the learning curve. But the truth is, I was probably never sharper than the day I graduated as a college sailor.

* * *

The duties of a coach are broad and range from studying the opposition to enhancing the synergy of a crew. It's no accident that professional sports teams rely heavily on coaches. Sailing is more challenging because a coach can't communicate with a competitor during a race. In contrast, a football coach often calls every play. To me, this would take the fun out of sailing if decisions were made off the boat!

Sailing coaches have a ways to go to catch up to the sophistication of NBA or NFL coaching, but many people are making a living as a sailing coach. Today professionals work with young Opti sailors at yacht clubs and at the highly elevated collegiate level. Dozens of coaches assist crews at Key West Race Week, NOOD Regattas, and even in strictly amateur classes like the J105.

Sailors need to be cautious using a coach. An amateur class could easily drive competition away if the top group has coaches and the majority does not. From my helicopter vantage point over the racecourse in Key West, Chicago, Miami, and Newport this year, I was surprised at the large number of support craft floating in the starting area and around turning marks. This is an issue that race committees should consider when writing Sailing Instructions. Twenty coach boats racing to a windward mark affects the action.

Although I spent five years as a professional coach at Kings Point and the U.S. Naval Academy, in many ways I've been a coach on and off the water for 40 years. I have learned that you are most helpful as a coach when you give only a few tips at a time, always deliver your message in a calm manner, and ask questions. It's also helpful to get sailors on the same boat talking about specific techniques on how to improve. And sailors have to buy into the concept that coaching is helpful and therefore must be receptive to advice.

Crews can self coach too. Designate one member of the crew to take notes during the day. After returning to shore, talk over the list. If there is not an easy answer go seek advice. I find that most top sailors are happy to help. At the other end of the experience spectrum, young sailors need to be coached with great care. This is no more disheartening sight than an Opti parent (or coach) screaming at a confused 10-year-old. The priority for young sailors should be that what you learn is far more beneficial than how you finish.

I sailed a Formula S with the striped sail on the right in the 1975 Yachting Magazine One-of-a-Kind Regatta off Newport Beach, California.

The Laser: My Other Boat

I've sailed a lot of different boats in my career: Olympic-class dinghies all the way up to 12 Meters and 80-foot Maxis. But I've always considered the singlehanded Laser dinghy my "other boat"—for as I look back over the last four decades, the nifty Laser has been my one constant in sailing. I've always kept one at the ready, hanging in the garage.

My Laser career got off to a rocky start. In 1970, the Laser's designer, Bruce Kirby, gave a lecture at Maritime College. After the talk he invited me to Rowayton, Connecticut, to try out a new dinghy he had designed. Originally known as the Weekender, it was later renamed the Laser.

A few days later I found my way to Rowayton and launched Kirby's flat-decked dinghy off the float. The boat had the number 100 on the sail, which designated that it was the first one built. Within seconds, I felt at home. My 6-foot-2 frame seemed to fit the boat perfectly. How fast I sailed was an exact function of how hard I hiked, as I leaned out the windward side of the boat in a perennial sit-up position. Handling the mainsheet and tiller simultaneously seemed a little tricky, but the boat was simple and fast and gave me a sensation I'd never felt before on a dinghy. I could have sailed it all day.

On the way back to the dock I saw a stake in the water with an arrow on it. Was the arrow pointing toward a rock to avoid, or a deep channel? It turned out, it indicated a rock. I went inside the stake and promptly ran aground, taking a chunk out of the boat's centerboard. Back at the dock Mr. Kirby wasn't worried at all about the bruised centerboard. He really wanted to know how I liked the boat. "It's great," I said. Now, many years later, if he asked me the same question, I'd give him the same exact answer.

I have since had many memorable moments competing in a Laser, such as sailing the O'Day Singhelanded Championships in 1972 on San Francisco Bay, in strong afternoon thermals of 30 knots plus. Screaming into the reach mark, I was in third place and knew that a jibe would be very risky but the best way to turn the corner. I jibed and got my boom caught in the water and promptly capsized. I was incredibly upset, but then realized every other boat in the fleet had capsized as well. That heavy-air regatta would be won by the sailor who could right his boat the fastest after a capsize.

A few years later, the Laser class was getting ready for its first official World Championship. I was one of 188 competitors who descended onto the Royal Canadian Yacht Club in Toronto to sail in the class's North American Championships.

The top four boats would qualify for the Worlds in Bermuda—and the competition was intense and came down to the last race. During the pre-race tune up I noticed that boats coming out of the port side of the course were always gaining and crossing ahead of the boats on starboard. I figured out that a weird wave pattern made steering difficult on starboard tack. About three minutes before the start, I broke away from most of the fleet that was clearly maneuvering to start near the starboard end. At the gun, I flipped over to port tack and crossed the entire fleet by six lengths. It was one of the most thrilling moments of my sailing career. I went on to race in Bermuda, finishing a respectable 11th.

Recently, I entered a Laser Master's Regatta (I am actually a Grand Master). By that time, sailors had discovered many new, cool ways to rig the boat, so I picked up a tuning guide to figure it all out. With my boat on the dolly, I laid out the printed instructions and started leading the lines. I noticed a competitor video recording my procedure. "What are you up to?" I asked him. "Oh," he replied, "I just thought it would be fun to show my fleet how you need instructions to rig a Laser." Ouch!

No matter where you sail there is usually a Laser fleet nearby. Many of the competitors don't sail any other boat, yet they are very competitive and there is a special camaraderie that exists amongst Laser sailors.

Today I enjoy daysailing a Laser as much as racing it. To push away from the dock and trim in gives me the same thrill I had in 1970, when I first test drove Bruce Kirby's Weekender. Leaning out against the hiking straps gives me a sense of power, strength, and freedom. Lasers are forever.

I sailed my Laser, *Barnegat Arrow*, at the North Americans in Toronto, Canada.
I finished 4th out of 188 boats, which qualified me for the Worlds in Bermuda
later that year. I would finish 11th out of 127 boats in Bermuda.

I endorse the concept of using a coach, particularly during practice sessions. But sailors improve most rapidly by making their own decisions on the water, while using a coach to recognize trends and give helpful ideas.

* * *

College sailing is a vital part of the sport, and it has always been an important chapter in my life. But after I returned from racing in the America's Cup and started coaching at the Naval Academy, I knew deep down I was in a rut. I always had an entrepreneurial streak, and I wondered when the time would be right for me to strike out on my own and use my sailing as the basis for my own business.

On those days when I felt too deeply entrenched in the intercollegiate racing scene, I thought back to the day in 1976 when I bumped into Ted Turner at the Chicago Yacht Club. We were there for the annual meetings of US SAILING, the sport's national governing body. It was at the yacht club that Turner asked me to join the *Courageous* crew. After the meetings, we ended up on the same flight traveling from Chicago to Baltimore.

As we sat together, Ted pulled out the in-flight magazine and the map in the back of the United States, and he told me his game plan for becoming a billionaire. It was a heady thing to be sitting with someone a decade older, with the brains and guts and wherewithal to turn these big dreams into reality.

As we flew back to the East Coast, Ted pointed to Atlanta on the map; there were no sports teams there, and he talked about buying sports teams and his business ideas and his vision for providing news 24 hours a day—and I sat and listened, overwhelmed by his grand plans. The conversation then turned to my professional life. "So, how much are you making now?" Ted asked me. I sheepishly gave him the answer: $14,000 a year, which was probably a lot for a sailing coach in those days.

"Well, we'll get you a lot more than that," Ted laughed. "You'll see. You'll do better."

And on that flight we made a pact: I would help Ted in sailing and become his tactician; in return, he'd guide me in my career. By early winter after our Cup victory, it was time to take Ted up on his offer.

I first went to Atlanta over the Christmas holiday in '77. In his lifetime, Ted Turner has owned several major tracts of land, but back then he and his wife Jane and their kids were living in a large house in a subdivision of Atlanta.

The holiday week between Christmas and the New Year is a quiet week for most people—but not for Ted Turner. There were lunches every day, at which several sides of Ted's business life were represented: network VPs, real-estate men, officials from his sports teams the Hawks and the Braves. It was typical of Ted to deal with more than one topic at a time, and typical for him to juggle several different appointments almost simultaneously, racing from one to the next.

I sat in on board meetings, listened in on sales calls in his office, and just quietly observed. I watched how Ted operated and saw how strong he was as a businessman. I had never seen someone like Ted operate, and I saw how intense he was and how his leadership came into play and how he'd just go, go, go. He had a genius for dealing with people, driving everyone hard and getting them focused both on the details and on the high-end vision. Those days in Atlanta had a huge impact on me.

After the Cup, Ted got an offer from the publisher Simon & Schuster to write a sailing book. So Ted asked me to be his co-author. We would discuss the shape of the book and the ideas, and I would write it. Ted gave me two-thirds of the book advance and we would split the royalties. The book we wrote, *The Racing Edge*, was a logical, straightforward book on sailing technique—and I was able to make good use of all those notes I kept growing up on the Toms River and racing at Maritime. Ted also proposed me for membership in the New York Yacht Club and the Annapolis Yacht Club.

Anheuser Busch had also asked Ted to be a spokesman for Michelob. Ted declined the job, but he recommended me. So by the spring of '78, I suddenly had a book contract and a job as spokesman for Michelob. And those two things together were paying me more than I was making as a college sailing coach. One of my mentors was Arthur Wullschleger. I had raced with him in three Southern Circuits. He gave me inspiration at this critical point in my career to make the most out of my Cup experience. His encouragement was a big help to me.

I left the Naval Academy in early June to work out of my house. Janice was concerned: I was giving up a steady income and our health insurance. But if I was ever going to strike out on my own, I knew then that it was time to give it a try.

In sailboat racing, when you sail away from the pack on a long tack in the hopes of finding more favorable wind or current, you call it *taking a flyer*. Sometimes flyers pay off big time, and sometimes they fail miserably and put you in last place. But at that point in my life, that is exactly what I needed to do: take a flyer and set up a business that would be completely original and like nothing anyone had ever tried before. There was no model I could follow, for there was no one who was making a living promoting sailing. I had to be creative and write my own rules.

Ted had also given me some advice on how to promote myself, to go around to yacht clubs and junior sailing programs and do lectures. I had done many clinics and talks on technique, but after the America's Cup, sailors were asking for something different. They wanted to hear the stories about the America's Cup and racing at the grand-prix level. So I started a lecture circuit—and that lecture tour got me in contact with people from all over the country and provided me with a great network of friends. Those associations frequently presented business opportunities or ideas.

In 1979, I did 56 lectures that drew just over 7,000 people. And the circuit just grew from there, with years when over 30,000 people came to hear me speak about the sailing world. I never looked back and never stopped booking lecture dates—that is, until I was diagnosed with lymphoma and my life took a detour that would test me in ways I could never have imagined.

.5.
STORMS

Cancer wards are strange places. It's not like going to the local yacht club—a place where you want to be, because you can do something you are passionate about. You are at the cancer ward because you have to be there. It's life or death.

———————— ▬ ————————

Going into the ward is an experience you never quite shake from your memory. When I was there to be treated for lymphoma, I couldn't help looking around at all the other patients. They were just like me: crumpled up and hairless.

I remember one woman who had lost all her hair, and that was hard to see. She caught me staring at her. I looked away and instantly knew what she was thinking: Why are you looking at me? But you can't do anything about it. You are either bloated from steroids or skinny, and none of us are exactly ourselves. Some of us are fighting hard and are going to make it. Some are battling but will still lose the fight. And for some, you just see it in their faces: they have already given up.

Everyone at the cancer ward is painfully aware that we are all facing tough odds. And even though everyone around you is sick and you want to be compassionate, you can't really afford it. You have to focus on yourself. Otherwise, this thing consumes you.

Getting diagnosed with lymphoma was a shock, but when the time came to start my treatments, I was ready and my attitude was pretty good. Of course, maybe it's easy to say you are going to keep your spirits up when you begin. But then you start and the effects of the treatments kick in, and there you are: lying on the couch, not doing a thing. It's hard to do something as simple as walk or even lift your arm. Sometimes you are doubled up in intense pain.

The first treatment that spring really threw me and tested my fortitude to maintain a good attitude. A week after that treatment, my belly was killing me. It was still distended, the way it was in New Zealand. I figured, it's just the chemo. I am going to tough it out. And I spent three days in excruciating pain, crumpled up to the point where I couldn't take it any more. Glenn Robbins—my sailing friend and the doctor I had asked to be on my team—just happened to call to check up on me. I described the pain and he could hear it in my voice. "Get yourself to the emergency room," he said. "I'll meet you there . . . And call Markan."

I quickly called Dr. Markan, the doctor who had given me my diagnosis, and on a Sunday night, at 10 pm, I walked through the emergency room doors. Soon, all these doctors were swarming around me, doing a battery of tests. Turns out I had something in addition to lymphoma. I had pancreatitis and would have to stay in the hospital for several days. They gave me synthetic morphine, and let me tell you—that takes away all the pain. So I stayed in the hospital until I was in good enough shape to go back home.

After the first few rounds of chemo treatments, I took an inventory of my deteriorating body. Eleven things were hurting me: pain in my chest, sores in my mouth, joints that ached like crazy, blotches on my skin that were beyond itchy, and others. Any one of them would make most normal people want to to to bed, but I had 11—and rolled all together, they were nearly unbearable. Every ache, every pain was amplified by all the other things coursing through my body. During this time in my life, I learned to really dislike the nighttime, because you think about death a lot.

As tough as the treatments were, and as much as they took the wind out of me, I had the hardest time sitting still. After years of jetting from regatta to regatta, from lecture to lecture, that is just my nature—always on the go. So I figured after my first few treatments, I would get outside for a bit. I was still bent over, walking slowly and breathing hard, but I figured I could manage a drive over to my office in Annapolis to collect my mail. The truth was, I had no business driving a car.

I made it to the office and parked for a few minutes alongside the post office while I ran upstairs. I say *ran*, but those three flights up to my office were slow and tough—my personal Everest for the condition I was in. The *Washington Post* keeps an office in the building, so I stopped to catch my breath before I could say hello to the folks who worked there, then I completed the trip to my office, got my mail, and headed back to the car. The trip up and down the stairs took about 15 minutes, but it wiped me out. As I made my way out of the building, my only consolation was that I'd soon be in my car, heading home.

At least that's what I thought.

I have been in the same office for over 25 years, and in that time my car has been towed once. Just my luck, that day was my second tow in all those years. The postmaster of my office neighborhood is the overzealous parking Nazi who sits there with a stopwatch and calls the tow truck the minute someone is parked too long. So when I arrived to get my car, there was just a sign that I had been towed to a place about a mile away. So I walked down West Street at an excruciatingly slow pace—drooling and breathing hard—only to learn the towing service had moved about two miles away. I thought, you have to be kidding me; this is like a bad movie. By now, I literally had foam coming out of my mouth, tears coming out of my eyes. I looked like a derelict—over 30 pounds under my normal weight with my clothes hanging off me.

I shuffled over to the taxi stand, lugging a big wad of mail, and arrived at the tow place totally out of gas. "You guys towed my car, and all I did was get my mail," I managed to say as I tried to catch my breath. A young man with a stack of earrings and an equal number of tattoos manning the lot took one look at me and just handed over my keys. I'm sure he thought, "This is lawsuit material, this one." I paid the price for my little adventure. I was in more pain and had several days of hell to pay.

One thing that helped me get through my treatments was connecting with other lymphoma survivors. Timmy Larr, a sailing friend who was one of the sport's top racers in her day, introduced me to her husband, David. Having survived lymphoma once, David's disease had returned. But when he told me about the treatments, his attitude was so matter-of-fact that it made me feel okay. Knowing he could get through these treatments a second time gave me confidence: when it does come back, you can battle it again. David gave me guideposts, such as on Day 18, your hair starts to fall out. And just like clockwork, on Day 18, I saw my hair whisk down the drain.

By summertime, I was feeling well enough to travel again, and so I did what I now call my victory lap. It wasn't just a lap, but several trips with good friends who kindly hosted me for some R&R. I spent a week with Ted Turner at his ranch in Montana—although I got sick there and Ted flew me back home and to the hospital on his plane. I spent a week in Nantucket with my friends Norwood and Marguerite Davis. I also visited Jack King, in North Carolina. My friend Elizabeth Meyer, who restored the classic J-Class sloop *Endeavour*, invited me for a week of sailing on this big historic boat. Now *Endeavour* is special: it's stunning to look at, meticulously restored, comfortable down below, and a dream to sail. By this time Elizabeth had sold the boat—but she chartered it for a New England cruise and invited me to join her other guests. With a professional crew, it was a perfect way for me to go sailing—to pitch in if I wanted, but to rest on the boat's comfortable berths if I was feeling tired. It was one of the best weeks of sailing in my life.

Since the time I was diagnosed, I had received thousands of emails and cards from friends and colleagues, and so I sent an update telling them all that my medical numbers were better and things looked encouraging; that I had already had multiple surgeries, rounds of chemo treatments, and my share of setbacks; that I was 38 pounds lighter with a new hairdo (none); but that I was walking every day and feeling optimistic that I could finish the treatment regimen in August. I thought it would be that simple.

Labor Day came, and I was still feeling good. I went to a Redskins game in early September with Douglas and Bernadette Bernon, good friends who are cruising sailors and writers. I remember that summer sky as I walked across the parking lot and looked skyward toward a beautiful landscape of blue and thought to myself, I'm going to be alright.

Later that month, I traveled out to the West Coast to do some commentary for the Outdoor Life Network with Dawn Riley—a woman racer who has broken new ground as a big-boat sailor and now mixes sailing with television commentary. I was back into the full-production life of a TV journalist, with several days of commentary and a grueling schedule. It would have felt great to be back in the saddle, except the pain came back, now worse than ever. I was on the phone to my doctor, to get a prescription for some painkillers, and Dawn took one look at me and immediately called an ambulance.

The hopes I built up that summer about being on a solid road to recovery were quickly dashed, and my life as a journalist was instantly traded for one of a hospital patient as soon as the ambulance arrived. After three days I was stable enough to fly home. The next step was a bone marrow transplant.

By the time I went to New Zealand in 2003, my wife Janice and I had separated. As a former oncology nurse, Janice understood what I was going through, and she was supportive. Still, deep down, I knew I was fighting this solo.

The day I got home from the West Coast, I headed right to the hospital. My assistant Kathy gave me a lift. When we arrived at the entrance, I got out of the car and closed the door behind me with a thud. I will never forget that walk by myself from the car to the hospital doors. It would be a month before I'd smell the outdoor air again. I never felt so alone.

The faces in the cancer ward, they haunt you. But even though it's a terrible place to be, there are lessons. Some people simply give up and get angry. I will never forget one day, standing in line to get a shot. This is the shot you get after a chemo treatment. I called it the "Saturday morning shot"—and we all lined up that morning and waited to get in.

A lady stood in front of me one day as I waited for my shot. "Why me?" she asked in anguish. "I can't believe this happened to me. What did I do to deserve this?" And I came to a realization: I hadn't asked, Why me? I did not think I was the target of some cosmic conspiracy. No, my attitude was different. This was simply the worst storm of my life.

As a sailor, I knew about storms—the times when you are out on the ocean, it's rough and no fun, sails are tearing and things on the boat are breaking. You have to sail through it. You just can't end it, can't call a helicopter and get off. You're seasick, your crew is seasick, nobody onboard is motivated. But you still have 300 miles to go before you get anywhere. So you simply have to keep going.

It takes a lot of inner strength to keep sailing through the worst conditions— and that is one of the hard lessons of the sea. But sailors know something that gets them through the most difficult times: Tomorrow we'll sew up the jib, tomorrow the seasickness will pass, tomorrow the seas will be calm again.

The 1979 Fastnet crew aboard *Tenacious*. We won Cowes Week and the Queen's Cup. Little did we know about the storm we would face a few days later.

A bleak view off the stern of *Tenacious* heading into the 1979 Fastnet storm. Jim Mattingly is at the helm.

* * *

In the summer of 1999, all of us on the crew of Larry Ellison's *Sayonara* worked together to race this sleek 78-footer around Fastnet Rock—an eerie jagged peak with a lighthouse about 8 miles off the coast of Ireland. We were not racing around just any lighthouse in this 605-mile race: we were rounding a tragic symbol to sailors of just how fierce the sea can become.

Twenty years earlier, this same race around Fastnet Rock off the west coast of England turned into "one of the most vicious summer gales in the twentieth century," as writer John Rousmaniere dubbed it in his book, *Fastnet, Force 10*. Not only was the weather that summer during the Fastnet violent: it developed into the deadliest storm in yacht-racing history.

Ted Turner, his son Teddy, and I were three crew on *Sayonara* who were haunted by the memory of the historic '79 Fastnet. Along with other crew, the three of us raced Ted's 61-foot Sparkman & Stephens *Tenacious* 20 years ago in the infamous race. We knew how bad this patch of ocean could get—even in the midst of summer.

The crew on *Sayonara* also carried their ghosts. Most of them had raced in the deadly 1998 Sydney-Hobart Race. Only nine months earlier they had sailed through a brutal storm that battered the fleet as they raced from Australia to Tasmania. Six sailors in the fleet died. Ellison and his crew were still marked by the experience, clearly not anxious to sail again in similar weather.

Before the Fastnet on *Sayonara*, I noticed how everyone paid strict attention to the pre-race safety meeting led by the boat's captain, Bill Erkelens. Prior to the race, every boat was required to sail through a gate with storm sails set, to demonstrate that these sails for rough weather were on board and the crew knew how to use them. The procedure seemed a bit comical, since there was no wind. But everyone onboard knew exactly why this test was necessary, and no one questioned the importance of the procedure.

Two days before the start of the race, we attended a memorial service at Trinity Church in Cowes for the fallen sailors of the '79 Fastnet. It made the memory of that deadly storm even more vivid, and my mind went back to the worst part of it: the middle-of-the-night watches 20 years ago when we were in the midst of this vicious weather system.

"Don't let anyone else steer. You're the only helsman!" Ted Turner shouted above the din of raging winds and seas, as Ted finished his watch and I took the helm of *Tenacious* that terrible August night. Ted has a big voice, but it was even hard to hear him above the sound of the weather. The waves felt huge and the sound of the wind was deafening.

John Mecray painted this image of *Tenacious* surfing downwind as daylight breaks during the infamous 1979 Fastnet Race.

"Take your hat off. It's the only way you can tell what's happening," Ted yelled. I sure could have used some protection on my head, since the spray stung like needles. But I didn't need my hearing muffled by foul-weather gear; I didn't need my sight blinkered by a hood. I needed all my senses to thread *Tenacious* through the steep waves. With no visibility, feeling the waves and wind proved to be the solution.

A fleet of 303 boats started the race, and we were among the larger boats in the fleet. The first 300 miles of the race seemed easy after we started in winds that reached about 15 knots in the afternoon as we sailed generally southwest down the English Channel, then turned northwest to cross the Irish Sea and round Fastnet Rock before returning to the finish line. We knew we were in for bad weather as we returned across the Irish Sea. The forecast called for a storm that would pick up to Force 7, and then diminish to Force 5. Instead, the wind just kept coming, stronger and stronger until it reached Force 10, which is 48 to 55 knots on the Beaufort scale and near hurricane conditions.

Ted is a strong leader. When the weather forecasts came in, he made sure everyone had a hot meal and those who were off watch were getting their rest. After we rounded Fastnet Rock, I drove the boat for three hours. At midnight, Ted took the helm and drove four hours through what was probably the worst of the storm, when the gusts hit 60 knots.

At 0400, when I got back on deck to helm again, I was almost glad to be back topsides. During my off-watch hours, I kept popping my head up to see if I could help. But Turner wanted the off-watch crew to rest and kept ordering me below. Frankly, life was no picnic below decks. We were getting tossed around like a toy boat sailing inside a washing machine. The crew was thrown all over the place and everyone was getting seasick.

As bad as the weather was, we kept focused on racing—and I enjoyed keeping *Tenacious* in a very narrow groove. If we sailed just a few degrees low, we might not make our next turning point at the Scilly Isles, and if we sailed too high, our small jib would luff violently, risking a tear. It was a fine balance, but the challenge was compounded by dozens of smaller craft that were well behind us in the race, limping toward Fastnet Rock. For some, the wind was so high that they could not carry any sail at all and the prospect of a collision was frightening.

As I helmed in the dark and low visibility, a red light would appear ahead and then disappear as the waves rose and fell. Then a green light would appear and vanish behind a wave. These were the bow lights of the smaller boats heading toward Fastnet Rock that we had to be so careful to avoid. Our boat responded slowly as I altered course, but with luck and a lot of concentration, we were able to avoid the kind of collisions that could have proven deadly.

It wasn't until daybreak that I realized how large the waves were. Bigger than huge—a liquid mass the size of the Maryland State House, looming over our deck. Luckily, most of the waves passed underneath our hull. But there were those that didn't. They crashed on deck, washing green water over the crew who were strapped in with safety harnesses and huddled on the windward rail.

As we drew closer to the finish line, the radio reports came in. Several yachts were sinking and a number of crew had been washed overboard. I wondered, Could it happen to us? I decided that it wasn't going to happen. We just needed to keep racing. Little did we know then that we were racing for our own survival, that by the end of the race, 15 sailors would be dead.

Tenacious won that race. By the time I stepped aboard for the 1979 Fastnet, I had sailed over 25,000 ocean miles and crossed the Atlantic five times. Never again did I see conditions as bad as we did that August, 20 years earlier, and the only positive development after the tragedy was that sailing authorities put measures in place to tighten up safety regulations.

Tenacious approaches Fastnet Rock several hours before the storm hit the fleet. The rock is about eight miles off Cork, Ireland. The Irish call this lighthouse "Tear Drop" because it is always sad to be leaving home.

Looking back, I consider winning the 1979 Fastnet Ted Turner's finest hour, and it was a victory he felt was even more impressive than our 1977 America's Cup win. He was a strong leader that night—so strong, in fact, that as bad as the weather got, I was never truly frightened. I figured, if Ted's alright with this, then things must be okay.

The brilliance of Ted's leadership was that he never had us panicked and focused on mere survival. We had a goal. We kept racing—and it kept our minds focused and kept us motivated. If we had stopped to think about the severity of the weather, the fact that boats were struggling and people would die that night, all of us on *Tenacious* could have had a different outcome. As Ted told *The New York Times* after the race, "We were more afraid of being afraid than anything else." So the push for victory in the '79 Fastnet was a good thing. It kept us from realizing that terrible night that we were, quite literally, racing for our lives.

* * *

The thing about storms at sea is that you know they are coming. The forecasters detect the signs, and then you prepare as you watch the barometer drop, watch the seas build, and feel the winds grow stronger and stronger until you are in the thick of it. But the problem with a storm that blows through your life is that there aren't any forecasts: there is no warning that you are headed for troubled waters.

When I turned 50 in 2000, I totally missed the signals of the weather I was heading for. Reaching 50 gave me a sense of accomplishment, a feeling of freedom, and a sudden license to do things I had never before contemplated. In a word, I went *nuts* at a time when my health was perfect, my family life secure, and my business thriving. It was easy to take it all for granted. Turning 50 made me feel entitled to change my universe.

There had been bigger birthday celebrations. My surprise 40th birthday party attracted 200 friends, family members, and business associates from across the country. During the decade of my forties I watched my kids grow up, my reputation in the world of sailing advance, and my net worth shift from substantial debt to significant assets.

With all this good fortune, the obvious question would be, Why change anything? But in the three years after I turned 50, my world did change—for the worse, at every level.

At the helm of *Tenacious* the morning after the Fastnet Storm.
It was still blowing 50 knots at 0700 when this picture was taken. My hands were raw.

Things were shifting at home. My wife Janice had embarked on a new career as a teacher. She was busy and had her own sense of independence, while still looking after our three active daughters. The girls spent increasing amounts of time doing their own thing—and so I too went off in my own direction.

In 1999 alone, I wrote 50 articles and a book. I traveled over 200 days and attended 42 board meetings, gave 63 lectures, and was honored with the Nathanael G. Herreshoff Award for my contributions to the sport. The work was exhilarating but my personal life was another story.

In 2001, Janice and I separated, and in the next two years my life became wrapped around my career: travel and television shows, lectures, sailing. There was a sense of excitement about a new life. But deep down, the pain of Janice and me unwinding so many years of our life together was tearing me apart.

As the 2003 America's Cup in New Zealand approached, I even changed my look. I went a little loony and stopped getting haircuts and got an earring. My friends were exceedingly polite, but I am sure they thought I was deep into a midlife crisis.

And then, gray skies socked in over my life at the 2003 America's Cup, when the signs of my cancer started to keep me from living life as I had known it. My diagnosis followed after I returned home to the States, and then I also learned that ESPN, my most important client for 16 years, was canceling their regular coverage of sailing.

Looking back today at the last event I covered for them, the 2003 America's Cup in New Zealand, maybe I should not have been surprised. We had the best coverage of the worst sporting event: weather delays and waiting for wind clearly upset the ESPN executives. And Cup fans were turning off their TVs in droves. Still, the fact that ESPN was leaving sailing was disastrous for me—both financially and emotionally.

The period of my life after my diagnosis was the equivalent of a Force 10 storm: two years of endless medical procedures, a stem cell transplant, numerous setbacks, excruciating pain. I couldn't walk. I was constantly drugged. My body was a battlefield where the enemies just kept coming back at each other. I had no idea which side would win, and I could feel myself slipping away and depression setting in.

Writing helped me survive. I worked on another book, *Championship Sailing*, with my assistant Kathy. It's a book that today I am very proud of, since it compiles all that I've learned about racing sailboats over the course of my life.

Kathy and I worked on it together, bit by bit. It helped me relive all those years of being on the water, and the tactics of how to reach the finish line first. It was a lesson too: through the pain and confusion of drugs and cancer I could still be productive.

During the worst of my illness, I received many of my career's top honors. In October 2003, I was inducted into the America's Cup Hall of Fame—which includes a collection of individuals recognized for their outstanding contribution to the America's Cup, housed at the Herreshoff Marine Museum in Bristol, Rhode Island. It includes skippers, crews, syndicate managers, designers, organizers, and chroniclers of the event, and the honor ranked me amongst some of the greats: Russell Coutts, Ted Turner, Charlie Barr, Dennis Conner, Sir Thomas Lipton, Buddy Melges, Olin Stephens, and T.O.M. Sopwith—to name just a few. There was no way I was going to miss out on the dinner in New York to accept this honor. But the date of the dinner fell just around the time I was due for a stem cell transplant, so I worked with my doctors on the timing.

Rather than looking for a donor to match me, my doctors decided on an autologous stem cell transplant where they would harvest my own stem cells. The injections of Neupogen to prepare for the harvest were painful—not the injection itself, but the aftermath—and I got those several times a day. But I was lucky: I had a good harvest—collecting enough stem cells to use for the transplant, with some spares to keep on ice in case I needed them in the future.

The bone marrow recovery takes about a month to process, so my doctors harvested the stem cells a few weeks before the dinner. Then they worked to help me recoup and prepare for my trip to New York, boosting me up artificially so I could make the journey to New York.

A friend sent his private jet to fly me from Baltimore to New York—and let me tell you, that is one good way to travel. I made it to the dinner, albeit totally bloated from steroids and with no hair. But I made it.

My three families were there: Janice and the girls, my ESPN colleagues, along with the entire crew from *Courageous* and our '77 Cup win. A lot of people traveled a long way to get there. During one of the low ebbs of my illness the previous summer, I received a get well card, signed by every member of the *Courageous* crew. In it, one of the crew, Richie Boyd, wrote that after all these years, we are still a team. Those powerful bonds were evident that night.

Before the dinner, I reserved my strength so I could get up and make an acceptance speech. I talked about my first encounter with the America's Cup as a kid on a family visit to Newport, and later sailing and covering the Cup. I thanked

Ted and I at the 2003 America's Cup Hall of Fame dinner hosted by the Herreshoff Marine Museum. I was in between treatments at the time. Alan Bond was inducted with me that night.

all those individuals who have been a part of my path in the sport. And I told the audience that I was on the road to recovery and would continue to promote the sport we all loved.

It was humbling to be included in this group of Cup greats—and it was quite a night. But it was important well beyond my sailing career: it was the beginning of rebuilding my life with Janice. She had been such a part of my success and so tolerant of all my globe-trotting and time away from home. It's hard to woo your wife back when you are in such wretched shape and bloated and bald. Still, I thought if we could get back together again, that would be my life's biggest accomplishment.

Ted had encouraged Janice and I to begin anew. He spoke with us separately. It was important to me and I was ready to try again.

Just three days after the dinner in New York, I returned to the hospital in Maryland. The chemo treatments to prepare for the stem cell transplant were harsh. After 23 days I arrived home in mid-November in an extremely weakened state. It was hard to even sit up without being out of breath. This procedure was by far the

At the Leukemia & Lymphoma Society event in my honor in Baltimore, I was hurting.
This was the low point in my life. Luckily Janice was there to support me in my time of need.

most difficult I had yet endured. I wondered how much more could I go through. Lymphoma was a hard disease to get rid of.

My whole system needed to rebuild. And if all went according to plan, in January I would start a series of scans to see if the cancer was still around. I wrote to friends and supporters when I returned home. I updated them on my condition and offered them this thought: "Take a deep breath every morning; say thank you for your health. The alternative is unbelievably tough. I am hanging on, but finding it tough."

I was lucky to be assigned to Dr. Aaron Rapoport. He had been on the sailing team at MIT. After graduation he attended Harvard Medical School and then completed his residency at the University of Rochester. It was my good fortune to have one of the finest doctors in America quarterback my treatment, one who has led breakthrough research teams in the quest to cure blood cancers.

My immune system was weak and in March I got a vicious zoster virus that was extremely painful. I was back in the hospital, just when I was looking forward to another dinner to recognize my achievements. The Leukemia & Lymphoma Society was holding their annual fundraising event in my honor. And I was determined to go.

On the day of the dinner in March, I was still in the hospital. This round of treatment was debilitating. I had begun to wonder before I went into the hospital that winter, Is this it? I had all my papers in order. My first priority was making sure my family was taken care of. Then I began asking myself all the questions I needed to ask before checking into the hospital: Is there enough money in the college funds? What stupid things do I have lingering? What do I do with my Redskins season tickets? I started thinking about what I had done in my life and realized I had done everything in racing I set out to do. I wanted to do more cruising, or maybe coach again. And I thought about how I would be remembered—hopefully as someone who made sailing interesting to a non-sailing audience. Twenty years later, that is what I wanted people to remember.

On the afternoon before the Leukemia & Lymphoma Society banquet, I decided to stop taking pain medication so I could be completely in the moment at the dinner. But I felt so sick, it was unbelievable. I could not walk independently. I had a splitting headache, an awful earache, and nausea. I felt like somebody took a fist and smashed the side of my head. I had chest pain too—just as if someone put a belt around my chest, put both feet on, and pulled with all his might. I knew, though, I'd get back on the pills after the banquet and hopefully get some relief.

That day I dozed and preserved my energy. My friend Doug Bernon kept me company. He was writing a profile on me, so we talked as I fell in and out of sleep. We talked about my life, my illness, my sailing. About two hours before the dinner, my assistant Kathy drove us to an apartment I owned in Baltimore. I rested there a bit more and tried to get some broth down before I had to get dressed for the banquet. Janice and our twins soon arrived, and they kept asking, Do you really have to go to the dinner? Doug told me, You don't have to be Superman. Staying in character, I told them: "Yeah. Kryptonite. It gets ya every time."

As much as I was involved with the Leukemia Cups, as much as I had read about cancer as part of my work directing that regatta series, and as much as I had family—my grandfather, my father, and both of Janice's parents—who died of cancer, I didn't really know what cancer was before it invaded my body. After I had it, I did learn how it overwhelms your body and takes you away. But I learned through all that pain that I'm a fighter. I don't give up.

As evening arrived, I managed to get a shower and get dressed for the banquet. I had to use a wheelchair, and as we traveled to the dinner I had to hold a bucket in my lap in case I puked.

We arrived at the dinner, and as I was ready to go in I turned to Doug and told him: "Man, you're about to watch one miraculous comeback. I've spent the last thirteen days getting ready for the next five minutes."

Janice led the procession and Kathy rolled me in. And as soon as my wheelchair rolled through the door the crowd erupted into wild applause. As I rolled past all of them it grew louder and louder. After my introduction, I was able to rise from my wheelchair and tried to quiet the crowd. But they'd have none of it. Waves of applause just kept coming. Finally, I was able to quiet the crowd and introduce the sailing film I was about to show. Mustering all the strength I could, I told the crowd, "OK, let's roll the tape . . ."

* * *

It was a difficult night and a wonderful night—all at the same time. Talking to Doug about the profile the afternoon of the dinner pushed me deep into my own thoughts. Through all the pain and agony of cancer, I didn't get lost in the suffering—even though I thought this transplant the winter of the Leukemia & Lymphoma Society dinner might be it.

During that bout of treatment, I'd lie on the couch and know it would be five days of agony, then four and a half days, then four. I'd just bear it out. When you feel that bad, tomorrow is a long time away—and days, weeks, and months of suffering can almost destroy you. But just like sailing through a storm, you keep going. You keep searching for blue sky ahead.

Through the haze of all that pain I kept thinking about returning to a special place. During those days, lying in bed, I'd imagine McGlathery Island. It's a remote and rugged island off the coast of Maine. There are not many boats around, and the only structures on the island are trees. I wanted to get back there—to the wind and sun and magic of the kind of sparkling blue day you only find in Maine.

People ask me where my inner strength came from, and I think it was knowing that I needed to do things in the future. I wanted to do some extended cruising. I wanted to make things right with my family again. I wanted to continue promoting sailing.

My biggest goal in 2004 was to cover the Olympics in Athens. It was a struggle to be healthy enough to make the trip, but Dr. Rapoport infused me with more stem cells in early July, preparing me for the start of the Olympics in early August. I just made it. I will always be grateful to NBC's Dick Ebersol and Molly Solomon for being patient and allowing me to make the trip. Geoff Mason came as our producer, along with the assistance of John Wilson. We produced reports for 15 straight days.

During those dark days before the Leukemia & Lymphoma Society dinner, I felt so close to giving up. That dinner was a turning point. I realized my mission wasn't complete yet and I couldn't even imagine what the finish line would look like. All I did know, deep down, was that I certainly hadn't reached it yet.

.6.
REACHING A WIDER AUDIENCE

1983 In September 1983, something big happened in sailing. Actually, it was more than big: it was seismic. After 132 years, America lost the America's Cup. It happened in Newport, Rhode Island, in the final race of a best-of-seven series, when the American crew on the 12 Meter *Liberty*, skippered by Dennis Conner, match-raced *Australia II* with John Bertrand at the helm.

$$\longleftarrow \quad \blacksquare \quad \longrightarrow$$

By the numbers the boats had even odds, and they went into that final race tied at 3–3. The Australians had some early equipment problems in the series, and Dennis and his crew were able to gain ground on *Australia II*—a boat that was clearly fast and branded by its battle flag of boxing kangaroos sailing from the land Down Under. But even though Dennis had evened the score as the boats sailed into that last race, there was a sense of foreboding on the docks: Could this be the year the Americans lose the Cup?

Despite the ominous mood, with the light and shifty winds blowing for the final day of racing, Cup watchers knew that anything could happen. I was doing live radio commentary back to Australia with journalist Bruce Stannard, and so I had a close vantage point during that last race from the press boat. It was a see-saw battle: Dennis won the start but *Australia II* got the lead, but then threw it away by not covering their arch rival. On the fourth leg of the race, Dennis seemed to extend his lead by sailing from one wind shift to the next, and by the time the boats reached the next mark, Dennis had a 53-second lead. It looked like the Cup was going to stay in America.

Downwind the two Twelves went. The press boat rolled lazily as the Americans and Australians locked into their final battle. Dennis jibed frequently downwind. On a 12 Meter you lose about two-thirds of a boat length every time you jibe, compared to a competitor who doesn't jibe; *Australia II* seemed to stay on a steady course. Dennis had his motives: he was desperate to find windshifts and more wind to maintain his lead. But the Australians kept charging, sailing lower and faster, a difficult combination to combat. At one critical moment, Dennis jibed away from the Australians, putting *Liberty* on the west side of the course while the Australians occupied the east. This was the decisive moment: when the two boats finally came together, the Australians had the lead.

The Australians had a lead of about a boat length at the leeward mark, but they looked nervous, spinning their boat too quickly and over-steering on every tack. Dennis was remarkably smooth, but his *Liberty* just didn't have the juice.

Australia II crossed the finish line in first place. It was the gunshot heard around the world: these sailors had overturned the longest winning streak in sports history. After the finish, bedlam reigned on the racecourse and the mood continued on land. The Australians were jubilant; Dennis was distraught. Dennis did his best to keep his chin up that day, but the tears eventually flowed.

During that Cup summer, the Australian boat had been under cover, draped with a "modesty skirt" from deck to ground when the boat was hauled from the water. But when the Australians hauled their boat after the final race, her skirt was gone. Alan Bond finally showed the world his secret weapon: a highly controversial keel that was later revealed as one that did not have a traditional dagger-like shape but was an appendage with wings. It was a magic moment in sailing, but a devastating one for Dennis, his crew, and the team that worked so hard on the campaign.

New York Yacht Club Commodore Bob Stone graciously handed the America's Cup over to the Australians the next day. It was a solemn moment for the Americans, yet the whole world cheered. The Australians had done something that no one else had been able to do in 132 years. But for Dennis Conner, it wasn't over: that bitter defeat sowed the seeds of an amazing comeback that would happen only 40 months later.

Something else happened on that September day that also had a powerful effect on the sport. The final race was scheduled for a Saturday, but when the winds were too light, the race was rescheduled for a weekday. At the time, I was commentating for ABC's *Good Morning America* and *Nightline*, but they did not offer live coverage. With no one else to televise the finale, a young, four-year-old cable network named ESPN took the feed from the local network WJAR. There was a blimp shot, a helicopter, and cameras on land. In those far-away shots, the 12 Meters looked like toy boats making chess-like moves on a big sea. But the drama of the bloodless war on the water and its significance was not lost: the story was catnip to sports fans, and ESPN got its highest ratings to date for a non-primetime show, by a huge margin.

After that race, a young ESPN producer named Jed Drake found himself thinking, "Hang on, this could be something, this America's Cup that is going down to Australia. Maybe we should engage . . ." And of course, they did, making ESPN the pre-eminent network carrying sailing coverage in the 1980s and '90s. It launched a career for this young network.

At that history-making time, I was not yet part of the ESPN fold. In fact, that prospect was not even on my radar screen. After Conner's loss in '83, the tide of opportunity blew wide open. Who would win the Cup back? One of the men who had put his hat into the ring was Wisconsin-born-and-bred Buddy Melges and his *Heart of America* syndicate.

I had already done three Cup campaigns as a tactician: winning with Ted Turner in '77; racing again with Ted in '80, although we lost the defender selection;

The late Tom Blackaller at a press conference in 1987. Tom was colorful and a gifted, natural sailor. I had great fun as his tactician in the 1983 America's Cup trials. He died of a heart attack racing a car on a track in California in 1989.

Tom Blackaller sails *Defender* upwind prior to the 1983 America's Cup Trials. We had a great crew, including Paul Cayard, Rod Davis, Mike Toppa, Peter Stalkus, Bruce Epke, John Mulderig, Dana Timmer, Ken Keefe, and Jim Plagenhoef.

and serving as tactician in '83 with skipper Tom Blackaller. We lost the Selection Trials in both 1980 and 1983. Turner and Blackaller—who died tragically in 1989 from a heart attack—were complete originals. But in some ways, they were cut from similar cloth. Like Ted, Tom was not an East Coast denizen of the sailing world. He was a West Coaster, a man's man with a bold penchant for speed (which he also put to good use in the race-car world) and strong opinions, a colorful character with magnetism that ran in overdrive. He was not one to shy away from controversy—and his shock of gray hair and a gleam in his eyes were his trademarks.

Buddy Melges was of a different mold. He was a home-grown hero from the small Wisconsin town of Zenda on Lake Geneva—and for as long as I've known, he's been called the Wizard of Zenda. It makes him sound like a Star Wars character, and in many ways his ability to sail fast on the water is just as other-worldly.

To me and to many sailors, Buddy was a living legend. And so I signed on with my childhood hero and his *Heart of America* syndicate. What an opportunity it was, to chase after the America's Cup with a sailor I had long considered to be one of the greatest in our sport.

Back in the 1980s, being an America's Cup sailor was not a professional gig for me. I was also writing books and articles, spending time on the road promoting sailing in lectures and slide shows, and working as an advisor to companies interested in using the sport as a marketing and promotional tool. Sailing had a lot of glamour, so in 1984, I helped create an event in New York Harbor called the Liberty Cup. I talked Ted Turner out of retirement to join a celebrity lineup of skippers. Star power coupled with the city's strong media market made the Liberty Cup the first event of its kind, tailor-made for the New York media. The sailing magazines dubbed it "Metro Sailing," and it was very cool.

The event also caught the eye of a young executive at ESPN named Steve Bornstein, who called to ask if I'd be interested in doing some work with ESPN. I instantly said yes and got a tryout, doing interviews and voiceovers. I was nervous, but the work was not a stretch for me: by that time I had been talking and writing about the sport so much that I could quickly launch into commentary on any facet of sailing with a moment's notice. Soon, I was packing my bags for Australia for three weeks to cover the 12 Meter Worlds in Australia for ESPN with Jed Drake and another young producer, Jamie Reynolds. It was great fun.

ESPN was gearing up to cover the next America's Cup more fully than any other television network, and they invested the time up front to educate their viewers on what the Cup was all about and to prove to viewers that 12 Meter racing was bona fide athletic competition. A new head producer, Geoff Mason, joined the team and the network had an ambitious lineup of shows: a half-hour show on each of the American syndicates heading to Australia, coupled with an historical retrospective on all the past Cups using archived film footage from places like Mystic Seaport.

After the Worlds in Australia, I got a call from Geoff Mason, asking me to play a larger role on the ESPN team. That moment sticks in my mind to this day, for his call was a door to a huge opportunity—a chance to cover one of the biggest stories in the history of sailing.

In the call, Geoff told me that ESPN wanted me to do the coverage of the '87 Cup, "but if you are going to sail with Buddy, we understand," he said. That was on a Thursday, so Geoff made a plan: "I'll call you Monday morning at 10 am. You're either going to tell me yes, you're doing the coverage with us, or, no, you're not. Either way will be fine."

I weighed the pros and cons of trading the role of an America's Cup tactician for that of a television journalist. Whoever won the Cup would be a gigantic hero, but the television commentator would be a secondary hero. And there were other things to consider too.

I was then in my mid-thirties. Janice and I had started a family and were now parents of one-year-old Kristi Lynn. Kristi arrived the winter after the momentous American loss of the Cup. Kristi was born on a cold day in late January, just days before I was scheduled to jet off yet again to sail in the Southern Ocean Racing Conference in Florida and the Bahamas. It was a long delivery and Janice was simply amazing. Our Kristi arrived with lots of black hair and—I have to admit—a striking similarity to ET. Being our first, I had no idea how strange babies look when they first appear. She made her own kind of entrance: Hey! Here I Am! It is just the way she is today. Enthused, smart, active, outgoing—that's Kristi.

Now that we were parents and Janice had left her nursing career to become a full-time mom, banking so much of my career on racing boats was starting to lose its luster. I thought back to a 12 Meter regatta on San Francisco Bay, where I was calling tactics for Buddy. We were racing against my old skipper, Tom Blackaller, who was then racing with Paul Cayard, a young and talented sailor from San Francisco Bay who has since gone on to become one of the world's top inshore and offshore racers. We got into an altercation on the racecourse and a shouting match ensued, and I'll never forget Paul on the back deck—screaming, with veins popping out of his head. And Buddy was screaming at Tom, and Tom was roaring back, and I was thinking, You know, I don't really need this. I went back to my hotel room that night, locked the door, and took the phone off the hook. I was getting tired of the race scene: the constant pressure to fundraise to go sailing, racing for wealthy owners, and being on boats where the mix of high-octane egos in pressure situations quickly turns explosive.

So I decided to give ESPN a shot. I flew out to see Buddy and tell him I was leaving his Cup campaign. He was very supportive, only asking me to keep my departure under wraps until the syndicate's new boat was launched. Geoff Mason called right on schedule. I told him I was in. It was a good decision, but it was also quite a weird feeling to be leaving sailing at that seminal time in the sport.

Covering the Cup in Australia with ESPN made the transition from the cockpit to a TV crew well worth it. Filming the action and making the Cup come alive for thousands of viewers turned out to be as fun and challenging as racing on a 12 Meter. Geoff, Jed, Jamie, and I were joined in Australia by commentator Jim Kelly—and when Dennis Conner won the challenger selection, the Cup story had

A Bad Night

On a mid-September night in 1982, our America's Cup crew had just ended the summer practice session—and skipper Tom Blackaller and I decided along with the rest of the crew to celebrate in a proper way. First stop: the famous Candy Store, for refreshments. We got pretty well lubricated. At this point, Tom, who I was calling tactics for onboard *Defender*, and I had the bright idea to go to the movies. We saw *Rambo*, then stopped for a greasy fast-food burger and fries. From there, we traveled back on Route 138A, and, well, we were driving mighty fast. In fact, we were going 110 miles per hour—and we got stopped.

Tom was not only fast on a sailboat; as a race-car driver, he was also fast behind the wheel of a car. Tom was in race-car mode that night and he got the ticket. But somehow I smoothed it out enough so we were able to go on our way. We continued on for about two miles, and we got stopped a second time. But this time, Tom was really angry with the police; and when the policeman went to grab the keys, Tom started driving away, the policeman with his hand still in the window.

A second cruiser arrived with dogs, and the dogs were barking like crazy and Tom was screaming bloody murder and with that, the handcuffs came out. Off we went to the local jail.

a perfect bookend: Dennis, the skipper who lost the Cup to Australia, now had a chance to vindicate himself and win it back. We knew it would be a huge story.

Jim Kelly and I spent our days commentating from a 120-foot catamaran named *Sun Bird*, and by the time the Defender and Challenger sailed into the Cup, our ESPN crew had become like family. Jim and I had good chemistry on the air—and we would need it. During the races, we commentated live for over four hours. We cut in interviews and special features, and we also thought of novel ways to explain America's Cup racing to the masses—including having me jump into a pool with two model Twelves, to push the boats around the water and explain sailing's tactical moves. The production had become much more sophisticated than what viewers watched in Newport in '83, and we mixed on-the-water shots with onboard cameras and the wide views from a helicopter.

Me, I was the quiet one and went into a jail cell with about 20 other misfits who had also misbehaved that night. Everyone was smoking cigarettes. It stunk. It was dirty. And it was weird. Blackaller, on the other hand, made such a tirade that they bounced him around a little bit in the bushes before bringing him into a cell. Tom's last act of defiance was throwing a shoe at the officer. Take that!

The next morning all of us in handcuffs were brought into the courtroom to go before the judge. The guy brought in before Tom and me had apparently raped a nun; I am sure he's still in jail. Then Tom and I stood before the judge, and he looked down at us over his glasses.

"What in the world are you two doing here?" he asked. The judge no doubt recognized us from seeing our photos in the sports pages. We got released on about a $100 bond—and all I can say is that it was a bad night. Since that time, every time I do an ocean race, I query the crew: "How many people here have spent at least one night in jail?"

The ratio never varies from race to race, from boat to boat. At least 50 percent of an ocean racing crew have spent at least a night at government expense, at some point. Everyone has their own weird circumstances. But it just seems to be a trend: half the sailors around the world have also had a bad night.

A big personal event that happened during the '87 Cup was the arrival of our twins, Brooke and Ashleigh. Janice flew down to Australia in September 1986, but it was a one-way trip. She was too late in her pregnancy to head back home, and so our girls were born in Australia just days before the America's Cup Finals. The TV stations thought it was a great story, so they came to visit once the girls had arrived. Most of America watching *Good Morning America* got to meet our girls. Joan Lunden was so excited about the story she did the voiceover: "This is Brooke . . . This is Ashleigh." Years later, it is still a fun clip for all of us to watch together.

I had to learn how to juggle television and fatherhood during those first days with Brooke and Ashleigh—and once again, Janice was an amazing mom and took it all in stride.

Junkyard Jobo

It is a sad moment when America's Cup teams are eliminated from the competition. Once a syndicate is out of the running, the team packs up quickly for home and the compound that was once busy with activity and full of hope becomes a ghost town; with the boat pulled apart, the crew solemn, and bits of garbage blowing around the waterfront.

One day I had a bright idea for our TV coverage to mark this sad exodus: we ought to do a junkyard sale. And with that, the character of Junkyard Jobo was born. I put on a straw hat, red bowtie, stripped shirt, and cane and took our camera crew into a closed-down compound and pretended to sell off the used parts. "Hey, I'm back. It's Junkyard Jobo . . ." I used my best used-carsalesman voice. The music played in the background: *Catch a wave and you're sittin on top of the world* . . . "Hey, come with me," I'd say as I looked around the compound to scout out things to hawk. "Ahhhh, look at this beauty!" Old sails, hardware, bits of rigging: all these pieces of a campaign that were once valuable and essential were now obsolete, I hawked them all.

It was a nice bit of levity and it made people chuckle. But deep down, it was a way to mark that sad time when you are suddenly not in the game any longer.

During the America's Cup, the Fremantle Doctor was a major player. The Doctor is not a local medical celebrity but the wind itself. It typically arrived with strong blows in the afternoons and was just as much a character of that Cup as Dennis Conner was. The most astounding shots during the regatta came from our onboard cameras when the Doctor appeared, showing Conner at the helm and bowman Scott Vogel, awash in big seas as he worked the foredeck. And we had sound: the waves crashing, sails crackling in the big breeze, the voices of the crew in the heat of the battle. The sports world was riveted by this American team sailing the regatta of their lives.

With the time difference between Australia and the United States, fans on the East Coast were setting their alarm clocks and waking up after midnight to catch the live action from Down Under, and the ratings grew and grew with each race.

I share a laugh with Jim Kelly and John Bertrand during the 1987
America's Cup before shooting a show open.

Some 320,000 households tuned in for Race 1. By the sixth race, the viewership had escalated to 640,000. Those numbers were double what ESPN had expected.

In the final race, Dennis and his crew sailed the upwind legs deftly, edging away from *Kookaburra III*. The smoky-blue *Stars & Stripes* with its upturned ends did not look as sleek as its Australian nemesis and was maligned as the "banana boat" when it first arrived in Fremantle. But not that day. *Stars & Stripes* stood straight up in the building breeze and kept *Kookaburra* on its tail. The Australians made gains downwind, but Dennis played the wind shifts upwind and led to the finish to bring the Cup back home. I was the only journalist to hop on board and get his reaction. What a great moment that was.

Dennis came home a hero, to a ticker-tape parade and a visit to the White House. But it was clear, even from faraway Australia, that the Cup frenzy that raged in America came down to one simple reason: patriotism. America had recaptured the America's Cup.

A Conversation with Jed Drake

Jed Drake was a young ESPN producer at the start of his career when the network covered the '87 America's Cup over 20 years ago. He has spent his career with the network and remembers that first America's Cup as the best event in his entire ESPN career. In this conversation, he takes us back to the network's first involvement with the Cup and the impact the landmark event had on the network.

Gary Jobson (GJ): What inspired ESPN to get involved in the America's Cup in the first place?

Jed Drake (JD): It was just one of those deals where you had to be at the right place at the right time. As you know, in Race 7 in 1983, there was not enough wind to sail on Sunday so the race got moved to a weekday. ESPN, a four-year-old cable network, just happened to be there where nobody else could televise it, and so suddenly we were finding ourselves with Race 7 of the America's Cup on our network, taking local coverage from WJAR, and—as we all know what happened—the world changed rather dramatically for the yachting world at that moment.

GJ: So how was the rating on that Monday afternoon?

JD: It was the highest rating that we had ever seen on any non-primetime show by a huge margin. I think we got a 2.4 that afternoon, and it was just good luck and good fortune that we were able to get it. And what that did was it propelled us, saying, oh, hang on, this could be something, this America's Cup that is now going down to Australia; perhaps we should engage. And, of course, we did.

GJ: So off to Australia, a very patriotic event.

JD: It was the kind of thing that when you lose something after 130-plus years . . . then all of a sudden the country wakes up and says, Oh my God. And Dennis Conner had been the guy who was sort of not well liked until he lost it. And remarkably when he lost it, he became much more well liked. So he went to Australia with his team of Americans and everybody was dressed in red, white, and blue in a sea of yachting that was really unparalleled at that time. Challenger Harbor was just a magnificent scene every morning. It was a very patriotic scene. The Italians were there, the Kiwis were there, the French were there, Dennis was there. It was a remarkable time.

GJ: Going back to '83, Race 7, I think there is a blimp picture, I think there was a shot on Castle Hill and there was some commentary. There wasn't much.

JD: There was precious little—and it spoke to where yachting was in terms of its interest and appeal . . . Also, it was right on the outside edge of where technology was really starting to come into its own, in terms of being able to televise these events with the kind of technology that would allow us to get inside. And we all know what we're talking about here, which are the onboard cameras. They changed everything.

GJ: When did you realize that having those onboard cameras would make this television event special?

JD: I realized the onboard cameras would change everything the moment I saw those pictures. Now, when we went to Australia, as you recall, the onboard cameras were already on *Kookaburra*. They had been there for some time because it was all funded; it was Australian and, you know—one for all and all for one in terms of the Aussies and the cameras and everything else. When we put our own camera on Blackaller's boat that very first time and saw pictures coming off of that, to us in the television compound it was like seeing a man walk on the moon. It was like, Oh my God, we can actually see pictures from these U.S. boats . . . The interesting thing is that that camera itself is nothing more than a relatively inexpensive, off-the-rack camera that would just happen to be mounted in a waterproof, Plexiglas tube. You could put the tube in the Smithsonian, because for the America's Cup, for the U.S. audience, it changed everything.

GJ: And not only did we have pictures but we had sound.

JD: And the sound was equally interesting. It was a confluence of so many different things that worked for television. It was the onboard cameras, it was the venue, Gage Roads where the winds whipped . . . It was these 12 Meter yachts that sailed so magnificently in those heavy seas, and it was the audio. We used to ask you and your colleague Mr. Kelly to pipe down just a little bit: We're getting a lot of good audio off these boats here; let it come in . . . One of the most memorable moments to me of all the America's Cup races was the pre-start of Race 4 in 1987, when Dennis clearly had a huge boatspeed advantage . . . So the only question was whether or not he was going to win this start. And with about three minutes to go, we've got the mics on and Tom Whidden—and you can hear him clear as a bell—says, We're going

Geoff Mason (left), Jed Drake (right), and I on ESPN's announce boat during the 1992 America's Cup off San Diego.

to win this start. And from that moment, I knew the America's Cup was done—because once they won that start, case closed. And as we know, it was pretty much a parade from that point.

GJ: And when Dennis Conner won it, he became a national hero.

JD: I think it was kind of surprising to him that he would be as well liked—going to see Ronald Reagan, getting the parades, bringing home the Cup on the big plane, and the whole deal. It changed a lot. Quite honestly, for those of us who had been involved, this was the pinnacle in 1987 as we look forward. I remember we hung a sign outside our compound in Fremantle as we left for the last time; there were a lot tears. They always say the best events are the ones that feel the worst when they are over. And this one felt really bad to be over. There was a piece of plywood up there and Jamie Reynolds and I sprayed on it, "Last one out, lock the door. See you Hawaii!" We thought it was quite likely the America's Cup might have, in the next incarnation after '87, gone to Hawaii.

GJ: What did the America's Cup on ESPN do for the network after the '87 match?

JD: When you think 1987, remember that ESPN was only eight years old at that time. And even in a few years prior to that, there were some skeptics who thought that ESPN might not make it . . . But what the America's Cup did was create this sudden, national interest in ESPN doing something really, totally remarkable in terms of televising the America's Cup. And with Dennis and the nationalistic pride and him winning the Cup and bringing it back, there were a lot of people who took notice of ESPN. And right at that time, Steve Bornstein was negotiating the NFL rights. Think about this, an eight-year-old cable network trying to negotiate the rights for the National Football League. Steve needed something to help get over the goal line. And what he had was the America's Cup. Because it happened at exactly the right time, it got him just enough juice to say ESPN is a real deal—and he convinced the NFL that we were. Once we got the NFL, it was like turbo-charging the rest of the network. And as they say, the rest is history.

As we packed up in Australia, our whole ESPN family was coming off the wave of a huge high, knowing a highpoint for all of our careers was over. The reality was, one of the biggest stories in international sailing was a once-in-a-lifetime thing. It was a tale that crossed boundaries, appealing not only to sailing fans but to many Americans who cheered for a home team in the middle of the night. ESPN knew such a story was rare fortune—and one that literally put this young network on the TV-sports map.

But I was raring to go again, so as soon as I got back to the States I got in touch with Steve Bornstein and told him, "Well, that was great! What are we going to do next?"

"Well, we don't have any other sailing events in the plan," Steve told me, "unless you want to learn how to package and produce." And so, I learned.

* * *

The 1987 America's Cup opened the door to my TV work. Soon after that historic event, *Boston Globe* sportswriter Tony Chamberlain dubbed me the closest thing to a yacht-racing media star America had ever seen. It was a nice tagline after my name, but the star potential did not lure me: it was the math. Before the '87 Cup, my articles were appearing in sailing magazines that had the potential to reach up to 100,000 readers. But TV was a whole new game, with hundreds of thousands of viewers to promote the sport to. It was tailor fit to everything I had done up to that point. But as much as the '87 Cup was a great entree, after that I had to cut my own path—learn the television business and then develop a standard for covering a sport that did not see much airtime in the United States.

My big break came quickly when I was contacted by an NBC executive named Michael Weisman about producing and narrating the sailing reports for NBC's coverage of the summer Olympic Games. Little did NBC know that I had never done any producing myself. But I had certainly been telling stories and putting slide shows together, so of course I said yes.

In the summer of 1988, I flew off to South Korea to cover the Olympics, and let me tell you, that was one tough gig. The international broadcast center was in Seoul, so I would fly back and forth each day from Seoul to Pusan, which is about an hour-long flight. I'd arrive in the morning, work with the crew to get footage of the racing, hit the docks to get my interviews, then head back to Seoul with footage in hand to cut the piece. I would usually get back around 7 pm, produce my piece, and get to sleep about 1 am—only to wake up and do it all over again the next day.

The '88 Games saw some wet and wild sailing, and as part of our coverage, we did a story about a heroic Canadian singlehanded sailor named Lawrence Lemieux. Like all Olympic athletes, Olympic sailors train four years, or more, to get one shot at an Olympic medal—and in the Finn class racing in Pusan, Lemieux was in striking distance of a bronze and winning the race in very heavy air when he spied a capsized, two-man 470 team representing Singapore. In the rough seas, he could see that one of the crew was seriously struggling and in risk of drowning. So Lemieux sailed over and pulled the 470 crew from the water—and of course, that disqualified him from the race.

I did the story, and it became quite a phenomenon. In the end, Lemieux got his accolade: there is only one sportsmanship award given at each Olympic Games, and he was crowned with the Pierre de Coubertin Medal for Sportsmanship in 1988. I got an Emmy for that Olympic coverage, and I am sure that story was a big part of the reason why.

Today's technology would transform the logistics I faced in Pusan. Our digital footage can now be dispatched electronically anywhere in the world. Back in those days, it wasn't exactly carrier-pigeon technology: it was just me, commuting 200 miles through the South Korean skies to get the story.

After the '87 Cup and the '88 Olympic Games, the luster of the America's Cup waned quickly. Michael Fay launched a surprise challenge with a 90-foot monohull instead of a 12 Meter, and Dennis Conner answered the challenge with a catamaran. ESPN covered the event live. But the legal battles surrounding the match-up and the fact that these two completely different boats did not make for exciting footage cast a long shadow over the event.

The America's Cup had turned sour. I searched desperately for a sailing story that would be dramatic and telegenic. One year later, a woman named Denise Norman from England contacted me about producing the U.S. coverage of an ocean marathon called the Whitbread Round the World Race. This event had all the elements of great TV: the dramatic conditions of some of the roughest patches of the ocean, big powerful boats, landfalls in faraway locales that served as stopovers between the different legs of the race, and lots of human interest stories about crews who took sabbaticals from everyday life to compete in a rugged contest where every decision could lead to triumph or tragedy.

For the first Whitbread I was involved with, in 1989–90, I took the Whitbread footage, re-edited it for a U.S. audience, wrote my own script, and created the show. And once again, this sailing event generated compelling stories and big ratings for ESPN.

That first Whitbread was the start of my long association with the event. As I got to know the Whitbread organizers I started playing more roles with the race, as a spokesman, as a member of the Advisory Board, as an MC at prize-givings. I floated the idea of allowing racers to send reports off the boats via satellite, and the Whitbread organizers bit. That idea blossomed in a big way as technology advanced—with racers doing their own blogs from the middle of the ocean before the word *blog* was in our daily lexicon. More and more people started tuning in.

I started lobbying as early as 1990 to get the race to stop in my home waters of the Chesapeake Bay. Annapolis yacht designer Bruce Farr—who had designed most of the boats competing in the race and had the ultimate street cred in Whitbread circles—helped a great deal. By 1998, this global marathon was making its way to Baltimore and Annapolis. I stayed involved with the race until 2006.

*   *   *

The Whitbread proved to be my third lucky break and helped me build a foundation for my career in television. By the time I boarded a plane for Key West, Florida, in January 2008, I was a seasoned veteran.

As I winged my way to Key West, dangling off the south tip of Florida, the island promised sun and blue water. But my exodus from the north was not simply a cold-weather escape. It was my annual mecca to Key West Race Week, where the world's top world-class racers go head to head against weekend warriors from around the globe.

Key West is a must-do event. If sailing is your line of work, as long as you are not training for the America's Cup or braving icebergs in the Southern Ocean in a round-the-world race, you are in Key West. So as my plane winged its way toward the island, anticipation ran high. Would conditions be perfect, with big winds and waves? Would we get in 10 races? Would all our pre-regatta planning come to fruition?

Our crew was flying south from all corners of the country, and when we all landed we gathered that evening for our traditional crew meeting. But we were not a traditional racing crew; we had a much different agenda. As the ESPN team covering Acura Key West Race Week, we had to deliver the excitement to our viewers—which is not an easy task. But by this time, 21 years after that first Cup in Australia, our ESPN team knew the right formula for taking raw footage and interviews and weaving them into a story under brutal time constraints.

Our 12-member team for Race Week—working both on- and off-site—was primed for the week ahead. Cameramen traveling onboard race boats, on chase boats, and in a helicopter would be our eyes on the course. I would direct the action from the helicopter during the racing. After the racing, it was a full-on offensive with impossible deadlines: chase the docks for interviews, edit footage, write the stories of the day, and package it all for a nightly report.

As we prepared for the 2008 Key West regatta, we had our slick technology all in place, but the job essentially hasn't changed. It's all about telling a good story. It took three months before the regatta to prepare for our mission in Key West of capturing the essence of the regatta, reporting its highlights, and making even the most casual ESPN watcher appreciate the great sport of sailboat racing.

The biggest challenge I faced that week in Key West was convincing owners to allow our cameras and microphones aboard their boats. For sailors, racing with onboard cameras takes a leap of faith, but most skippers in the end are happy with the results. At times there is salty language (which we bleep over), but viewers get to see first-hand what actually goes on during a race.

I always look for close action, and then edit from several viewpoints. In Key West, we shot from onboard, from the water, and from the air. The backbone of the coverage is shot onboard. Cameraman Rick Deppe is a highly experienced blue water sailor and a skilled cameraman. He's nimble and small and he knows what to look for and how to stay out of the way, which makes him a natural choice as an onboard cameraman. Our philosophy is to shoot both play-by-play race action and beauty—and Deppe always comes back with something unique.

Our on-the-water cameramen were Mike Audick, Vince Casalaina, and Keith Sandler. These guys have remarkably steady hands to get steady footage while shooting with 35-pound cameras attached to gyro lenses (a 16-pound, $15,000 unit and the key to getting footage that doesn't make you seasick).

For our aerial footage shooting from the helicopter, Steve Cassidy brings his $500,000 gyro camera with a special mount. Unlike the still photographers that buzz racing boats at close range, our chopper stays 500 feet above the fleet to get the steadiest pictures. My job is to ride in the helicopter and direct Steve and pilot Jean-Paul Robinson. I divide my time between looking at the shot on a small TV screen and watching out the window to understand what is happening on the racecourse. You can see a lot from the air, so I have to anticipate how a race will unfold so I can direct our flight pattern over the course. To coordinate with Deppe, we follow the boat he's shooting on, and all three cameras must shoot from the same side of the course for proper editing. We also have to keep the sun at our backs to make the boats look their best.

Steve Cassidy, J.P. Robinson, and I after shooting with Paul Barth's helicopter and a Cine-flex camera at Key West, Florida. We have shot remarkable images of sailing with this system.

After the last race is sailed for the day our crew hits the docks to interview the sailors. Win or lose, we always seem to find everyone in a good mood. In Key West in mid-winter, how can you not be? By 5 pm we are loaded with about 20 hours of footage from the day's racing. Video editor Scott Shucher, writer Roger Vaughan, and I convene in a closet-sized section of the media trailer to view the footage and produce our nightly Internet report. I lay the narration track at about 6 pm. Suzy Leech—a top racer who is also an excellent onboard shooter worked off-site that year, handling webmaster duties—got us online by about 8 pm each night. During the week, 375,000 visitors from around the world watched at least one of our eight episodes.

* * *

Ten months after returning from Key West, editor Rick Larmore and I are in the studio, searching for a soundbite for our latest film on the history of the New York Yacht Club. The room is all black and quiet, except for the hum of our equipment. The only color in the room pops from the video monitors.

The studio these days is like my second home, and after years of working in offsite spaces, Jobson Sailing now has its own editing suite. I installed the studio in the same building that houses my office in Annapolis, and what a treat it is to be able to run downstairs and work on a film, then run upstairs to catch up on other work and phone calls.

For the New York Yacht Club film, I conducted all 52 interviews myself. My assistant Kathy transcribed them all into a notebook that I read, reread, and then read again, so I know the content well. But right now we are looking for something elusive—a few words that mix the right tone, substance, and cadence.

"Good thought, but too may ums and kind of awkward," I say, as we view one possibility.

We view another, but it takes over 20 seconds to get out the complete thought. And then we find it: a short and substantive quote only a few seconds long. It is like striking gold. Rick edits it in.

The film is almost done, save for some fine-tuning; there is also more narration and audio to mix in, and Victor Giordano—a talented audio editor I work with who composes music for my films—is coming in today with the music track. We want it to be as close to done this morning, when Bob Towse, the rear commodore of the New York Yacht Club arrives to get his first look at a work that has been a year and a half in the making: 14 months of shooting at the club's New York City and Newport homes and at club events, 100 hours of footage, 1,500 images, 52 interviews, and about 4,000 audio edits. It had been a long and interesting project.

Sun Bird was the viewing platform for a few hundred spectators along with our ESPN announce team—Jim Kelly, John Bertrand, and I—during the 1987 America's Cup.

Great at some things, but not all . . .

In the fall of 1998, Ted Turner and I were invited to sail a long-distance race off San Francisco on Larry Ellison's Maxi *Sayonara*. Ted was considering chartering the boat the following summer, to sail in the 20th anniversary of the infamous Fastnet Race. So the night before the race, Larry Ellison threw a small dinner party, and Ted and I were invited.

That evening, Ted, Jane Fonda (Ted's wife at the time), and I arrived at Ellison's home, which had an amazing view of the Golden Gate Bridge. We were joined by Larry, his wife Melanie (then girlfriend), Steven Jobs, and his wife Laurene. As you can imagine, it was a fascinating evening spent in the company of people who are all great and accomplished in their respective fields.

After cocktails and a fabulous dinner, Steven Jobs asked us if we'd like to see a clip from his new film about to come out from his company, Pixar Pictures. Larry answered an immediate, Absolutely! So we retired two levels down to Larry's small movie theater.

Steven Jobs had a VHS of the film, but we had some technical difficulties. Larry couldn't quite get the VHS player to work, so Steven Jobs got up to help. The two of them continued to push buttons, but still, no film. At which point, Ted couldn't help himself and got up to lend a hand. But still, no film. After a few minutes of the three of them fumbling around, Jane Fonda got into the act too.

So there I was sitting on the couch between Melanie and Laurene, and the three of us watched the largest stockholder of the biggest media company in the world, the second-largest software manufacturer in the world, the owner of Apple and Pixar Pictures, and a two-time Academy Award–winning actress not being able to run the VHS player.

Soon, a member of the kitchen staff walked out, pushed about six buttons, and screens started popping up and we were soon watching clips of *A Bug's Life*.

We all laughed about it afterward. But it just proved to me, you can be great at some things, but not everything.

But it's not the only project we have going. Since Key West, I traveled down to Antarctica with the New York Yacht Club and produced a commemorative film of the adventure. We are working on a film on Maine-built boats, to help promote an industry that is important to this coastal state. We are in the final editing stages of a film on the legendary Chicago-Mac race, the 100-year-old, 333-nautical mile race that is the longest freshwater sailing contest that runs from Chicago to Mackinac Island. The Chicago-Mac project involved lots of planning and coordination, including getting onboard cameras on 11 boats during the race. Putting all those films together since Key West required seventeen cameramen, four writers, three editors, and a sound technician.

For all the films I produce, the first critical step is the idea itself. Lots of people say, Oh, you should do a film on this regatta, or on this club, or this boat. There are a lot of good ideas—and some have legs. I don't have a big Hollywood staff: it's only me in the beginning of a project. I pull in the cameramen and production crew, writers, film editors, and sound editors once the project is established and underway.

Once the idea is solid, I have to figure out how to fund it—and that's never easy. Sometimes I sell it to a network like ESPN and finance it by selling advertising; sometimes it's a sponsor-funded piece; sometimes it's funded by an organization. The formula is always slightly different. I have to admit that I suffer from my own enthusiasm and often end up putting more time into a project than budgeted. But I am too quality conscious to shave back once I see the potential we could reach with some extra effort.

By now, I've just accepted this is something that happens. I have to come away with quality I can be proud of, for the films are a record of our sport and our time, of events that will never be recaptured again. It is important to me to leave this legacy, and I want someone 20, 40 years later to look at one of our films and say, These people really did their homework. I think about that all the time.

When I document an event or an organization or an expedition, I do not start with a blank sheet of paper and go off and create scenes. I go as an observer and get people talking, and through them, I can tell the story. I like to be thoughtful, not flash. I don't like MTV quick-cut editing flashing all over the place. I like a film to flow and move and tell a story along the way.

Every documentary needs voices, and I like to have a lot of them. I insist on doing all the interviewing myself—and I never compromise on that for good reason. As I am interviewing people, I can respond to them and ask questions and get the thoughts in each interview feeding off the other interviews. When it comes to visuals, I develop a vision of the final project in my head as I work, and I scout out scenes with our cameramen: we need the yacht club flag flying, the race committee coming into the dock at sunset, the regatta scene in the morning when bleary-eyed crew are coming to their boats with coffee in hand. The difficult thing with a documentary or event coverage is you don't know the story yet: What are people going to say? What's going to happen on the racecourse? The story is never clear until the end of the project, so I grab the images and interviews I think we will need. In the end, we take that enormous stock of footage and interviews and essentially cut it up into small pieces, then piece them all back together in a different order to make the narrative. That is the part I like most: the editing. Because you are telling the story and putting it to pictures. I learned to do that at a young age, when I put my slide shows together to take on the road. I'd lay my slides out and study the images and figure out how to sequence from one image to the next to tell a story. It is the same process, only the film images are moving and the technology is so much more advanced than working with three carousels of slides!

It may be unusual in the film world to work as the producer, to direct, to work as talent, to edit, and to write and co-write. But I had the rare opportunity at the 1987 America's Cup to be a part of the whole operation and see how it came together. Back then, I played a smaller part as talent, but my impressions of the operation were solid. So when I learned that to keep making sailing films would require me to step up and tackle the whole project and not just the talent part, it tasked me with an enormous challenge—but one that has made my career fascinating and unique as an observer of sailing in our time. At the end of the day, none of these films would have ever flickered across a screen if I didn't just go out and do it. Far from being a daunting task, I have found it a rare opportunity to take sailing to a wider audience.

.7.
NEW FRONTIERS

 My heart is pounding. Standing on the edge of an icy shelf, I lean back and begin the rappel down the 300-foot cliff. My weight on this sheer of ice is held by a skinny line the size of a Laser mainsheet, anchored to a ski buried three feet in the snow. Safety or disaster depends on that thin line. I hope it holds.

Everything around me is white and frozen. My shipmates who have joined me on this sailing expedition to Antarctica look Technicolor in contrast. Sailing adventurer Skip Novak, world-class climber Alex Lowe, cameraman Alan Hughes, and I have come ashore to explore an ice cave, leaving five other crew members onboard Novak's 54-foot steel-hulled sloop, *Pelagic*.

The long rappel is our only passageway into the cave. But once there, we are rewarded with a magical scene: a grotto of ice illuminated by pale blue light cascading off the cave walls.

I look around the cave and think about the explorers who have been known to live in caves like this for extended periods. Our berths onboard *Pelagic* are warmer, but no less compact.

There is limited space on a 54-foot boat, but Novak cleverly stowed the enormous amount of food and equipment we needed for this six-week expedition. After years of operating *Pelagic*, Skip has the routine down to a science and uses a computer program to specify the provisions. On this expedition, *Pelagic* was prepared to serve 1,215 meals. Every ingredient was purchased from a food wholesaler in Ushuaia, Argentina, 87 miles north of Cape Horn. On provisioning day, 50 kilos of potatoes, 30 kilos of carrots, and 25 kilos of onions came aboard. Two slaughtered *corderos* (lambs) were hung from the boat's backstay. Every meal was started from scratch and required a lot of time and patience to prepare on the boat's simple two-burner stove. Every piece of garbage we generated stayed with the boat. The food scraps were dumped 20 miles offshore on our return sail. As permitted by the Antarctic Treaty, our gray water was released overboard.

How did I end up here in 1996, exploring under sail in a desolate region many refer to as the end of the earth? It all started in the relatively balmy climate of San Diego, during the 1992 America's Cup.

I reported on the '92 Cup for ESPN, when Bill Koch's *America³* beat the Italian boat *Il Moro di Venezia* and won the venerable trophy. Then in my early forties, I began to think about the choices I had made in my sailing career. I raced with Bill as tactician on two of his maxi boats, *Matador* and *Matador²*, between 1984 and 1990. It took some time for me to appreciate his relentless pursuit using advanced technology to improve boatspeed. In 1990 *Matador²* won the Maxi World Championship. There were many top-name sailors racing in the maxi class at that time. Koch's successful research inspired him to launch an America's Cup defense syndicate for the 1992 match. Once he got rolling, he handily won the America's Cup over Italy that year. Bill Koch, like many America's Cup leaders, has a tremendous desire to succeed and will go to extremes to achieve success.

My life had been focused on racing at the top level, and I wondered about other types of sailing that were, for me, still unexplored.

Bill Koch sails *Matador²* to windward off Newport, Rhode Island. The boat was a breakthrough design and won the World Championship in 1990.

The *Pelagic* crew are all smiles after rounding infamous Cape Horn. From left, me, Peter Isler, Mike Audick, Julia Crossley, Dan Wellehan, Jamie Reynolds, and Norwood Davis.

I started to think more about expedition cruising and exploring remote areas of the world under sail. Two contemporaries of mine, Skip Novak and Elizabeth Meyer, were both big influences on what I began to see as a new direction to add to my sailing life. Both Skip and Elizabeth are highly motivated sailors, but where they differed from me is that they had focused their lives on cruising. They have each gravitated to different types of boats and different types of voyages, but they share a common desire: to see the world from the deck of a sailboat.

Skip Novak is a modern-day adventurer who thrives in extreme environments; his steel-hulled *Pelagic* is a strong, utilitarian boat that takes him from one place of adventure to the next. Elizabeth has restored a number of beautiful classic yachts— including the stunning 1934 J-Class sloop *Endeavour*—that are all head-turners. Many credit her with sparking a renaissance in the world of classic-boat restoration, but Elizabeth does not restore these yachts to be museum pieces: she uses them as her platform to see the world, and she sails them hard in all weather conditions. For Elizabeth and Skip, cruising is structured, rewarding, and ambitious, and they both have had a big impact on my desire to see new frontiers. I am lucky to have cruised with them both.

After the light winds of the '92 America's Cup, I wanted to produce a film about a place that was *windy*. I took the idea to John Wildhack in programming at ESPN, first with the thought of heading to Cape Horn, the remote and forbidden land mass that juts deep into the Southern Ocean at 56 degrees South latitude. This point of land satisfied the windy part of the equation: the Horn is the windiest place in the world, where gale-force winds blow one out of every ten days. In 1993, I made my first trip to the region, sailing with Skip and a crew of eight onboard *Pelagic*.

It took a year to plan the first expedition—and just getting to our departure point in Chile was a major undertaking. The flight from Miami to Punta Arenas, the largest town on the Magellan Channel, was 11 hours. From there, we took a two-hour flight on a charter plane to the Chilean Naval base, Puerto Williams. The desolate town was the starting point of our 15-day expedition on *Pelagic*. The town's population—mixing sailors, officers, and the local population of native Indians—is around 2,000. The town looks like a Hollywood stage set for a Wild West movie: all dirt roads and wooden sidewalks.

Our next destination was 60 miles west of Puerto Williams at an *estancia* named Yendegaia, where Novak knows the ranch owner and the *caballeros* who work the land. There was no electricity, running water, telephone, or television. Everyone worked from dawn to dusk and lived off the land. With winter coming, the snow covering the peaks moved lower with each day, and we lived under a constant drizzle of rain. Daytime temperatures were in the 40-degree Fahrenheit neighborhood and dipped down into the 20s at night.

As we sailed west from Estancia Yendegaia, we saw 50 knots of wind that derailed our expedition while we waited 14 hours in a small cove for the wind to subside to a milder 35; driving rain followed by magnificent rainbows; glaciers that ranged in color from blue to white to jet black; williwaws that swirled the snow on the mountains and the spray on the water; and seals and birds and dolphins and wildlife of many kinds. We climbed up a 5,000-foot mountain that traversed through foliage as dense as a jungle, hiked over a spongy bog where our boots sank half a foot with each step, steep rocks, and ice; and slept through dark nights at anchor that were like living inside a bottle of black ink. On those dark, spooky nights with no visibility, our imaginations got away from all of us. I imagined Indians sneaking up silently in canoes and snatching me off the boat—and everyone else admitted to similar bizarre fears during those pitch-black nights so far from civilization.

The most important part of our expedition was the long-awaited rounding of Cape Horn—a place of shipwrecks, monstrous seas, powerful winds, and dangerous jagged cliffs. The Horn is the focal point between the Atlantic and Pacific Oceans. The transition creates massive waves and confused current patterns. Seas as high as 100 feet have been recorded, yet 10,000 ships made the trip during the age of sail. The island archipelago surrounding the Cape Horn region is devoid of most foliage other than peatmoss: it is simply too windy for roots to take hold.

To reach the archipelago, we sailed across the Gulf of Nassau, a long, dangerous stretch of open water. The wind piped up to 40 miles an hour. Luckily for us it was downwind. I kept thinking, What is it going to be like to go back the other way? But Novak didn't seem worried.

The night before our rounding, we anchored off Wollaston Island, situated eight miles north of the Horn. It was a time of great anticipation, thinking about all the people who had rounded the Horn before us. Many never made it, and our thoughts were of them. The next day would be our chance.

Pelagic steams through a fiorjd called the Gerlache Strait on a rare, windless Antarctic summer day.

We approached the Horn from the north sailing downwind. The wind was blowing between 28 and 42 knots. The waves were huge, extending the length of a football field from crest to crest, measuring about 16 feet high. The breaking waves on the rock became our gauge in estimating the size of the waves. Naturally everybody wanted to spend time at the helm as we rounded the Horn. The sail took two hours and maneuvering was difficult, but our rounding was an unforgettable transit between two oceans.

This region could be brutal, but it was beautiful and serene. Visiting there had its great rewards. I knew once I left that '93 expedition, I would someday return.

The Joys of Simply Sailing Around

Well before my first adventure to Cape Horn in '93, I knew something was missing from my sailing life. After years of grand-prix racing on America's Cup yachts and giant Maxis manned by an army of crew, I became acutely aware that I was missing simply sailing around. Janice and I had our three daughters by that time. In 1987, our twins Ashleigh and Brooke joined their big sister Kristi Lynn. I felt the few valuable days I could muster time to go sailing should be spent encouraging the girls to enjoy the water—and so a seed was planted: it was time for a new family boat.

The next question was, Which one? We were not looking to do expeditions as a family but wanted to start with a daysailer, a small boat for heading out just for a few hours of sailing. Plus, we needed a boat that could handle the firm winds of the Chesapeake's fall and spring seasons, and one that would ghost along in the light summer breeze that blew over the Bay waters that were a stone's throw from our house in Annapolis. And I wanted a boat that was well built—and definitely one that had character.

It took a year of searching, and then, one day, out of the blue, I discovered a 28-foot, 1932 design by L. Francis Herreshoff called a Stuart Knockabout. The boat was fast, it could fit eight people, and it had low freeboard, keeping you close to the water and giving you a thrilling sense you are a part of the sea. Luckily, a builder in Marion, Massachusetts, Bill Harding, was producing these boats. I took a trip up to Marion to have a look, and the Knockabout was just what we needed. My order followed immediately.

The boat arrived in April, and Janice and I loaded the girls on board. It took some encouragement to get everyone on board. After I allowed the Barbie dolls and teddy bears as extra crew, off we went.

Ashleigh, then three, needed to steer before we even got away from the dock. Brooke, on the other hand, found a quiet place underneath the spacious foredeck where her Barbie dolls could be unpacked and enjoy the ride. It was a windy day, but two extraordinary things happened: we didn't hear one complaint from the girls, and everyone enjoyed being out on the water together.

On that first sail, the reaction to our little Knockabout, which we named *Whirlwind*, was extraordinary. People cheered for this beautiful little classic: we had found the right boat indeed. But in time, kids grow, lives change—and so too did our needs for a family boat. Enter, *Silver Heels*.

Our family on the bow sprit of *Silver Heels* in Stonington, Connecticut, in 1994. The twins are seven and Kristi standing is ten.

Brooke sails *Golden Ankles*, our dinghy for *Silver Heels.*

My first glimpse of *Silver Heels* was a stunning photo in a brokerage advertisement—and her beauty captured my imagination. She was classic, purposeful, inviting, well-proportioned, and unique, and I clipped out the picture and showed it to my longtime sailing friend, Jack King. His response equaled mine: "Let's go sailing!"

We found the boat on the Damariscotta River in Maine. She was in immaculate condition—thanks to Bruce MacNeil, who had been *Silver Heels'* owner for six years. Designed by Murray Peterson and painstakingly built by highly skilled Maine craftsmen, the boat still looked stunning 32 years after she was launched. After a brief sail, Jack and I shook hands, acquired the boat, and became 50/50 partners in—what I believe—is a true masterpiece of American craftsmanship.

My sailing had mainly been on modern sloops, so learning to sail a schooner had its comical moments. It took me and Jack King an hour and 18 minutes to set the topsail for the first time. I was amazed at the power and extra speed generated by the fisherman sail set between the spars. On a reach, a schooner is magic. Even at 42,000 pounds, *Silver Heels* parted the water with the strength of a nuclear submarine, with a motion that was rock steady and barely a heel.

At 41 feet on deck, *Silver Heels* was big enough for long family cruises. We transited by day from port to port, and as our three daughters grew, they took over a considerable amount of the load, hoisting sails and working the anchor. I thought cruising was meant to be a way to slow down and relax. But when we traveled as a family, we found time passed swiftly while we lived onboard. And with that boat, Janice and the girls and I started our tradition of taking month-long summer cruises as a family.

More growth spurts came in the girls' teenage years, and we considered a bigger boat. One summer—when our oldest daughter was 16—we chartered *Southerly*, a 56-foot ketch designed by the great Olin Stephens and built by Paul Luke in East Boothbay, Maine, in 1973. Around the time period of *Southerly*'s launch, Stephens had drafted several fast ocean racers that are now famous: *Running Tide*, *Dora IV* (later renamed *Tenacious*), *Yankee Girl*, and *Charisma*. *Southerly*, however, was quite a departure from the other designs, with a centerboard and a ketch rig. The boat needed at least 8 knots of wind to sail efficiently—and the windier it got, the happier we were.

Our family aboard **Southerly** on the Saint John River in New Brunswick, Canada, in 2000. The girls were teenagers at this time.

We planned an ambitious (for us) 28-day, 25-port cruise along the coast of Maine, Nova Scotia, and well up New Brunswick's secluded Saint John River. This cruise would be our fifth month-long trip. During those family voyages, it was fascinating to watch our three daughters adapt to life onboard as they grew. When they were younger, it was easy to gather everyone and go. But I knew that the teenage years provide a lot of opportunities: friends, jobs, parties, sports, movies, camps, and hanging out. Luckily, everyone was game.

Every landfall on the rugged coast we sailed along on *Southerly* was different, but special. We usually anchored before dark, and spent our days underway rotating steering and sail-trim duties, reading mounds of books, watching the sea life, and breathing in the fresh air. And as we made our way along the coast and sailed to increasingly remote areas, sightings of sealife and birdlife became the most exciting events of the day. The dolphins, seals, and birds we saw were fun, but the whales were best. Big, graceful, and likeable, they instantly brought everyone on deck. But whale watching took patience: they kept their distance, so we had to keep an eagle eye out for them.

At sea, the weather, sky, seascape, wave patterns, atmosphere, and wind all seem to change within minutes; life is never constant but always in flux. During some of our daily 50-mile legs, we experienced what felt like all four seasons (it is funny how frequently you change clothes to keep up with the weather).

The fog rolled in often, and when it did, I navigated while the girls steered. At times, we had zero visibility, ships all around, and a strong adverse current. During one particularly hairy ride into Yarmouth, Brooke helmed the boat and did particularly well. But thanks to GPS and radar, fog is no longer feared, as long as you pay strict attention to your location. Rocks, however, are another matter.

We hit North America head-on, just once—in the form of a mud flat outside a buoy on the Saint John River. I felt like moving the buoy to account for the shifting bar of land. Even with the engine at full rev, the sails up, and using the dinghy as a tug, we were stuck hard in four feet of water. This was a first for the girls; they were remarkably patient although curious about our one-hour delay. Lucky for us, my America's Cup colleague and good sailing friend Ted Hood happened to be in the area on his 47-foot powerboat, *Sea Robin*, and he dragged us off the mud. With the crisis over, we rafted alongside *Sea Robin* for the evening. One of the greatest American sailors and innovators, Ted was still thinking about better ways to spend time on the water, and we talked at length that night about design ideas and his thoughts on a potential breakthrough concept for an America's Cup boat.

The Bay of Fundy is notoriously cold, but all that changes on the Saint John River. Sixty miles north, Grand Lake features 75-degree fresh water. The girls swam for hours. Canada is beautiful and the people we encountered were the most friendly and helpful in the world.

As we visited one diverse port after another, we developed a comfortable routine onboard. Morning was for clean up, hiking, and exploring. We sailed in the afternoons when the wind filled in. Unfortunately, we were forced to motorsail frequently, but anytime there was wind, the sails went up.

Anchoring was always our preferred way to spend the night. Occasionally moorings were acceptable, but busy marinas were out. We wanted to cruise on the rustic side, to appreciate the topography and culture of the coast.

It was work on my part to keep the girls focused on the ever-changing events around us—the passing shore, other boats, sealife, even weather changes—and of course I had to compete with video games and books. It was also my job to make sure everyone had a specific job—for when that happened, my young crew was happy. No one likes to be left out, so I had to make sure that each job had its own importance.

Belowdecks, life was energetic. After dinner and clean up, we played dice, boardgames, and cards every night. A particular favorite was Greed, a dice game where you get more points for taking bigger risks. After 28 days, Ashleigh beat me by one point. The girls also played the venerable "Old Bachelor" card game (I remember it as Old Maid) card game. The chess set was untouched—but I was enjoying the girls' enthusiasm for game time.

As our days turned into weeks, our routine became second nature. The nights were magic. Under clear nighttime skies, far away from the bright lights of land, we took time to contemplate the stars. Shooting stars seemed to appear every few minutes—and many times we tried counting all the stars, even if looking up at all those pinpoints of diamond lights made you feel small and lonely.

During that cruise on *Southerly*, we never drove a car, flew in an airplane, tied up to a marina, or turned on a computer. We did walk a lot—and when you are moving slower, you meet more people. The girls particularly enjoyed meeting kids on other boats.

On our final sail, we made our way back upwind to Camden, Maine, where we had started our adventure a month earlier. Before we even reached Camden, our thoughts already turned to school, work, and rejoining the fast-paced world we left behind. We would all miss *Southerly*, so I told the girls I was going to install all the toilets at home with pump handles—just the way they were on the boat—so they wouldn't get homesick for our floating home. It was not a popular idea.

On our last night onboard, we kept the ship's clock wound up, just as we did every night, and listened to the bells every half hour. They were a soothing reminder that we were living on a boat. And during the wee hours of that last night, they were a cue of the constantly changing weather and tides that had become such a part of our lives. Soon, those natural forces would seem so far away; soon, we would be home and *Southerly*'s bells would sadly be silent to us.

*   *   *

During the 1995 America's Cup in San Diego, I wondered about producing another expedition type film like we had done at Cape Horn. John Wildhack, the Vice President of Programming at ESPN, suggested finding a place even more dramatic than Cape Horn. Where could that possibly be? The answer came to me quickly—Antarctica!

On my 1996 passage through icy polar waters with Skip Novak, our crew sailed with a distinct purpose. Our mission aboard *Pelagic* was to explore this remote region, climb the peaks of the surrounding terrain, and experience Antarctica from a sailboat. We set three priorities for the expedition: safety, filming a high-quality production for ESPN, and having fun. Our eight-man, one-woman crew included two expert climbers, three filmmakers, and four sailors.

But this expedition had a theme: a sailor and a mountain climber experiencing each other's world. World-class climber Alex Lowe had never been on a sailboat, and I had never climbed rock walls or ice cliffs. We decided to head to Antarctica to experience our new sports in this extremely hostile environment.

Our first sighting of Antarctica was more dramatic than any documentary or photograph could ever capture. Two years of planning did not prepare me for this overwhelming moment. The jagged, icy cliffs of Smith Island off the northern tip of the Antarctic Peninsula rose 7,000 feet straight out of the ocean. It's unusual to see mountains of this magnitude meet the sea. To borrow from Yogi Berra, "Antarctica was even better looking than it looked."

Antarctica is a dynamic land with the icy features of the landscape constantly changing. It holds two-thirds of the world's fresh water, which is trapped as ice and covers 98 percent of the continent. The ice cap is so heavy, scientists theorize, that the Antarctic tectonic place would rise more than 500 feet if the ice melted. For 35 days this frozen wilderness would be our home.

Our expedition to Antarctica in '96 was Novak's sixth trip to the region. Unlike the early polar explorers—Scott, Amundsen, Weddell, Shackleton, and Ross—we had the advantage of modern technology aboard *Pelagic*, including GPS, a diesel heater, email communications via Comsat, and radar. Those who came to the region long before us had to take the weather as it came, but we could anticipate and prepare for the worst. Nevertheless, we found intuitive decision making to be our guide. Many of our charts were decades old and not always reliable. Just one example of the challenges of using the charts of the area was this: what were thought to be islands actually turned out to be peninsulas!

141

Alex Lowe climbs an iceberg several miles off the Antarctic Peninsula.
There were no safety ropes on this free climb.

Pelagic navigates around ice floes near Petermann Island on the Antarctic Peninsula.

Our expedition was no vacation. It was cold, with temperatures ranging from 5 to 35 degrees Fahrenheit. The wind blowing over the ice on shore made the climate brutal. At one point we spent nine days waiting for the weather to clear. Living with nine people in close quarters on a small yacht is challenging, but our crew did well by staying focused on our mission.

Crossing the infamous Drake Passage is serious business. Novak's mantra, "Just get across," continues to ring in my ears. When the wind went light, Novak would fire up the engine to keep the boat advancing at 6 knots. From experience, Novak knew the Drake's fury. Images of the horrific 1979 Fastnet Race flashed through my mind. The extreme weather that blew through the fleet after the start in England still stands as the deadliest storm in yacht-racing history. Haunted by the memories of that race, I was happy to share Novak's assessment and minimize our time in this most treacherous stretch of ocean. Two weeks before our departure the wind had been clocked at over 100 miles per hour at Cape Horn.

Once in Antarctica, every day was filled with adventure and surprise. *Pelagic* is able to venture deep into uncharted waters, thanks to a lifting keel and rudder. The toughest assignment for our two camera operators, Mike Audick and Alun Hughes, was staying disciplined to film one thing at a time. At any given moment, whales would appear without warning, and Mike and Alun had to be ready.

The extreme cold was tough on our camera equipment. Everything had to be handled with care. Our director, Jamie Reynolds, a veteran of four ESPN America's Cup television productions and our ESPN expedition to Cape Horn in 1993, always tried to shoot from a unique angle. These angles ranged from Mike sitting in a bosun's chair dangling at the end of the spinnaker pole over frigid water and menacing leopard seals, to Alun Hughes hanging from a thin line atop an iceberg while Alex Lowe climbed straight up its face. Both moments provided remarkable video.

Climbing the face of an iceberg has major risks. The saltwater below is freezing and a berg can roll over or break apart at any moment. During a 35-knot blizzard, Alex picked a berg to climb in the Gerlache Strait. With an ice ax in each hand and crampons (spikes) on his boots, Alex launched off the bow of *Pelagic* and scaled the 90-foot face in 14 minutes. Lowe—who is, to this day, considered one of his generation's finest all-around mountaineers—was also one of the world's top ice climbers. His long list of achievements included successfully climbing Yosemite's El Capitan 18 times and Mount Everest 3 times. Even with these experiences, Lowe was apprehensive about climbing an iceberg. Falling in the water could be catastrophic. Just in case, we kept the Zodiac dinghy close by.

We were all surprised by the frequent loud sounds of the terrain and icebergs. The Antarctic ice pushes down from the center of the continent under immense pressure and eventually breaks off into the sea. During summer, when the weather is relatively warm, there is a lot of ice activity. Every few minutes you could hear sounds like thunder as ice walls collapsed and bergs broke apart, always in tune with the restless whistling of the wind. Half the time during our journey, the weather—with subfreezing temperatures and 50-knot winds—was too rough for exploration. But on our rare nice days, we were able to film 16 hours straight thanks to the continuous light of summer. At 65 degrees South latitude, the sun set at 11 at night (2300 hours in nautical parlance) and rose at 2:30 in the morning.

Life on *Pelagic* changed dramatically when nine days of storms lashed the region. Illness and injury slowed the crew down. John Thackwray developed a bad infection in his right hand. Chuck Gates suffered a staph infection. I had an inflamed knee after a climb. Our reading list was diverse: how the atom bomb was made, Warren Buffet and his billions, Franklin and Eleanor Roosevelt, how longitude was first calculated, and various exploration books.

We also kept in contact with the outside world. With our Comsat Mobile Communications, each member of the crew was able to send and receive daily emails. Our communications officer Suzy Leech—an accomplished racing sailor who worked the bow on *Mighty Mary*, the all-women America's Cup crew that competed in the '95 Cup—was able to transmit video images of our activities. As an aside, Suzy married Jed Drake a few years later.

During good weather we navigated around and through the ice with the goal of reaching the Antarctic Circle. But the ice was too thick. The most southern point we reached was 65 degrees, 20 minutes South, 75 miles short of our goal. The key to navigating in ice is to stay away from the leeward shore. Pressure on the hull could collapse *Pelagic*, just as it had done to Shackleton's wooden ship back in October 1915. In spite of the cold, the wind, and the rawness, the wildlife of the Antarctic has found unique and creative ways to survive.

The bottom of the food chain is krill, a small crustacean that resembles shrimp. Almost everything else feeds off the krill. The biomass of krill in Antarctic waters is far greater than the biomass of the entire human race. Krill are taken by seals, whales, birds, and penguins. Areas with bare rocks were inhabited by penguins, with the rocks being warmer than the ice.

Alun, our Welsh cameraman, explained that the word *penguin* is Welsh for *white head*. What pictures never show is the putrid smell of penguin droppings on the rocks. Skip refers to the odor as a fine perfume but to me it smelled like a cross between an East River garbage scow and a cattle ranch.

Against a backdrop of Alpine peaks and huge, menacing icebergs we witnessed penguin babies carried off by hungry birds called skuas, and fur seals meeting their demise in the jaws of Orca whales.

While crossing the Drake we were consistently escorted by an albatross and petrels and entertained by a pod of humpback whales. I watched the albatross for hours. It is a bird of amazing grace and persistence. With a wingspan of 12 feet, the bird is able to soar without flapping its wings for minutes at a time. It uses the contour of the waves to gain lift and then zigzag across an area about 100 yards wide.

Occasionally, the albatross lands and sits tall in the water. Taking off requires effort, but once airborne, this magnificent bird flies at speeds of 40 miles per hour in search of fish, squid, and krill. The Beatles song "Free as a Bird" fits the flight of the albatross.

We did encounter human civilization at the British Antarctic survey base at Faraday. We delivered four ice-bound Faraday residents back to their base after finding them holed up in an abandoned hut 20 miles north. The British base at Faraday is famous for discovering the ozone hole in the mid-1980s. Ozone is a gas three millimeters thick spread through the atmosphere. But in Antarctica, in the winter, the ozone is only one millimeter thick and allows dangerous ultraviolet light to filter through. Back then, Jon Shanklin, one of the three scientists that discovered the hole, was reporting that the hole is shrinking and may be gone in about 50 years.

We explored an abandoned survey hut at Cuverville that proved to be a time capsule. We entered the wooden structure through a hatch underneath. I was surprised when my head popped up through an opening that turned out to be a toilet seat. We found magazines inside with cover dates no more recent than 1958.

Several countries including Chile, Norway, New Zealand, and Argentina have large territorial claims in Antarctica. But the continent is protected by a treaty extending until the year 2041. Under the treaty, all development, mining, and fishing is banned. Claims of sovereignty are not disputed or confirmed. The treaty has been signed by two dozen countries, but the United States has yet to endorse the document. Scientific research and tourism is allowed. America's National Science Foundation is involved in the most activity, although funding is rapidly drying up for these activities. Due to lack of funds, the British turned Faraday over to the Ukraine just a few weeks after our visit.

There is an international proposal to designate Antarctica a world park. This is a policy worthy of study. The region's remoteness and harsh weather will fortunately dampen any major development, but environmentally sensitive tourism and continued research should be encouraged.

Tourism is already growing rapidly in Antarctica. When we visited in 1996, converted research vessels and small passenger ships had doubled their capacity in the previous two years. Around the same time, it was estimated that 8,000 people visited Antarctica in the 1995–96 time period. During our expedition we were aware of seven other small cruising boats in the area. While I would encourage everyone to visit Antarctica, I would also caution that time spent there is not easy. It is a strange and alluring place, yet one filled with danger for the unprepared. For those of us sailing with Skip Novak, exploring this little-understood land was an opportunity of a lifetime. What made this special voyage possible was Skip's *Pelagic*—the small, rugged sailboat that carried our crew to this remote and magical corner of the globe.

Tragically, three years later, in October 1999, Alex Lowe was lost in an avalanche on a mountain in Shishapangma, Tibet. His loss hit our *Pelagic* crew hard. Alex had talked about the risks of mountain climbing. During an interview I did with him during our 1996 expedition, he told me how intrigued he was by sailing and how it compared with mountain climbing. "Passion is a wonderful thing. Climbing digs up that inner fire. I see the same thing in a sailor's eyes and I see it in my climbing partner's eyes. I don't know where that comes from. I am basically a neurotic, restless, individual with a lust for adventure. I can't turn down a good adventure. I don't know whether that's a character attribute or character flaw, probably goes both ways actually. But I tried to be normal for a few years and sit at an engineering desk. That didn't work. I sort of outgrew the desk too quickly and now I'm comfortable with who I am. I know I'll always be seeking places like Antarctica and the greater mountains of the world, which is sort of where I find myself. I really sort of come alive there. I've known that for a long time and I've been very fortunate."

I returned to Antarctica with Janice in February 2008, aboard a small ship with 100 members of the New York Yacht Club. While it was a more comfortable experience than being on a sailboat, Antarctica was still dramatic. We visited several of the same places but I was surprised to find how much recession had taken place on many of the glaciers. Climate change was clearly having an impact on the frozen continent.

.8.
MAKING A DIFFERENCE

**1993** When I served on the committee for my first Leukemia Society regatta, I witnessed a scene that was—by this time in my life—so very familiar. All the boats from my home waters of Annapolis had put their best crew shirts on and were heading out to the starting line for a day of racing, except there was something dramatically different about their motivation for heading from land. Sailors race their boats for a lot of reasons: the challenge of sailing faster than the next boat, the competition, the opportunity to interact with the elements, or simply fun and camaraderie. But at this regatta, competitors had a deeper reason for going sailing: a good cause.

←————— ▪ —————→

By the end of that regatta, hosted by the Eastport Yacht Club, we had raised $30,000 for blood-cancer research, and once it was over I was already thinking bigger: why couldn't this same format work on a national scale? After all my traveling—giving lectures and making connections in the sailing community across the country—I was in a perfect position to knit sailing communities together under a common cause. So when I was invited to be the honorary chair of the national series for the 1994 season, I did my due diligence, and, liking what I saw, I jumped in with both feet to work alongside Marty Siederer of the Leukemia Society's home office and their regional chapters. As I write this, we've grown to over 40 annual events nationwide. Today, a total of some $40 million has been raised to find cures for leukemia and blood-related cancers, and to improve the quality of life for patients and their families. Some 11,000 sailors race in the series each year.

There is a strong tradition amongst sailors to take care of the community they've built together. Sailors have always given generously to fund sailing programs for young sailors, Olympic sailors, and others. But as American sailors have become more aware of people afflicted with diseases and disabilities, charity regattas have also become a popular way to express moral and tangible support—and many different entities have found a way to contribute.

In the Leukemia Cups, corporate sponsors such as Mount Gay Rum, *Sailing World* magazine, North Sails, West Marine, Offshore Sailing School, and others have helped the cause by serving as sponsors. Companies such as Ken Gardner Model Maker and individuals such as the marine artist John Mecray—have donated auction items that have had a big impact on the events' fundraising results. I have even been auctioned off at Leukemia Cup auctions, the winner getting my expertise on the racecourse the next day.

To host an event, a local Leukemia Society chapter and a yacht club generally join forces and work together. Each year, we have a national conference where all the chapters and participating yacht clubs send a representative to compare notes and plan for the upcoming year. Through the exchange of information, we have been able to greatly enhance our fundraising results.

There are many other good causes sailors go to the racecourse to do battle for: multiple sclerosis, cerebral palsy, hospice care, the American Cancer Society, the Jimmy Fund, blind and disabled sailing, the American Heart Association, Hope Funds for Cancer Research, and many others. But the Leukemia Cups are unique as the largest organized circuit of national charity regattas in the United States. Each Leukemia Cup has its own personality, but they are all built around common elements: incentives for the top fundraising boats, good parties, auctions, and the satisfaction of helping people in need.

Of course there is an irony in the role I play with the series. In the 1990s when I accepted the chairmanship of the Leukemia Cups, I had no personal connection to serious illnesses like leukemia and lymphoma. Business was booming and my career had taken off: I had become ESPN's go-to man for sailing commentary, each year I was turning out more books and lectures and articles, and in the early '90s, I made my first foray into adventure cruising, organizing an expedition to Antarctica and using the trip as the basis for a feature film and articles. Life was good. Still, something in my gut inspired me to get involved with this worthy cause. Little did I know I would someday be one of those patients who would benefit from all the fundraising work that sailors around the country have done. Today, I joke with the folks organizing the Leukemia Cups that they get a twofer with me: both a lymphoma survivor and a spokesman.

I am, however, not the only sailor with a personal connection to these illnesses—and in my work with the Leukemia Society's mission, I have gotten to know some amazing people who have made these charity regattas what they are. They are fascinating, committed, and passionate people, and their involvement gives them a way of creating meaning out of loss.

There was an Annapolis sailor whose connection to this national series was strengthened by a family tragedy. He lost a three-week-old granddaughter to leukemia, but he pulled something positive out of the ashes of that loss: he named his Tartan sailboat after his granddaughter and went racing in the Leukemia Cups to help find a cure for the disease that took her life. One California long-distance cruiser raced exclusively in charity events, but not only did he help the cause as a participant, he worked to make the events more fun for other cruisers like him who generally cruise for days to reach a destination as opposed to doing short races around buoys. He reached out to individuals and sponsors to fund a portion of his cruise. People made donations for each mile of sailing. I met cancer survivors who were faithful participants in Leukemia Cups, feeling that this was their way to give back and to give thanks for surviving the disease. And there were those who had sadly lost family members or friends to blood cancers, and racing in these events was a way to honor the people they loved who were no longer with them. It takes courage to ask for donations. Leukemia Cup participants are inspired people who want to help.

Becoming involved with the Leukemia Cups has been my way to acknowledge my good fortune and give something back—but my purpose with the series deepened after being diagnosed with lymphoma. The one constant through all those years of being involved is the inspiration gained from being around other people who are also dedicated to this series. Through 2010 I had attended over 260 events in person. My involvement touches a part of me that makes me feel worthy. But for everyone involved, one participant sums up the spirit of this great national series best: "Everyone instinctively knows it's not about winning. It's about living."

* * *

Many sailors make a difference in the sport, and not just those who sail for charity causes. If you don't sail, you might assume sailing is a singular sport: one crew, one boat. But it is far from that, and sailors have a way of pulling together. It takes an entire community to keep the sport running smoothly, and many of the individuals who do the work are volunteers running yacht clubs, running races, and attending meetings that focus on key issues in sailing—such as administering the racing rules, selecting the boats to be sailed in the Olympics, creating new opportunities for sailors with disabilities, and other issues.

Each year, about 150 volunteers travel from their home waters to the annual meeting for US SAILING, the sport's national governing body of which I now

In 2005 I was on my way to recovery after two years of battling lymphoma.

serve as president, to attend several days of meetings and hammer out these important issues for the sport. A smaller contingent travel from the United States to the meetings of the International Sailing Federation (ISAF) to do the same on a global scale. It does, indeed, take a village.

Sailing may be tiny compared to the participant and fan base of the ball sports that are so popular in American culture, but small a sport as it is, sailing has a diverse following. Some sailors prefer to travel solo, crossing oceans on lone ocean passages; some are drawn to racing small dinghies in big fleets where the social life and dock talk are as active as the competition; some enjoy lazy summer days sailing with friends and family on home waters; and some enjoy the adventure—cruising away for a weekend or even taking a year or two off for blue-water voyaging and a circumnavigation of the globe. As diverse as sailors are, there is one type of organization that knits the community together: yacht clubs. These organizations are the backbone of the sport.

The number of active clubs in the United States is hard to pin down, but US SAILING lists over 1,000 active clubs in its online directory. When you consider the cost of waterfront real estate on our rapidly developing coastlines, it's a miracle that so many clubs exist today. During my lecture tours, I've had the opportunity to visit hundreds of clubs and can state from first-hand experience that each club has a unique personality based on where they are located and who their members are.

The largest clubs may have professional managers, sailing directors, and restaurant staff, but the driving force are the members who volunteer as flag officers and board and committee members. And these volunteers have big issues to grapple with: aging membership rosters, declining participation on the water, growing regulatory restrictions, budget deficits, rising insurance premiums, the need to upgrade facilities, and policy questions of governance. It is enough to make your head spin, yet my travels have proven to me that these volunteers—no matter what size club they belong to, or where they are located—all have a deep desire to do things better and a curiosity about how other clubs are handling the tough issues.

Many clubs have the desire to not just look inward at their own membership and facilities, but to look outward. "A yacht club needs to interact with their community. Public access is important," says David Elwell, one of the more thoughtful and involved sailors on the East Coast who has served as a flag officer at both the American Yacht Club in Rye, New York, and the New York Yacht Club.

Elwell spent considerable time in New Zealand during the 2000 and 2003 America's Cups and notes, "Sailing is not elitist there; it is a public access sport.

We can learn from their example." The New York Yacht Club puts that ethos into play by strong cooperation with Sail Newport, the public sailing facility that is a waterfront neighbor to the club's Newport home, Harbour Court.

Many clubs in the United States take on leadership roles in the sport, not only reaching out to the community to gain water access but also developing the technologically complex handicapping rules that allow different types of boats to race against each other. They participate in fundraising events that raise support for entities such as our U.S. Olympic sailing team, as well as create novel ways to keep young people in the sport, such as economical membership schemes for young adults, investing in one-design racing fleets so members who don't own boats have access to racing, and hosting local high-school racing teams. Clubs even create signature events that draw sailors to our shores from around the world. The Long Beach (California) Yacht Club, for example, hosts the annual Congressional Cup. To run the regatta requires the help of over 250 member volunteers, and this event is one of the most important match-race regattas in the world.

Walk into any yacht club in the United States and you'll see a repository of history—and deep pride in that heritage—as soon as you pass through the front door, with displays of photos chronicling the club's past, perpetual trophies, burgees, half-hull models of owners' boats, and other memorabilia. Some clubs even have the means to house significant libraries, like those at the New York Yacht Club and the San Diego Yacht Club.

Keeping all these organizations thriving and intact takes the energy and passions of thousands of volunteers. So if you want to find the people who are making a difference in the sport, look for them at yacht clubs across the United States.

Every year our top fundraisers get together for a weekend sailing event. In 2010, 140 sailors raced off Charleston, South Carolina. Each person had raised or donated at least $8,500 to participate.

Helisara has a good windward position at the 1981 Maxi Class World Championship. Von Karajan painted the boat silver and red. Silver for a sword and red for blood. He wanted to invoke fear in his competitors.

Our New York Yacht Club Swan 42, *Mustang*, sails upwind off Newport. We named the boat *Mustang* as a tribute to Rod Stephens, who named all of his boats *Mustang*.

Alex Lowe and cameraman Alun Hughes have just climbed an iceberg near
the Antarctic Peninsula. The rest of our crew watch from *Pelagic*.

The ESPN Sailing Team covered the America's Cup live from New Zealand in 2000 and 2003.

Our family at the 2007 *Courageous* crew reunion.

Bill Jorch, Ted Turner, and I share a light moment aboard *Courageous* in 2007.

Jack King's *Merrythought* had a frequent presence on the podium at many regattas.
I joined *Merrythought* for racing throughout the USA, Europe, and the Caribbean.

Ashleigh and I sailing a Beetle Cat off Mystic Seaport on a layday during
the New York Yacht Club Cruise in 2009.

Tenacious, with Ted Turner at the helm, blasts to windward off Miami in the 1978 SORC. Ted was named Yachtsman of the Year four times in the 1970s.

Jack King, Roger Vaughan, Claire Davies, Stephen Davies, and I at Magdalenafjord Glacier, Svarlbard, at 79 degrees North latitude in 2001. Jack holds a gun in case we encounter a polar bear.

I take bearings of the competition while Ted Turner steers *Courageous* in 1977. Note the light touch he has with his hands on the wheel.

Our family on the L. Francis Herreshoff design *Whirlwind* on a chilly day off Annapolis, Maryland. The name *Whirlwind* refers to my lifestyle and is a tribute to L. Francis, who designed a J Boat named *Whirlwind*.

The *Courageous* crew attending our 30th Reunion in 2007, in Newport, Rhode Island.

Ashleigh, Brooke, and Kristi after hiking around White Island, Maine, in 1997. Ashleigh later graduated from the University of Maryland, Brooke from NYU, and Kristi from Harvard.

CNO Admiral Gary Roughead; National Maritime Historical Society Chairman Ron Oswald; me, President US SAILING; and Commandant Admiral Robert J. Papp, USCG, at an awards dinner in April 2010.

I interview Wendy Jordan during the production of a documentary on Outward Bound. I've learned to listen carefully to an interviewee's comments to formulate good questions. Aaron Webster worked sound, Roger Vaugan takes notes, and Mike Audick shoots with the camera.

Daniel Forster captured this remarkable shot of *Stad Amsterdam* in mid ocean. Cameraman Mike Audick recorded the scene on video. The wind blew 30 knots and the waves were 15 feet high.

Jim Kelly and I aboard *North Star* commentating on the 2000 America's Cup races from New Zealand for ESPN. He was very helpful to me when I first started commentating. I returned the favor by helping him understand sailing.

When the Whitbread Round the World Race visited Annapolis in 1998, the Bay Bridge was closed to traffic. While 50,000 spectators watched from the bridge, 6,000 boats were on the water. The start was carried live on ESPN. The locals were cheering for our own entry, George Collins' *Chessie Racing*.

After a bad race aboard *Courageous*, Turner gives me a pep talk so the same mistake is not made again.

I was 21 years old as Head Sailing Instructor at the Toms River Yacht Club in 1971.

A happy day for the *Courageous* crew after winning the fourth and final race of the 1977 America's Cup.

Leo Burnett, the ad agency for Dewar's Scotch, proposed that I sit in a bathtub for this profile. It was a little weird but got a lot of play all around the country.

Here are the weight jackets I used at the 1972 Finn Olympic Trials. The sweatshirts and sweatpants added 60 pounds to my 180-pound frame.

The great yacht designer Olin Stephens (middle) and I were honored by the National Maritime Historical Society with the Distinguished Service Award in October 2006. Olin was 98.

Brooke, Ashleigh, and Kristi are all smiles after a full day of sailing. The girls loved climbing the rig and swimming around the boat.

Etchells sailing on a breezy day off Annapolis. Onboard with me is Jud Smith and Rob Erda.

Silver Heels, at anchor, in Frenchboro, Maine.

Richie Boyd trims the main as I steer *Mustang* off Newport in August 2009.

Kristi is happy at the wheel of *Whirlwind* cruising in Maine in 2005.

*   *   *

When I raced with Ted Turner in the 1977 America's Cup, Ted and I made a fair trade. I would help him with the sailing side of his life, and in turn he'd help me with the business aspect of my life. At the time, I was a young college coach—but with a sense I could somehow use sailing as the basis for a career and a business of my own. And so in the winter after we won the Cup in Newport, I had traveled to Atlanta and simply observed how Ted operated. I learned important lessons—not only about how he ran his business but about how he ran his life. And there was one lesson that had a deep impact: it pushed me to expand my commitment to being an active volunteer and serving a number of diverse organizations as a board member.

One afternoon, Ted and I traveled to a meeting of one of the local boards he sat on. There were about 20 people in the room, and there was a little controversy brewing. I simply observed and saw how Ted helped steer the conversation and engineer an outcome. On the way home from the meeting, he told me his philosophy—how you can have a lot more impact serving from the inside, as opposed to being on the outside. "Me," as Ted put it, "I prefer to be on the inside."

I took that advice to heart—and today I joke with friends: I used to sail all the time, but now I sit on boards. Before I joined Ted's 1977 America's Cup campaign, I had already started volunteering as a member of US SAILING's Olympic Sailing Committee, which steers the Olympic sailing program in the United States. But my volunteerism has since expanded, and I have sat on the boards of a diverse group of organizations, many of which focus on education and healthcare, as well as sailing.

Serving within the sailing community has always been part of my life. I have served with the US SAILING Olympic Committee, on the US SAILING board, and as the president of US SAILING. I have also served with my alma mater on the SUNY Maritime Waterfront Committee, the U.S. Coast Guard Foundation, the National Sailing Hall of Fame in Annapolis, the International Yacht Restoration School, OpSail, and the U.S. Naval Fales Committee, as well as the Annapolis Yacht Club, the New York Yacht Club, and some boards of other yacht clubs of which I am a member.

I have also branched out beyond the sport to become more involved locally, serving on boards such as the State of Maryland's Tourism Board, St. Mary's College of Maryland (which has an excellent sailing program), and the Annapolis Community Foundation. I became involved in healthcare and served on the

Blue Cross/Blue Shield Board of Virginia for 15 years. As a lymphoma patient, I gained a great deal of insight into our healthcare system. I was treated for lymphoma at the University of Maryland's Marlene and Stewart Greenebaum Cancer Center. The University medical system maintains a network of hospitals across eastern Maryland, trains many of the state's doctors, and is one of the largest employers in Maryland. I have since served on the board of the University of Maryland Medical System and most recently joined the Anne Arundel Health System.

At this writing I have been working hard to establish a Chair for Dr. Aaron Rapoport at the University of Maryland Medical School. I'm grateful to the many friends who have donated to this cause.

To some, that list may seem like an eclectic grouping, but these organizations are all tied to the things I both care about and have experience with: the sport of sailing, my local community in Maryland, and the healthcare system.

Getting recognition isn't why I volunteer so much time—but when the kudos come, it's a nice acknowledgment. So in 1999, when I was named the recipient of US SAILING's Nathanael G. Herreshoff Trophy, it was a great honor. The award is given each year to an individual who has made an outstanding contribution to sailing in the United States. Named after Captain Nat Herreshoff—the legendary yacht designer born in 1848 and known as the "Wizard of Bristol" for his technical and aesthetic genius that produced boats that are still restored and admired and sailed today—the award is typically considered a lifetime achievement award. Only one other person was younger than me when he won it, and that was my hero, Buddy Melges. That award meant a great deal to me.

The spring of 2008, I went to the Connecticut coastline to do a talk. The venue for the presentation was a nifty lecture hall, and then we were all off for dinner at the Pequot Yacht Club. If you wanted to make a movie about a summer in a New England yacht club, Pequot would be the place—with its clubhouse of weathered brick, its grand waterfront porch, its skinny harbor filled with boats that juts like a long finger from Long Island Sound, and a view across the harbor of emerald green marsh backdropped by grand historic homes. Many friends were there, like America's Cup colleague Dave Dellenbaugh, and Dave Perry, a racing rules expert who is a master at nurturing talent in other sailors. I had a chance to go around the room and connect with a lot of people, and as I headed toward the door to drive home, I had this great feeling that life was so full—that all the time and effort spent promoting the sport and celebrating it with other sailors had been a worthwhile road to follow. Until I was stopped at the door by a sailor with a problem.

At that time, US SAILING had floated the idea of making membership in the organization mandatory for racing sailors. Now, as I write this, an individual adult membership costs only $60, and most sailboat owners easily drop that amount at the bar after a race. The organization does a lot—coordinating the Olympic program and youth development programs, administering the racing rules, training race officers, creating opportunities for disabled sailors, and a lot more. The national governing body is essential to the sport, and in my opinion, all sailors should be members.

But here was this gentleman, his finger pointing in my chest and railing against the mandatory prescription: "You have to make me *want* to be a member, not *make* me be a member . . ." He ranted on, and I graciously offered to take any letter he wanted to write to the board. But the damage was done. The mood of the evening completely deflated, as if his finger-in-the-chest gesture was a sharp pin in a balloon. I had several hours of driving home that night in the car, and the man's attitude bothered me deeply, all the way down the long stretch of the New Jersey Turnpike.

With time, I put that night into perspective. Maybe there are two kinds of people: those who prefer to criticize from the sidelines and expect others to do the work and fix the problems of the world—whether those are issues of the sport or dilemmas of the globe at large—and those who prefer to jump in and be part of a solution. As for me, I have to agree with Ted Turner. I like being on the inside, making a difference.

.9.

ONE NATION, UNDER SAIL

 The wind was spotty, the waves were choppy, visibility was diminished, and the stakes were high for the medal race in the Laser Radial class at the 2008 Olympic Games. American Anna Tunnicliffe went to the starting line with a shot at the Gold medal, but she had to finish fourth or better in the random, fickle winds that blew over Qingdao, China. And as sailors are all too well aware, in those types of winds, anything can happen.

No American woman had won an Olympic Gold medal in sailing since 1988, when Allison Jolly and Lynne Jewell took a gold in the 470 class in Pusan. So history was riding on the shoulders of 25-year-old Tunnicliffe. Several thousand fans lined the sea wall, to scream for their favorites in the 10-boat field of contenders who had progressed into the final race. Among the fans were USA team leader Dean Brenner and other members of the U.S. Sailing Team. In patriotic American style, they cheered for Anna from a nearby sea wall like Super Bowl fans.

All this high-tension sailing would have been easier in big winds—when things are crashing around and adrenaline is racing through the body. But racing for an Olympic medal in light winds is a nerve-wracking game of chess on a moving board: every single action must be precise and measured. The singlehanded Laser Radials are identical in every way, and these women all knew how to maximize their speed. Every sailor's medal chances were riding on nerves and determination.

From my vantage point in the NBC studios in the United States, the start of the race looked confusing. It seemed as if the competitors were not sure whether to attack each other, or go for a clean start. At the starting gun, an individual recall flag was flown to signal there were early starters. An early start would be death: if that boat did not return and recross the starting line, they would be disqualified from the race. Any hopes for a medal would evaporate with that one error.

On the world feed microphone, I heard the race committee say that one boat was over early. To my eye, it looked like Jo Aleh from New Zealand jumped the gun. But Anna Tunnicliffe immediately turned back to restart, and so did three other boats—just in case.

Anna was playing a numbers game now, but so were the other sailors. Lithuania's Gintare Volungeviciute needed four boats between her and Anna to win the Gold. Complicating the math a little more, China's popular Lijia Xu was also in the medal sweepstakes.

After the start Gintare took an early lead with Lijia close behind. By the time the boats reached the first mark of the four-leg race, Lithuania was first, China was third, and the USA was eighth. The Gold was slipping way from Anna, but it got worse. Tunnicliffe tried sailing high on the downwind leg and got caught away from the mark, causing her to slip back into ninth place, with just two legs and about 20 minutes of sailing to go.

The fleet rounded the mark and headed back upwind. Now, the Australian and New Zealand boats sat on Anna's wind. The fleet leaders tacked to the right-hand side of the course, because there seemed to be more wind over there during the first leg of the race. At first, Anna thought about going that way too. But off in the distance, she saw something: a new wind, developing from the left. She split with the leaders. It was a gamble, but time was running out.

Olympian Anna Tunnicliffe proudly displays her Gold medal after the 2008 Games in China.

And then, like a miracle, a light puff of wind that was only about 5 knots filled in from the left. The breeze also shifted about 30 degrees in that direction. Suddenly Anna was sailing over the top of China and passing six boats. She rounded the last mark in third place, with Lithuania leading. But Gintare needed four boats between herself and Anna—and now she only had one. At that point, my balanced commentary took on a patriotic edge.

This was a race that was not only historic, it was an edge-of-your-seat contest. I found myself cheering "Go Anna go!" as she wore down her competition for the Gold medal. I didn't realize it at the time, but tears were welling up in my eyes.

Anna got another gust of wind and sailed right over the top of Australia's Sarah Blanck, and her fans went crazy. She finished the race in second place, and with that, Anna Tunnicliffe earned her Gold medal to become the first U.S. woman sailor to capture Olympic Gold in 20 years. It all happened so fast, it was hard to believe it was true.

The thrill of victory, the agony of defeat: Jim McKay coined the excitement of sports competition best with those great words. And for U.S. sailors at the 2008 Games in China, there were equal measures of both.

The thrilling victories belonged to Anna Tunnicliffe and a young Finn sailor named Zach Railey. The day of the Finn class' medal race, the wind was strong, up to about 20 knots. Railey had to face four-time Olympic medalist Ben Ainslie, a British veteran who was dominating this singlehanded fleet. Ainslie is pure joy to watch in a boat. The man is a machine, working this punishing dinghy upwind through big waves. But Zach means business on the racecourse. I had watched his career for many years (and when I wrote a book on Optimist sailing in 1997, Zach was the young sailor on the cover). He has worked as hard as anyone who has campaigned in the world-class ranks. As a young junior sailor, he was known as a hothead for a time—but as the years passed, he matured. So too did his drive to win an Olympic medal.

That day in Qingdao, Zach's drive was in high gear. And although Ainslie captured the Gold, Zach earned Silver in a big win for this first-time Olympian. Better yet, age is on Zach's side: at 24, he came close to striking gold and most certainly will be back. At 31, Ainslie will have a difficult time maintaining his dominance in this athletic boat.

Now here comes the agony. For the four years leading up to the 2008 Games, U.S. Yngling sailors Sally Barkow and her crew Carrie Howe and Deb Capozzi were singleminded in their quest to win a medal for the United States. Former world champions in this class, they went to Qingdao as the golden girls—one of the world's top Yngling teams and America's great hope for a medal performance in this three-person keelboat class.

But as always, four years of blood and sweat and dreams all came down to a single race. And in that final Yngling race, the wind was blowing 20 or more knots and visibility was extremely limited. Still, the Americans got off to a clean start, sailing fast on the first leg with their rivals from Spain comfortably behind after a few minutes into the race. Things were looking good.

Approaching the windward mark, Sally tacked a little early, just short of the layline, the direct course to the mark. But the current was ripping hard, forcing the United States toward the mark as they approached. With two boats blocking them directly to windward, the American women could not tack. As they luffed into the wind to clear the buoy, the women from the Netherlands blocked their wind and Barkow and her crew slipped sideways, right into the turning mark. With that error they had to perform a penalty turn and lost more distance.

And still, the Americans fought back.

As Barkow approached the windward mark for the second time at the end of the third leg, medal hopes were renewed: they had caught up to Monica Azon's Spanish boat and that of Greece's Sofia Bekatorou. But once again, the Americans tacked just short of the windward mark and had to make two quick clearing tacks to avoid hitting it a second time. And that was it: a heartbreaking error and four years of hard work were over.

Yet American sailors had captured two medals, a Gold and a Silver, and the excitement in China was Olympic racing at its best. It is not only the thrill of victories and the agony of defeats, but our Olympic sailors go to the racecourse with an entire nation behind them. Even if American sailing fans have only a vague recognition of who these racers are, they are rooting for them all the way. There is a purity to this kind of patriotic contest.

I am passionate about the Olympic Games because it's pure nationalistic competition. And while nationalism can be a dangerous thing on the world political stage, I believe it helps elevate the importance of sports—and it encourages a country to generate high level talent.

Now, it's great for a nation to have good sailors who win medals. But there is also a ripple effect: a sailor with high-level talent is likely to inspire others. So for that reason, I believe the Olympics play an extremely important role in sailing.

A Conversation with Anna Tunnicliffe

At the 2008 Olympic Games in China, 25-year-old Laser Radial sailor Anna Tunnicliffe became the first U.S. woman to win a Gold medal in sailing in 20 years.

Several months later I was the MC at the Rolex Yachtsman/ Yachtswoman of the Year Awards ceremony at the New York Yacht Club. Anna Tunnicliffe was the female recipient for her Gold medal performance. In her acceptance speech she made reference to how I had helped her by suggesting that the key to winning was to have a good average over the course of a long regatta and not take chances. Anna never won a single race but her consistency helped her prevail. It was a nice compliment.

Gary Jobson (GJ): What is it about sailing that makes you so passionate about this sport?

Anna Tunnicliffe (AT): I think it's just that fact that you go out everyday and it's something different and you're out in nature. There's no wave that's ever the same. There's no puff that is ever the same. It's not like going onto a basketball court and you say okay we're going to run Play 3. It's not the same every time. And yes you might do the same moves but you're going to do the same moves in different wind conditions and different seascapes so there's a lot more to it as well. And then just being outside. I love being outdoors. I love being on the water. All of that together I just love it.

GJ: How did you contain your emotions during that final medal race at the Olympic Games? Over the line at the start, at least perceived.

AT: That race was quite difficult. Going in I knew I had a medal but I didn't want just a medal. I wanted to win the Gold. At the first leeward mark I'm in ninth and in Bronze medal position and I'm well, this is not what I want. I've got to do something. I couldn't let my emotions get involved. I've got to find something so I can pass through and get to the top. I found that left shift out there whether it be a lot of luck or whether I did see pressure.

And it worked out. All week long my competitors had be going to a side, getting a shift and coming back even though I buried them off the start. They'd always end up back in the top five. I'd sail a conservative race and be right there with them and it's not fair, how'd they keep getting this? So I thought at least once it has to go my way right? And it did. Just kind of kept focused on what the goal was.

GJ: When you got out there on the left side of the course and the wind came in a little and you got a life, what did that feel like at that moment? Oh, my gosh this might actually work.

AT: I think I said a lot of prayers at that point. Thank you God. And then just like wow, this is kind of working. Good pressure and then it shifted more and I was like good shift, and it shifted more, and I'm like okay there goes half the fleet. This is fantastic. At the top mark I rounded in third and needed to get to the finish line. No yellow flags. Just let me get there. And I have never sat so still in my boat. Ever. And just had to drift down that downwind leg to make it to the finish line.

GJ: So when you crossed the finish line you knew you had the Gold, how did that feel?

AT: Amazing. Just kind of relief. Excitement. Thankfully these four years are over and I've achieved my goal. But at the same time it's a dream come true. I just couldn't wait to see my coach and celebrate with him and see my family and hug them. Give them huge hugs and thank them for supporting me and getting me to where I am today.

GJ: So Anna you've had a chance to talk to lots of young people who look up to you quite a bit now, what's it feel like kind of being an inspiration to younger people?

AT: I think it is great and I'm really happy that I can influence people and try and inspire them to achieve their goals. For me, I never really had . . . I had people that I'd looked up to but I never had the opportunity to meet them and so I think it's great that I get to meet young kids and they tell me about their goals and dreams. And I can be like, yes, look, follow them and you'll achieve it if you put the work in. It's just a great feeling. I love doing it.

GJ: You've been at this for a long time now, does it get easier or harder as time goes by?

AT: I think it definitely gets harder. The more you do, the better you do, people are going after you. It's just a lot of work and the whole time you're putting your whole life towards this. Sometimes you might want to go do something else and you can't. You've got to totally commit to this the whole time. But it is a lot of fun and I love it so I'm going to keep going.

Olympic Gold medalist Anna Tunnicliffe and I at a fundraising event at the Riverside Yacht Club.

In terms of that Olympic fever, I am a case in point. I watched closely when two sailors from Barnegat Bay—Carl van Duyne and Gardner Cox—represented the United States at the 1968 Games in Mexico City. The sailing was held in Acapulco, and something happened there that left an indelible impression on me as a young sailor. Van Duyne hit a mark of the course, and in those days, if you hit a mark, you were disqualified from the race. No one witnessed him hitting the mark, but he reported it anyway, and with that one act, his medal chances went up in smoke. But to me, it was an inspiring example of how the game of sailboat racing should be played. And so in 1972, I campaigned in the singlehanded Finn class. In the United States, you have to win the Olympic Trials regatta to make it to the Olympics. I did not win the Trials, but I was hooked on Olympic sailing.

That same year, I watched my local hero Sam Merrick try for the berth in the keelboat Soling class. He didn't win, but a midwest sailor, Buddy Melges, did. And his story had inspiration written all over it. After having a bad race and a broken mast in the Trials, Buddy fixed his boat during the regatta and won the next five races to win the U.S. berth in the Soling class. Then, he went on to Germany and won the Gold medal.

In '76, I tried again for the Olympics, crewing for skipper Art Ellis in the two-man Flying Dutchman. We did not win the Trials, but that same year, when I was 26, I was invited to be a part of the country's Olympic Sailing Committee. And so, as a competitor and as a college sailor and a coach, I brought my ideas to the table, proposing three key things to the committee: we need to go out and recruit sailors for the Olympic classes; we need to do seminars and exchange information between all classes, from 12 Meters to the smallest Olympic dinghies; and we need to beef up the coaching aspect.

Those ideas were pretty revolutionary at the time, so acceptance took time. But once I started doing clinics and big-name sailors like Tom Blackaller and Bill Buchan, who was a giant in the sport, thought those sessions were useful, the Olympic Committee started to pay attention.

From 1988 on, I added the role of television journalist to my involvement with the Games, first covering the '88 Games in Pusan, South Korea. I could not entice NBC to cover sailing in 1992 and 1996, but NBC was enthused by the sailing in Sydney Harbor in 2000 and I was back onboard as a commentator and producer. The 2004 Games in Athens were spectacular and I got to cover the Olympics again. In 2008 I covered the races live but did it from the NBC Studios in Connecticut and on the Internet. Even though the action was 12 time zones away, we had a substantial audience during the early morning hours.

Over the years—as a competitor, a spokesman for the U.S. team, a fundraiser, a member of the Olympic Sailing Committee, and a racer with strong ideas on coaching and training and recruiting—I have noted a fascinating trend: that it is very difficult for one nation to dominate these sailing contests. There was a time when the United States might have been seen as doing just that, and from 1984 to 1992, the Americans won 21 medals out of 25 classes. But in the last four Olympics from 1996 to 2008, we have won a mere 10 medals out of 43 classes. That is a big difference. Just study the more recent stats from the racecourse, and you

A Conversation with Nick Scandone

Californian Nick Scandone started sailing at age eight in his native Orange County, but college sailing was where he fine tuned his skills as a member of the sailing team at the University of California, Irvine.

Scandone won the 470 North Americans and was an Olympic hopeful in that class, but did not win the Trials for the '92 Games. In 2002, Scandone's life took a dramatic detour when he was diagnosed with ALS, commonly known as Lou Gehrig's disease, a progressive neurodegenerative disease that affects the nerve cells in the brain and spinal cord. After his diagnosis, it took time for Scandone to reach the starting line of a disabled sailing regatta—but when he did, he quickly rose to become one of the world's top disabled sailors. In 2005, he won the 2.4mR World Championship, a singlehanded class that draws able-bodied and disabled contenders, and was crowned US SAILING Rolex Yachtsman of the Year. In 2008, he represented the United States at the Paralympic Games in China, as skipper in the doublehanded SKUD class, and won the Gold medal.

ALS claimed his life a few months after his win in China. During his final years, as his physical abilities waned with the progression of his disease, competitive sailing gave him incentive to carry on. I spoke with him before he went to China for the Games.

Gary Jobson (GJ): You had a pretty good collegiate career. You guys won the Nationals if I remember, with Irvine back in '88. How much has your collegiate sailing helped you with the SKUD and the 2.4?

will see why it's hard for one nation to lay claim to Olympic sailing fame: at the Games in Athens, there were 126 races, with 76 individual boats winning at least one race; that trend continued at the Games in China, with 117 races and 69 different boats winning at least one individual race.

But every nation has to ask itself: what is the goal? Winning medals, or using the nationalistic inspiration of the Games to build more participation in the sport? As long as there is Olympic sailing as we know it, that dilemma will exist for every nation mounting sailing teams for the Games.

Nick Scandone (NS): I think the college sailing was a big help in my sailing career. I felt that without college I wouldn't be where I am [today]. The difference that college makes is you sail so many races over such a short period of time, you almost can't not get better. That would be one of my prerequisites for anyone to get into Olympic sailing is to make sure that they try their best to have a good college career.

GJ: Being named the 2005 Rolex Yachtsman of the Year, that must have meant a lot.

NS: Yes, it was definitely a big surprise. From where I've come—growing up sailing, doing college sailing, and then having to get what I call a "real job"—to suddenly being back in the sailing scene and then getting the highest award that US SAILING puts out, the Rolex Yachtsman of the Year, I was actually quite astounded. Even to this day, when I get announced as the Rolex Yachtsman of the Year, it still puts a smile on my face.

GJ: ALS, tell me a little bit about this disease that you have.

NS: Well, it's an awkward disease. It's a little different than most of the other disabled sailors and people with disabilities in general. ALS is, from what I understand, a slow progression toward total paralysis. So the big difference between someone like me who has ALS and someone who has lost a limb . . . is that I'm not stagnant. I am in a progressive stage, where they've had their accident and now they're stable. The hard part about having ALS is continually trying to figure out, Well what's going to be normal today? Because normal a year ago is not what normal is now.

GJ: So what will normal be by the time the Games come along?

NS: Well since I've already lost most of it in my legs, come Olympic time will probably be fairly similar to where I am now, but maybe just a little weaker . . . I've been fortunate; a lot of times the disease progresses very rapidly and mine's been somewhat of a slow progression. I've had it over five years now and most people don't last five years with this disease.

GJ: So having this Paralympic Games ahead of you has to be some incentive, to be prepared and ready and able to do it.

NS: The Olympics is something that I strived for when I was younger and I kind of gave up the dream years ago. And then when I got back into the game, it was something always to keep my mind off what is happening to my body—and something to look forward to. That's a big part of why I'm doing so well [with this disease] is that I always have something to try and grab for, something that gives you reason to carry on.

GJ: You told me a couple months ago that one of the great things is for disabled sailors to defeat an able-bodied sailor.

NS: What ends up happening when someone becomes disabled is after a while the reality comes into play, that you really can't do any sports and compete on the same level with anyone who

* * *

Look at America's Cup history, and you will see that patriotism was intended as an underpinning of this great event. The Cup's Deed of Gift describes the contest as "a friendly competition between foreign countries"—and sailing history has shown that if you win, your country earns the respect of the world. In today's America's Cup arena, however, this notion of one nation, under sail is slipping away from this great event, and the Deed's spirit of a friendly competition between nations has morphed into something else.

Today, America's Cup athletes switch borders to chase large paychecks. Look back at America's Cup history to understand what a detour from Cup tradition this is: how unthinkable would it have been if any of our past America's Cup he-is able bodied. But in the sport of sailing, with the right type of boat, you can compete against any able-bodied sailor out there. I can't go and bowl or play tennis or anything else, but I can actually do something physically to compete on the water with sailing. I think I'm fortunate to have had quite a bit of a sailing background before I became disabled. I'm just living the dream and having a good time doing it.

Maureen McKinnon-Tucker and Nick Scandone celebrate their Gold medal victory at the 2008 Paralymics in China. Nick passed away in January 2009.

roes—the likes of Bus Mosbacher or Ted Hood or even Dennis Conner—defected to a foreign nation's challenge? Or consider how the Olympic Games would be diminished in value if this practice of racing for other nations were allowed? And if you doubt the power of nations rooting for nations in international sports, just look at the soccer fans who follow the World Cup! Those scenarios give you some idea of the devastating results that occur in sailing when the nationality card is only a mere passport to allow sailors to play for other nations.

As I write this, the America's Cup has come off of one of the more bizarre chapters in its long history. In 2003, Swiss billionaire Ernesto Bertarelli, then in his late thirties, burst onto the Cup scene with his Swiss challenge *Alinghi* and won the trophy on his first try. Unlike countries like New Zealand and Australia, Switzerland is not a nation known to the world for its yachting traditions. But Bertarelli and his international crew blended many nationalities to build an impressive campaign that won the 31st America Cup and brought the event to Europe, where they defended in the 32nd America's Cup in 2007.

The next round of Cup action, however, escalated into an acrimonious battle. Extensive court action and litigation overshadowed the on-the-water contest between the Société Nautique de Genève, defending with team *Alinghi*, and the challenging Golden Gate Yacht Club and their racing team *BMW Oracle Racing*.

Unlike most sailing regattas, the America's Cup is a very public event. Since the first defense in New York Harbor in 1870, the Cup has generated huge interest. Go back to the newspapers of the era and you will find the front pages covered with America's Cup stories. While there was widespread disdain for the legal battles leading up to the 33rd Cup in February 2010, the media and avid fans kept a close eye on every development. And when the two giant multihulls finally met for the best-of-three race series, curiosity attracted hundreds of thousands of viewers to the Internet to watch. In the United States, this meant getting up as early as 4 am on the East Coast to catch the action. Still, a reported 656,000 unique visitors watched the live racing direct through the Cup's official website. And that figure doesn't include the viewership of the streaming broadcasting by 350 other Internet sites. I covered the event with catamaran-sailing ace Randy Smyth for ESPN3. The world watched as this one-on-one, Deed of Gift match was won by Larry Ellison's *BMW Oracle* team, 2–0. The Deed of Gift, orginally written in 1871, specfies that if no agreement can be reached between the parties, the series will be a best-of-three regatta.

New Zealander Harold Bennett was back as Principal Race Officer. He canceled the first two days of sailing due to unsuitable wind conditions. However, Bennett resisted the pressure from *Alinghi* to postpone racing on Day 3 and 4. Bennett got high marks from the racing community for running the races over the objections of *Alinghi*.

Ernesto Bertarelli's tenure as holder of this historic prize changed the nature of the America's Cup in ways never envisioned by the authors of the original Deed of Gift. Before winning the Cup in 2003, *Alinghi* did three specific things that were wrong, in my opinion. First was hiring international talent to compete on Bertarelli's behalf, which flies in the face of the Deed. Since 1958 most every individual crew represented their own countries (there were a few exceptions). Secondly, Bertarelli turned the 32nd Cup in Valencia, Spain, into a profit center. This goes against the spirit of the charitable trust of the America's Cup. No defender before *Alinghi* made the America's Cup a for-profit enterprise, nor should it ever be again. Third, writing a protocol that completely favored the Defender was disgraceful. The New York courts that ruled on the legal battles agreed.

The next item on my list is to increase participation. The cost to compete is so high, few teams could mount credible campaigns. A serious look by past America's Cup managers at how to reduce costs would be a first step. Ideas include limiting the number of boats that could be built, creating a salary or expense cap similar to other professional sports, limiting the time allowed for training and competing, and negotiating favorable leases for shore-side facilities with the host city.

It's time for a new America's Cup yacht, and the defenders have already announced that the 34th Match in San Francisco in 2013 will be sailed in large catamarans, 72 feet in overall length and designed to a box rule. The multihulls used in the 33rd Match certainly showed unbelievable speeds: these boats sailed three times the speed of the wind. The America's Cup has always been a designer's race—and I believe the future Cup should favor speed.

When the New York Yacht Club (NYYC) held the America's Cup there were always multiple defenders competing for the chance to race in the match, and the competition in the defense trials gave the NYYC the edge. The most interesting America's Cup seasons have featured a two-ring show, with both the Challenger and the Defender allowing multiple teams to compete.

The America's Cup is missing the boat with the international free agency that exists in the Cup arena today. If I was the czar of this historic contest, I would have the Americans on the American boat, the New Zealanders on the New Zealand boat, and the Swiss on the Swiss boat. In any type of sport, I think the world pays attention when there is something at stake for their country.

It is hard to envision what twists and turns the America's Cup will take over the next several decades. Hopefully, we are done with Deed of Gift matches, lawsuits, court hearings, and bad behavior. But one thing is clear: this venerable regatta needs to be returned to its former glory.

BMW Oracle sailed three times the speed of the wind defeating Switzerland's *Alinghi* in the 2010 American's Cup.

A Conversation with Dennis Conner

Perhaps no U.S. sailor is more identified with our country's history in the America's Cup than Dennis Conner. When he was skipper of the first boat to lose the Cup in 132 years in 1983, it was a tragic and devastating moment in Cup history—and in Conner's life. But he staged one of the greatest comebacks in sports history. Winning the Cup back in 1987 in Australia is seen by many as the last great American effort in the Cup game, when the sailors on *Stars & Stripes* went Down Under to win the Auld Mug for pride of country more than simply a paycheck. As Dennis says of that Cup campaign, "We were really racing for the passion."

Gary Jobson (GJ): When the long history of the America's Cup is written, you will be the most important character in the Cup: winning, losing, ups and downs. Do you now look back with satisfaction on all your America's Cup campaigns?

Dennis Conner (DC): Of course they are all special in their own way, a wonderful, big part of my adult life . . . Some great victories and tragic losses that turned out to be ultimately for the best . . . But I think one of the most rewarding things was that recently we had our 20th anniversary of winning in Perth. We had about 21 [members] of the team out here at San Diego Yacht Club for a reunion. I looked around, and there were only about three people whose lives weren't dramatically changed by that win in Australia . . . Life really changed in that one event. I think that was the one that I remember the most—and it was the most significant, bringing the Cup back. Not so much vindicating myself from the loss: it was more that it was a wonderful victory and kind of the last of the Corinthian America's Cups where we were really racing for the passion, for our yacht club and our country. And we were all Americans. Today, obviously, things have changed. People are doing this to make a living, just like any other professional athlete.

GJ: When you talk about having the reunion a couple of weeks ago and how it changed just about everybody in the crew's life, how did it change your life?

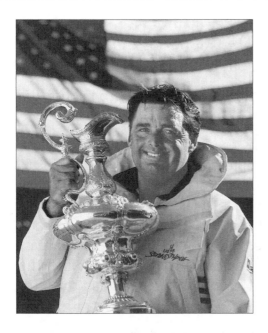

DC: Gary, I was basically making draperies for a living. If I made $75,000 a year, it would have been a lot. I went from being a drapery manufacturer to an America's Cup leader responsible for raising the money, staffing, and doing all the things that we see in running a big business today. That was a major change for me, to basically change careers. I always had sailing, but now I had a lot bigger responsibilities. When you go and borrow money on your house and pledge everything you own to get an America's Cup syndicate started, you have a little different perspective on life.

GJ: So in 1983 in Newport, you were up against an unbelievable boat, a secret keel that nobody had seen. You didn't know what you were racing against. And yet you took them right to the wire. How were you able to do that?

DC: Well, we were well prepared. We were fortunate. We got some winds that helped us a bit. We weren't that far off the pace. In a very, very narrow envelope—say 12 to 14 knots—we could go with them. We had a couple of races that helped us there. They had some bad luck in the first race, which they should have won: a breakdown on the halyard lock that injured one of their crew . . . We had some good fortune. They were well ahead in another race that was cancelled, because they ran out of the time limit. All in all we pushed them because we had a good crew. We sailed well with what we had. No excuses; we just got beat. If we want to talk about the boat and how the boat got to that speed, that is a whole other story. History shows that they won—and good on them. [It was a] wonderful victory for Australia, and in the big picture probably the best thing that could have ever happened for the Cup. I'll get killed by Bob McCullough for saying that, but it's probably the case.

GJ: I think one of the fun things is you became a hero in Australia [after the 1983 loss].

DC: You hate to be a hero by being the first man in 132 years to lose the Cup. They're wonderful people down there, as we all got to know later, not only in Perth, but in Sydney and Brisbane. They're great sportsmen and [the 1983 Cup] was a great, great victory for the Australian country. It changed their whole self-image and how they felt about themselves in a number of different areas. All in all, I'm sorry we couldn't have won for the NYYC and the members who supported us. But it was probably a good thing for the world of sailing.

GJ: Now in 1983, you're up three to one and things are looking pretty good. But they came roaring back and won the next couple races. Did you see something that turned around in their boat, that they were able to make a big comeback?

DC: Well, they had the fastest boat in anything other than 13 knots of wind. [In the] last race we started in a bit more breeze, and when the breeze died off they were just quite quick and basically sailed by. We had the feeling that they were going to catch us before we got to the weather mark as the wind was, as I recall, maybe 10, 11, 12 knots at the beginning and 7 knots by the time we got to the weather mark. We knew we were in trouble there. So it wasn't a matter of just covering them because they would have run us right down. So we took a chance and, as I recall, their side of the course may have had a little more wind. If they were two boats that were equal, you'd say for sure they had more wind—but they were fast and they slipped by around the leeward mark ahead of us, and we didn't want to just go in a straight line sailing. We knew what the answer was there. We would lose. So we engaged in a tacking duel and just hoped that something bad would happen to them, or to our good fortune. But it didn't work out that way. A lot of tears were shed that night.

GJ: Did you have a sense that history was being written at that point?

DC: We knew we were in trouble as far as defending the Cup from the get-go, before the series started . . . We had our hands full and it was going to take some good fortune to win this.

GJ: When you lost the Cup, that was a tough night: September 1983. And as you said, you were kind of devastated. But at what point did you sit up straight and say, Okay, we're going to come back and go get this job done.

DC: Emotionally I was distraught, returning to San Diego and knowing the unthinkable had happened . . . Here I was responsible for losing the Cup. Lots of bad thoughts. It was hard to be positive in that situation. But I think what happened as more countries started challenging for the Cup, I realized life was going on here. And it was going to go on with or without me. So I really had no choice. I could stay home and feel sorry for myself and watch it on, as we now know, ESPN, or read about it in *The New York Times*. Or I could pull myself up off my backside and see what I could do about winning it back. I knew it would be a tough struggle. I was under no delusions that the NYYC thought I was the greatest guy in the world, so show me the money. Of course, the money was always the key. You can be the best sailor in the world but if you don't have a boat, how can you win the Cup? The big struggle would have been, where's the money going to come from here? But I was on the board and to be commodore here, at the San Diego Yacht Club, and I convinced the board that I could indemnify them against any losses I might incur and asked for their permission to challenge. That is how I remember it.

GJ: Well it worked out pretty well. Looking back, you did some pretty clever things at the time. Went to Hawaii, with its big wind. Maybe it matched Fremantle a little bit, because they had some heavy wind. What made you think about going to Hawaii?

DC: Well the first step, I decided, was I'd better invest in technology—because I got beat by technology. We'll have to let history decide who really invented the winged keel, but definitely [there was] some Dutch involvement. It didn't come from seat of the pants. So the technology was a big part of our losing. So I decided I can't just do this pulling the feathers out of my head here, designing a fast boat. So with the help of John Marshall as our design coordinator and local company SAIC, and doing some predictions for us and the wind tunnels and Boeing and a number of technicians, we came up with the fast boat in the conditions that we expected to have in Perth. So that was the first step. The next key thing, as you mentioned, was to train in Hawaii out of the sight of the media and out of sight of our competitors. A long way off the beaten path. But most important, it had the conditions that we expected in the Gage Roads off Perth. Actually, bigger waves and consistently strong winds. So we were swinging a heavy bat practicing in Hawaii, with the water crashing over the deck. We had some waves that broke the windows out of the Bessie, our tender. The conditions in Hawaii were stronger than Perth. So once we got used to those conditions and we stepped into the conditions in Perth . . . we knew what to do when a headsail blew out. We had a chance to find out. So it was no accident that we knew what to do: we'd practiced in the strong waves.

GJ: So you get to Australia, there's lots of teams from all over the world, and other American teams, and it was pretty competitive in the early rounds. But as time went on, you just kept getting better and better.

DC: Well, it's comparative because our boat wasn't designed to race well in 7, 8, 10, 12 knots of wind. As the summer progressed—don't forget, it's 180 degrees from the United States—so in November the winds are lighter because you don't have the thermal breezes kicked up by the desert. So the light winds that we had in November and December weren't playing into the cards that we dealt ourselves with a strong, heavy-air boat. We didn't tack as well. We didn't accelerate. We weren't quick. So we had to win some races in the early going by sailing well. We weren't up against chopped liver . . . There was a lot of good competition, and when their boats were the same speed as ours, it wasn't just a walk over. As the summer built the winds came up and our boat came into its own—and also the crew and the sails that we practiced so long and hard for. It made all those sleepless nights and long days easier to stomach, when the conditions that we built the boat for started happening.

GJ: So, you go on to win the Cup back. It must have felt pretty darn good, bringing the America's Cup back to San Diego. Was it the highlight of your career?

DC: Surely one of them. The plane ride home—it was Continental Airlines at the time [that] gave us a plane, and we had the whole team there. I have a picture of the Cup sitting in the pilot's seat. Let's put it this way: it was a plane flight that whoever was there will never forget. I don't think there's going to be too many other plane flights like it either—with the restrictions we have now. But it was wonderful. We had the ticker-tape parade up 5th Avenue with Donald Trump and Mayor Koch. I'm told it was a nice parade; we were about seven blocks back, because the Cup was sitting up there with Donald and the mayor, so we didn't see much of the parade. Getting to go and see the president and having a private luncheon in the Rose Garden, and being on the cover of *Sports Illustrated* and *Time* magazine. Life was good.

GJ: During those races, did you have any sense of what a national phenomena your campaign had become?

DC: Not really, Gary. We had no idea people would be staying up at night watching these races. A little bit like when [the U.S.] won the hockey against the Russians: people were feeling good about themselves and good about America. It made them feel good and forget their problems. We had all Americans in those days. We didn't have any foreigners on our team. It would have been unthinkable: American designers, American crew . . . The broadcasts were good and exciting. There was some drama: people falling in and crashes and mast breaking, and the commentary was good and made for good theater like Nascar racing. People enjoyed it and it wasn't taking up much of their day because of the time schedule being the middle of the night in the United States. It all just fit—and it was very special.

A Conversation with Olin Stephens

Olin Stephens was the Designer of Record of eight America's Cup winning yachts: *Ranger* (1937) (with Starling Burgess), *Columbia* (1958), *Constellation* (1964), *Intrepid* (1967, 1970), *Courageous* (1974, 1977), and *Freedom* (1980).

Gary Jobson (GJ): You are one of the few people that understands what the skill level was on the J-Boat *Ranger* and all the great 12 Meter crews. You've seen the crews today of the modern America's Cup. Is the sailing skill level any different today than it was back in 1937 or in the '60s?

Olin Stephens (OS): I don't think it is. It may be in some ways, I know the crews of these boats and the skippers of the boats are at it all year around, year in and year out. That was not all together true of the 12 Meters. But I'm not sure that the 12 Meter gangs were not a little more intense about the whole thing than these. I hate to say it, but I think these professionals fellows are a little bit of the type, they've been there and they've seen it all and I have a little feeling about the crew frankly.

GJ: Remember the wing keels on *Australia II* back in 1983? There was a controversy about whether they were legal or not. Looking back on *Australia II*, do you feel that was a legal 12 Meter?

OS: I thought at the time she was legal. Actually I don't at the moment want to claim originality because in my case it didn't work. But we had tried an end plate across the keel on a model of *Intrepid*. It didn't look very good and we abandoned the thing. But they just did it again and did it a lot better. It was active in the aircraft field, so I thought it was okay at the time.

GJ: Did you borrow many ideas from the aircraft field?

OS: I was glad to borrow anything I could see. Actually at one time I said to my wife if I was a little younger I'd go to work in California instead of the East Coast because I think the aircraft people there were more aware of what was going on in fluid dynamics really. Its all the same in air in the aircraft and then air in the sails and the water and the hulls.

GJ: Of all the Cups you've been involved in is there one that stands out in your mind as the most satisfying?

OS: I was probably happiest with *Intrepid* as a boat that was a nice advance on what was state of the art.

A Conversation with Bill Ficker

Bill Ficker was the skipper of *Intrepid* in the 1970 America's Cup.

GJ: So how do you get everybody all working together? How do you put a team together in 1970?

Bill Ficker (BF): I had a theory of putting together a crew of people who weren't experts. I enjoy my hobby as managing and organizing things. I enjoy that and so instead of just getting my friends that I know are good sailors to sail with me, I decided I'd get a lot of young people that were good sailors, first of all so the grinder would know that the jib needed trimming and how far to go and he could just use his strength but his intellect as well. I interviewed about 70 people. They weren't just people I knew. As a matter of fact I knew virtually nobody in the crew except a couple fellas from my hometown. We had a very young crew. The average age was 22. I brought the average up to 26. I selected them by character too. I wanted people that were intelligent and that were flexible and really wanted to learn and sail on an America's Cup boat.

GJ: One of the key people with you was Steve Van Dyck. You guys seemed to have a very dynamic but close complementary relationship. How did that evolve?

BF: We had a unique relationship I think. I noticed on a lot of boats different individuals liked to be heroes. And that doesn't work in a team sport. And the America's Cup, particularly, really is the epitome of a team sport. You don't just pick up a crew and substitute people. I picked people for the crew that have competed in sports and understood that team work. And then I don't like to . . . once decisions are made start discussing, second guessing. So when I sailed in the America's Cup you really wanted a tactician that was very bright and could work with the navigator and the skipper and call the shots. We had very little conversation during races. Almost none. If Steve said we're going to go for another six boatlengths and tack, that's what we did.

GJ: One of the mysteries to me, you might not be able to answer it, but since the Australians had more sail area and were far lighter, why didn't they just tack you to death?

BF: We were surprised by that. It was light at the start and we didn't want to maneuver a lot and let them get their boat speed up so we took a timed start to make sure we were at maximum boat speed. They beat us at the start, the first time they crossed us they didn't cover us. We were kind of shocked at that. We would have been in a lot of trouble if they put us in a tacking duel. In heavy air we'd be fine, we were hoping for that, but not in the light air.

A Conversation with Ted Hood

Ted Hood was the skipper of America's Cup contenders *Nefertiti* in 1962, *Courageous* in 1974, and *Independence* in 1977.

GJ: How did you get involved with the 1962 America's Cup?

Ted Hood (TH): Don MacNamara and Commodore Anderson said let's do an America's Cup boat. So I designed *Nefertiti*. We didn't start until October designing. We had to build it in three and a half months, a wooden boat. I don't think anyone had done it

*   *   *

In August 1851, 16 yachts raced around the Isle of Wight in the America's Cup—and 150 years later, in the summer of 2001, 208 boats had traveled to England to honor that historic regatta at the America's Cup Jubilee in Cowes.

Attending the Jubilee reminded me of the days when passion was the driving force for amateur sailors to race in the Cup. Today's secretive Cup campaigns are fueled instead by massive budgets for professional sailors and lots of R&D. And that fast before. Double planked. Built it in Marblehead. I made the mast and rig. The whole thing was $450,000 start to finish. The boat, the housing in Newport, everything.

GJ: Did you do any tank testing for *Nefertiti*?

TH: *Nefertiti* was tank tested and all they did is move the rudder aft. We moved it back almost four feet. They said it was better moving the rudder aft. It's the only thing we changed in the tank. I think that added the wetted surface. It really made the boat slow in light air. She was probably the fastest boat in the breeze of all Twelves.

GJ: So you would have to race against the guys you were making sails for. That's pretty interesting. And then you teamed up with your friend Lee Loomis for the 1977 Cup. You had a unique campaign because you had the old boat *Courageous* and you built the new boat and then you were going to work together as a stable mate. That was a little different.

TH: Yes, we did a lot of work, a lot of testing. Actually we put a scheel keel on the bottom of *Courageous* in fiberglass, not the lead, and it made her faster than *Independence*. We should have put it on *Independence*, left *Courageous* the way it was. Full-size testing. We did an awful lot of full-size testing with good skippers out there. Turner would come up once in while. When he got ahead he'd never fall back so we could try again. So we had a lot of people to do a lot of full-size testing with all kinds of things.

as I spent time in Cowes that summer and saw Cup colleagues and all the famous boats that had made history, I kept wondering to myself: is this sense of racing purely for passion too difficult for today's professional sailors to comprehend?

The America's Cup Jubilee was living history at its best. It brought home the traditions of this great regatta and was, for me, the event of the year. Our British hosts joked that they were celebrating a "150-year losing streak." But together, the Royal Yacht Squadron and the New York Yacht Club did the sport of sailing a favor by organizing this ambitious, yet flawless week of racing.

The racing was competitive, but there was a friendly atmosphere on the waterfront. Cowes oozes history from every corner. One could feel what it was like 150 years earlier. Back in 1851, many of the buildings were already old. For example, the Royal Yacht Squadron castle at the harbor entrance was built in 1539. Today, from the water, the shoreline is relatively unchanged.

One quiet morning at the start of the regatta, I looked around the marina and counted thirty-five 12 Meters, a fleet that included former America's Cup winners *Columbia* (1958), *Intrepid* (1967, 1970), and *Freedom* (1980). That morning, many of the vintage designs had crews aboard who were veterans of past campaigns, methodically preparing their boats for a day of racing. Then suddenly, without a warning, a tender fired up its engines and blared the fight song of *Australia II*, the famous Twelve that ended the longest winning streak in sports history. "Down Under" by Men at Work broke the morning's silence, and the basin erupted in applause. At that moment, the America's Cup Jubilee came alive.

At the opening ceremonies, nine former winning Cup helmsmen were introduced to thunderous applause from 2,800 people. This was a magic moment for everyone. Just imagine nine Super Bowl MVPs appearing together. Simply walking along Cowes' High Street that week meant seeing one Cup legend after another. Dennis Conner was stopped repeatedly for autographs, and the story was the same for Bill Ficker, Ted Hood, Halsey Herreshoff, Alan Bond, Michael Fay, John Bertrand, Bruno Troublé, Sir James Hardy, Sir Peter Blake, Buddy Melges, Bill Koch, Dean Barker, Tom Whidden, and Russell Coutts. Ted Turner wasn't there, but ever present was the dean of American yacht design, Olin Stephens. Ninety-three at the time, he raced during the day and continually talked about new design ideas. And he still had time for the regatta's endless social whirl.

The highlight of the week was the 54-mile Round the Isle of Wight race. Yachts dating back to 1868 started first. Throughout the afternoon the faster boats passed close to the slower boats, rewarding everyone with a glimpse of what it is like to sail against yachts from different eras. It felt like a James Butterworth painting that had come alive. Never mind that the old heavy displacement vessels were slow compared to the 12 Meters, the beautiful J-Boats, and the present-day America's Cup Class. Each still looked magnificent, representing the swiftest designs of their day.

All thirty-five 12 Meters competed at the event. Russell Coutts' crack team topped the modern 12 Meter fleet aboard *South Australia*; Australian skipper John Bertrand, who made history in 1983 by winning the America's Cup for his country, finished second; I skippered *KZ 5*, owned by Edgar Cato, to a third place in the race around the island. Francesco de Angelis's *Prada* team beat the other Cup campaign teams in the International America's Cup class. But there was a certain atmosphere, on the waterfront and on the water, that this historic event was more important than the results at the finish line.

The replica of *America*, built in 1967, sat on a mooring off the Royal Yacht Squadron. Even at anchor, *America* looked like it was moving fast as the spring-tide currents gurgled past her topsides. With her aft-raked masts, *America* still looks fast and powerful; in the words of one observer in 1851, "She's frightening." The original *America* sailed around the island in 10 hours, 37 minutes, but today's boats sail around in half that time, showing how far design and technology have progressed. The evolution of yacht design has accelerated, thanks to space-age materials, innovative building techniques, computer prediction modeling, and wind-tunnel testing.

But the skill required to sail well endures and some things about racing in this region remain unchanged: the currents are swift, the winds are capricious, and the mark roundings are crowded.

In the United States, most sailors compete in a vacuum and crowds are rare. But on the English Solent during the Jubilee, thousands of boats carried countless spectators. On the shoreline, huge crowds of fans jammed every point of land. Normally I'm bothered by spectator boats cluttering the racecourse. But not here. I had to chuckle as many small boats anchored right in the path of the racing fleet. But to balance the obstructions, there was lots of cheering—and at this special event, winning was not as important as just taking part. Most boats sailing in the Jubilee have enjoyed their time of glory in the past, but on this day every boat shared the limelight equally.

The sesquicentennial America's Cup Jubilee created a renewed sense of excitement for the America's Cup, an appreciation for tradition, and an awareness of the evolution of design. For me, it also rekindled the basic principles of the Cup's Deed of Gift, of a friendly competition between foreign countries—of one nation, under sail.

GREATNESS AND MY HEROES

1966–2007

Greatness. It's just one word, but not an easy quality to define. To paraphrase a former Supreme Court Justice, "One thing we all know: we know it when we see it." In 1982, I had a chance to see a lot of sailing greatness, all on the same starting line.

◄———————— ■ ————————►

Imagine sailing against 15 of the world's best sailors, not only your contemporaries but the stars of the past 20 years. Picture yourself sharing the racecourse with your heroes—the sailors whose books have been your bibles since childhood and others you have long admired but never met, until now. The faces on the boats around you are intent on tactics and sailing well, and you can't help wondering, How did I get into this nightmarish position?

In 1982, *Yacht Racing/Cruising* magazine (now *Sailing World*) celebrated its 20th anniversary by asking readers to nominate the top 20 sailors of the past two decades. The winners were named to the magazine's Hall of Fame and invited to compete against each other at a regatta in Newport, Rhode Island.

The contenders in the fleet represented a remarkable array of talent, in terms of their racing skill and their seminal influence on the sport. I was surprised and honored to be included in the group and signed up for the regatta—although the prospects for success were unclear. Collectively these sailors had won 62 world championships, collected 11 Olympic medals, and logged 8 America's Cup victories.

I was heading to Newport to share a starting line with Arthur Knapp, Jr., Paul Elvstrom, George O'Day, and Stuart Walker: expert racers as well as theoreticians. Peers of mine such as Dave Ullman and Dennis Conner were there. Also racing were Buddy Melges, Hobie Alter, Lowell North, and dinghy racer Steve Benjamin. Rounding out the field were Bob Bavier and, surprisingly, Eric Tabarly of France, who paused long enough between long-distance ocean-racing events to come to Newport. Ten of the Hall of Fame group were missing: the late greats

Uffa Fox and Sir Francis Chichester, as well as John Bertrand, Tom Blackaller, Ted Turner, Ted Hood, Olin Stephens, Doug Peterson, Bus Mosbacher, and Bruce Kirby, who all had other commitments.

The regatta was held in Etchells 22s, and I recruited the best names in the class as crew. Etchells champion Dave Curtis of Marblehead was unavailable but he suggested his cohort, Jud Smith, whom Curtis considered the best Etchells sailor around. "If you take him, you'll win," Dave said. I took his advice, and I also recruited Hank Stuart of Ithaca, New York, an aggressive, all-around sailor.

On the first morning, the wind was light and our tune-up was going well. But as I watched the other members of the fleet practicing tacks and spinnaker sets, I suddenly had a sinking feeling: What if I come in last in this fleet?

Once I got started maneuvering for the start, all my abilities became focused on the moment. This was no time for internal doubt. I went for broke at the start, finding a big hole in the middle of the line of boats parading to the start, and sliding into it. I port-tacked the fleet and we began moving into the lead. It was then that the butterflies kicked in.

"We've got Melges by a half a boat length, and we're crossing Conner!" yelled Hank. I didn't want to hear the names of the legends so close around me, so I asked Hank to just call sail numbers.

Hank Stuart, Jud Smith, and I won the 1982 *Sailing World* magazine Hall of Fame Regatta.

Then Jud asked for an adjustment. "Ease the backstay a quarter of an inch," he asked. I did that, then retrimmed the mainsail. Jud never took his eyes off the jib. "That's better now," said Jud. I felt instantly calm. If Jud could tell that such a minute adjustment did the job, then we were in great shape.

Unfortunately, we overshot the first mark and went from first to fourth. It was hard to lose the lead; still, it was a good finish in that field of talent. The rest of the regatta was even better. We took a third and two seconds in the succeeding races, winning the regatta with Buddy Melges in second and Dave Ullman in third. Paul Elvstrom, the tough, bearded Great Dane who had been the number one vote-getter in the readers' poll, was fourth. The final race was both exhausting—and exhilarating. When we crossed that final finish line in second place, we knew we had won the regatta. It was one of the greatest moments of my life.

The Hall of Fame regatta was both nerve wracking and a definite highlight. So as challenging as it may be to keep company with the best of the best, I highly recommend it. Their company will improve your game, whether it's sailboat racing, another sport, or your professional field. In fact, one of my golden rules is to associate with successful people and ask them for their opinions and advice. That approach has always served me well.

How do you define greatness? For me, it's easier to define when you can think of examples. As I look at the people I consider great in sailing, they are a diverse group. But they all have one shining quality: they have a passion to be the very best—whether their goal is to win the America's Cup or cruise to some of the most rugged and remote regions of the globe. Here are my heroes, some of the great sailors who have had a deep impact on my sailing career, and on my life.

* * *

Sam Merrick opened a door of opportunity for me as a young sailor. A seasoned one-design racer 33 years my senior, Sam invited me to race with him on his E Scow when I was getting to be known on Barnegat Bay as a hot young racer. As I started to win more races in my own junior circuits, he began to seek my tactical judgment on the racecourse. Together, we scored a big win at the E Scow East Coast Championships in 1967. But it wasn't just Sam's willingness to trust my tactical advice on the water: he had a lot to do with my development as a young person by treating me as a fellow sailor, not just a kid.

Sam was one of the legends of Barnegat Bay. He had intense but friendly rivalries and was known among his peers as a skilled sailor and a racer dedicated to winning. He worked hard at his sailing, approaching it methodically and learning through books and trial and error on the racecourse. One of his rivals, the well-known sailor and sailing theorist Dr. Stuart Walker, summed up Sam's reputation best: "He believed in the game and believed in playing the game—to the hilt."

Sailing with Sam really boosted my confidence, and when we sailed, a relationship of equality developed on the boat. Off the boat we talked about our favorite sailing books, and we reached a point where I talked to him about my ideas and plans for the future while he told me more about his career in Washington, D.C., which he began as an attorney in the Department of Commerce during the Roosevelt administration. Over the years, we continued to sail together and our friendship matured beyond a mentoring relationship to one of two adults. We met as friends in the nation's capital each month for lunch and a good talk. For years, before he passed away in 2000, I sought his counsel.

To me, he was a great friend and a great sailor, but the rest of the sailing world witnessed his sailing prowess when, in the 1970s, he became involved with the U.S. Olympic Committee. At that time, the American Olympic sailing effort was a piecemeal operation without the kind of organized effort that characterized the strong European teams faced by U.S. sailors in the Games.

The United States had won medals over the years, but Sam had something else in mind: an American sweep of the Olympics.

I was deeply involved as a member of the Olympic committee at the time. So in preparation for the 1980 Summer Games in Moscow, he and I traveled the country and appeared at yacht clubs where clinics were held in Olympic classes.

The 1980 effort ended in disappointment for American athletes, when the U.S. government pulled out of the Olympics in protest against the Soviet invasion of Afghanistan. But Sam did not let the turn of events derail him. He was now chairman of the Olympic committee, a job I recommended him for, and in a position to put his ideas into place. Initially the chairman of the committee questioned my recommendation. Remember, I was only 26 years old at the time. But, happily, Buddy Melges endorsed my thinking.

Sam's approach was to concentrate on a small core of the most promising sailors. The top six crews in each class were chosen at national trials, and subsequently trained under coach Robert Hopkins. While Sam's approach was not without controversy, the proof was at the 1984 Games in Long Beach. The Olympic yachting team garnered more Gold and Silver medals than any other American team that year.

Buddy Melges at the wheel of the 12 Meter *Heart of America*, in 1986.

Sam downplayed his role, but the members of what is now US SAILING felt otherwise, granting Sam the Nathanael G. Herreshoff Trophy, for the individual who has made the most outstanding contribution to the sport. At the awards ceremony, Sam humbly turned the attention to his team in accepting: "In honoring me you honor the team and those fine sailors who missed by inches." And then, the following weekend, he did what sailors do—he went out racing his Soling, as if nothing ever happened.

*   *   *

I give Graham Hall, my coach at Maritime College, a tremendous amount of credit for my development as a competitive sailor. I first met Graham, who graduated from the U.S. Merchant Marine Academy at Kings Point in 1964, racing Penguin dinghies in Sea Cliff on Long Island Sound. When I visited Maritime, I liked what I saw. Graham, who was then in his late twenties, and I hit it off.

Even within the short space of my freshman year, Graham's methodical and organized approach to sailing helped me develop from a slightly better than mediocre sailor, to a racer who was far better than mediocre. Graham started me on the path to becoming a world-class sailor by giving me a strong foundation—a system for sailing that worked, no matter what type of boat you are sailing. Over the years, I have been able to build on those fundamentals. I still credit him with helping me perfect my starting techniques, and those techniques have worked for me over my entire career—in boats that range from small singlehanded dinghies to large Maxi boats with an army of crew.

Graham also helped me immensely with the mental aspect of the game, with keeping my focus on the things that mattered. As a young sailor, I needed reminding a lot of the time. "Let's not try and improve everything at once," he'd say. Or, "You need to have a good attitude." Or, "Just have fun and see how you do." It was almost as if he was inside my head and knew exactly what I needed to do to re-gear my brain for the specific situation I was facing. Graham left Maritime to work as a sailmaker in my senior year. I missed his counsel, but we stayed in touch and over the years he became a mentor and a good friend.

He passed away in 2005, at the age of 63 from cancer. I spoke at the service, and I remember his two daughters Whitney and Morgan—about whom Graham talked all the time—sitting there in the front row. I was glad by that point I had a lot of public speaking experience because it was hard to keep my composure, looking at these two young women who had just lost their father. What a sad but touching day. Naval Academy coach Pat Healy summed up Graham Hall perfectly, "Graham coached the perfect balance between racing hard and simply enjoying being on the water." Even now when I nail a start and position myself well for the rest of the race, I think, Thank you Graham. He is missed, but his wisdom about sailing and how to perform well on the water will stay with me, forever.

At age 15, my heroes were all local racers on Barnegat Bay, until the summer of 1965 when Buddy Melges arrived at Little Egg Harbor for the E Scow Nationals. Barnegat Bay was the eastern center of scow racing, and it never occurred to me that my local heroes could lose to a midwest lakes racer. That is, until Buddy Melges demolished the local fleet.

He was hard to miss on the racecourse: in the first race, he made an extremely audacious move, port-tacking the 85-boat fleet at the start and sailing on to win the opening race. His strategy downwind was completely different from anything the locals had seen before. When sailing on a run with our spinnakers, most of us pulled our spinnaker poles all the way aft and ran dead downwind. Melges showed up with a flat reaching spinnaker, and he did not sail straight downwind to the next mark but reached at sharp angles—zig-zagging back and forth, sailing a longer distance but at greater speed. It was a technique you might use on a catamaran or an iceboat, but Buddy proved it could work in scows. At that point, Buddy already had numerous iceboat championships to his credit, and you could see his cross-pollination at work.

After his victory at the Nationals, I made it my business to learn more about this great sailor from Zenda, Wisconsin, whom everyone called the Wizard of Zenda. His tongue was reputed to be as sharp as his sailing, and he was a hot ticket—probably the best dinghy racer in the country. He won an Olympic Bronze medal in Flying Dutchman dinghies in Japan. Later, in 1972, he arrived at the Olympic Trials for the Soling class on a windy San Francisco Bay, never having had much experience in the boat. He finished fifth on the first day, and on day two he was dismasted. Now most sailors would have packed up for home at that point. But not Buddy. He spent a good part of the night rigging a new mast, then went on to win five straight races to secure a berth for the Olympics. After that, he went to Europe to race the Olympic regatta in Kiel. And like a good ending to a fairy tale, he captured the Gold medal.

In the late '70s, Buddy decided his record would not be complete without a run in the Star class, a punishing, two-man sloop that demands peak performance from its crews. Buddy was a sailmaker as well as a boatbuilder, so he studied the sails, made some of his own modifications, and took himself and his new boat to the Star Worlds.

"It's too bad you have to sail with your own sails," said Dennis Conner to Buddy in the parking lot once he arrived, obviously thinking that Buddy's "home-made" sails stood no chance whatsoever against the sails of sailmakers who were actively racing in the class.

"Well, we'll just have to see what happens," Buddy told him.

Melges won that regatta; his record was so strong he did not even have to sail the last race. So after the regatta, he asked Conner, "Would you like to borrow my sails to race with? I know the guy who makes them, and I can get you a good deal . . ." There is no record of Conner's reply.

The biggest thing going in Zenda is Melges Boatworks, which has been doing business in town for several generations. Buddy is retired now, but his sons have carried on the family tradition of building the Melges brand of speedy one-design race boats that are known around the world.

Buddy is so good at sailing, with a natural feel for tactics and possessing great physical strength, that he has honestly earned the crown as the Wizard of Zenda. But beyond his great sailing ability, what struck me about Buddy from the start was his willingness to share his knowledge with the racers he sailed against. The first night of those E Scow Nationals, I wandered down to the docks. There I found Buddy showing some competitors how to trim the jib. I wondered, Why would you help your competitors? "The better my competitors are, the better it makes me," he said. I have tried to follow his example ever since.

* * *

Ted Turner has had a big impact on my sailing career, and on my life. He is amazingly smart and disarmingly direct, a person with bold visions. His greatness comes from the ability to rally people around that vision—to make them see it too, and to motivate them to work with him to achieve it.

Another of his winning qualities is loyalty: he gives it, and he inspires it. We first got to know each other during the *Courageous* days in Newport, but we have remained close friends. Once or twice a year, Janice and I spend several days at one of Ted's ranches in the United States or Argentina. Those visits are filled with horseback riding, fly fishing, bird hunting, and—of course— conversations about sailing always produce great memories.

In the summer of 2010, Ted and I sailed together in the 12 Meter North American Championships in Newport. Our friend Carol Swift had chartered *American Eagle* and invited Ted and I to sail aboard. We slipped back into our old 12 Meter roles, Ted on the helm and me calling tactics. We were having a spirited battle with *Columbia*, but Ted had not driven a Twelve in a long time. At one point I got frustrated and kept telling him to keep the bow down. Ted resisted my encouragement and the talk between us during that race got louder and louder.

"You're a lot grumpier than I remembered," said Ted after the race.

"Hey Ted, I am just trying to help you out here . . ." I answered.

Carol pulled me aside later, to tell me how much Ted really did look up to me. It was touching to have her tell me that. For all these years, I so looked up to Ted. It was nice to be reminded that it had become a two-way street.

The next day, our *American Eagle* crew sailed out to the starting line for the final day of racing, and we sailed home the victor in our division—racing in the fashion Ted and I had become known for long ago in 12 Meter circles.

Ted Turner and I aboard *Whirlwind*, my Sabre 402, off Hog Island in Penobscot Bay in 2004.

* * *

In the late 1970s, Herbert von Karajan—the conductor of the Berlin Philharmonic Orchestra—was one of the world's best known and most influential musicians. And he was a sailor too. When Dick Bertram, a fellow competitor I had raced with on the Maxi boat *Ondine*, suggested I contact von Karajan to help train his crew, I was intrigued. Not only was von Karajan one of the most powerful figures in classical music, he was a true sportsman who, even in his seventies, piloted his own jet, skied like a devil, and commanded his own racing yacht. I knew there was something I could learn from this gentleman whose concerts drew standing ovations everywhere he conducted.

Friends described him as tough (one would imagine he'd need to be). Still, I decided to write to him, and his letters back belied his tough reputation. He dictated them to his secretary at his office in Salzburg, Austria, during quick stops between concerts. "It would be a great honor to have the best sailor in the world giving us his advice and training," he wrote. And so, I made my way to St-Tropez to train with von Karajan and his crew onboard his 39-foot Ron Holland–designed *Helisara V*.

Herbert von Karajan at the wheel of *Helisara* and I discuss the next move off the coast of Sardinia.

St-Tropez, like much of the French Riviera, gets an afternoon thermal breeze. So the wind starts out at zero early in the morning and by afternoon, works its way up to a boisterous 25 knots. During my coaching visit to the Riviera, we followed a precise routine. I worked with the crew in the morning, and exactly at 2 pm, von Karajan came on board. We were back at the dock each day, at 6 pm sharp.

Each afternoon we threaded our miniscule 39-footer through the magnificent yachts of the rich and famous. In the stiff afternoon breeze, the crew was pushed to its utmost, practicing multiple jibes, tacks, spinnaker sets, and takedowns. By the fourth day, we were able to maneuver *Helisara* as well as any topflight racing boat. The week went fast, and my one regret then was that I was not able to spend more time with the maestro and get to know him better.

But our letters continued, and our friendship grew. In the summer of 1981, I was back in St-Tropez—this time onboard a new *Helisara*, von Karajan's beautiful new Maxi boat from the drawing board of the preeminent Argentine designer German Frers. Again, we sailed our precise afternoon schedule from two to six in the afternoon. On this trip, I had the opportunity to spend more personal time with von Karajan. Knowing his desire to excel, I broached the idea during dinner at his house one evening of entering his new race boat in the upcoming Maxi World Championships in Sardinia.

"It will give your crew something to really train for, a sense of purpose," I said persuasively.

"Yes! We'll do it," he replied, "if you come and help us."

So that September, Janice and I awaited the maestro's arrival at the Zurich airport. He was flying a group of us to Sardinia in his jet. When he arrived, he greeted us warmly, then pulled me aside.

"Gary, I think we are in for the battle of our lives," he told me.

When we arrived in Sardinia and traveled to the site of the World Championship, which was hosted by the Aga Khan at the posh Costa Smeralda resort, I saw the lineup of Maxis with their professional crew. Yes, we were in for a battle. "We are going to have to hustle," I told the crew.

In the first race, we were fifth out of thirteen. Not a bad finish in that top-caliber fleet. As the racing continued our performance continued to improve. The new *Helisara* was fast, and the crew was working together like a von Karajan orchestra. The final race was a long-distance contest. Von Karajan never left the deck during the entire 24-hour race. The wind was calm at night—the time when most long-distance races are won or lost. But the crew kept the boat moving, and we picked up some wind shifts and got free of the calm area.

At sunrise, we were about a mile behind the formidable U.S. entry *Kialoa*. All day long, as the breeze came up, we chased *Kialoa*. Little by little, we ground down her lead, and we got close enough to engage the American boat in a one-on-one jibing duel that lasted for 50 miles. The maestro loved every minute of it. There was a lot of yelling coming from *Kialoa*, and clearly, the more nervous they got, the more spirited we got. Three miles from the finish, we passed *Kialoa* and won the race by 55 seconds.

As we sailed across the finish line, the maestro's hands shot up into the air with clenched fists, and tears streamed down his face. "Bravo," he shouted. "Bravo!"

That night, there was a great celebration in Costa Smeralda, and von Karajan proudly received his trophy at the prize giving. This was a man who spent much of his life receiving applause. But on this night, the applause from those world-class Maxi sailors was somehow different.

Von Karajan is, sadly, gone now, having passed away in 1989. What an experience it was to sail with someone who had achieved such greatness in his art—and to watch him apply that same drive for excellence to a sport he loved.

* * *

I first met *CBS News* anchor Walter Cronkite in June 1977 when he came to Newport to do a piece on the America's Cup for *60 Minutes*. Walter loved sailing and owned a series of boats name *Wyntje*. As part of his assignment he went sailing with each of the American 12 Meters including *Courageous*. Soon after hoisting our sails Walter asked Ted if he could steer. Without missing a beat Ted shot back, "Sure Walter, I'll let you steer if you let me do the evening news." We all laughed and eventually Walter got some time at the wheel.

Four years later Walter and our mutual friend, Mike Ashford (who owns a popular bar in Annapolis called McGarvey's), invited me to race to Bermuda with them aboard *Wyntje*. As we entered the Gulf Stream on the way to Bermuda, the waves and wind kicked up. I ran around the boat reefing the mainsail and preparing to switch to a smaller headsail. Walter called me back to the cockpit and with a sly look on his face suggested, "If you want a smaller jib, why not roll this one up?" I have to laugh because up until that time I had never sailed on a boat with a roller-furling jib.

Walter Cronkite during the 1981 Marion to Bermuda Race aboard his Westsail 42, *Wyntje*. Mike Ashford is on the right.

When I first started commentating for ESPN, I called Walter for advice. He had one suggestion, "Make every word count! Only say something when you have an interesting observation or fact, or notice an item the viewers can't see for themselves." It was good advice that has served me well over the years.

In 2007 I spent several months working on a one-hour program on the history of the America's Cup for ESPN Classic. Geoff Mason suggested that I be an interviewee and not the narrator of my production. It took me a few days to agree, but then who should narrate my film?

I sent a letter off to my best candidate. Two days later his agent, Marlene Adler, called to say, "Mr. Cronkite would be honored to narrate your film."

At the studio on narration day, writer John Rousmaniere and I listened to Walter's methodical narration. John had written some brilliant text, and Walter has a beautiful way of enunciating words and phrases. Think of his voice as you read the following:

"Someone once wrote, 'The America's Cup is a synonym of things brave and big and famous.' To those words I would add one more: spectacular. No inanimate object is more beautiful than an America's Cup yacht in full flight in a stirring breeze, racing for glory, and sailing into our affections. And that's the way it is—and that's the way it was."

At that moment both John and I had tears in our eyes. This was the Walter Cronkite who brought us Neil Armstrong walking on the moon, and the assassination of President Kennedy, and was known as "The most trusted man in America." Our ESPN show on the America's Cup was the last program Walter Cronkite would ever narrate.

When Walter died in 2009 at the age of 92, Mike Ashford was asked to speak at the funeral service. He was one of only a few invited to offer some thoughts. Presidents Clinton and Obama were among the impressive list of attendees. Mike was nervous and called me for advice on speaking in public. I offered Mike Walter's suggestion, "Make every word count."

* * *

Elizabeth Meyer rescued the 1934 J-Class sloop *Endeavour*, the type of yacht that once contested for the America's Cup, from the mudflats of England. The boat was broken and derelict when she discovered it. But instead of seeing a decaying hulk, Elizabeth saw the bones of a majestic sailing yacht. She believed in her bold vision, and she got others to believe in it too.

Elizabeth managed a team of shipwrights and craftsmen and restored the yacht in England before sailing it transatlantic to Newport, Rhode Island. There, I helped her stage an event that would serve as the yacht's debut on this side of the Atlantic.

When *Endeavour* sailed into Newport Harbor—with her sleek navy-blue hull, graceful lines, towering rig with its broad Park Avenue boom, and handsome interior built to the highest level of craftsmanship—the yacht and the woman who restored it captivated the sailing world. No one else was undertaking such grand restorations in the 1980s, so she was truly a pioneer. If you could use only one word to describe this magnificent yacht, *stunning* just about summed it up.

I have had some of my most enjoyable days on the water onboard *Endeavour*. The sheer grace, beauty, and power of this boat make her a pure joy to sail. But there is so much more to a good day on the water than a great boat. A good day on the water onboard a large classic boat like *Endeavour* is also about inviting the right mix of personalities, organizing the itinerary, managing all the social aspects of sailing together and dining together, and making sure the boat is equipped to support all you plan to do. The fact that many of my most enjoyable days have been spent onboard *Endeavour* is a tribute to Elizabeth's brilliance as a cruiser.

Sailing with Elizabeth Meyer at the helm of *Endeavour* off Maine in 2003.
This was in between chemo treatments.

Elizabeth's cruising philosophy was developed during her years cruising in Maine on her classic 41-foot Concordia yawl. Sailing hard in all weather conditions is her fundamental reason for cruising, and she makes a plan for each day based on the weather and her geographic pursuits. Each day averages about six to eight hours of sailing, and the crew gets into a groove. When sailing with her aboard *Endeavour*, everyone wants to steer, and Elizabeth is careful to rotate the helm.

Unlike cocktail parties where conversations start and end at a breathtaking clip, people are relaxed and thoughtful on a boat. While cruising with Elizabeth, I watched her methodically spend an hour talking with each of her guests. She asked good questions and was genuinely interested in what people had to say.

Later that night at dinner, Elizabeth tied the day's conversations together and declared a dinner topic. Each night is different and fascinating; the crew gets to state opinions, speculate, inquire, teach, and—best of all—learn. During one cruise, our conversations ranged from the geology of Maine to the life of lobsters, the polarization of American politics, family heritage, and the America's Cup. Elizabeth has a nice way of making sure everyone participates equally.

When I wanted to explore new frontiers and mix more cruising into my sailing life, I looked to people like Elizabeth and my friend Skip Novak as examples of how it should be done. Both Elizabeth and Skip create boats that fit their specific goals: where Elizabeth is drawn to restoring classic beauties, Skip's wants as a cruiser are targeted at outfitting a strong, sturdy boat that can sail to remote polar regions. Both are well read and have put time and thought into building their onboard libraries—knowing that time to read is one of the great joys of cruising. Both know how to schedule downtime for the crew each day, how to organize a boat so it stays shipshape, and how to plan itineraries so there are built-in highlights during the passage.

* * *

Skip Novak is one of the premier modern-day adventurers—and he thrives in extreme environments. He has taken film crews, adventurers, and even Greenpeace teams to the ends of the earth and is a veteran of four Whitbread Round the World Races, where crews circled the globe in a race that traversed some of the most remote and wild regions of the oceans.

One way to know Skip is to understand what he considers his ultimate challenge. "I enjoy the extreme ends of the earth. For me, I would like to find a safe anchorage and spend a full winter in Antarctica. The boat would act as my base camp, allowing exploration and mountain climbing for weeks at a time. It would be great because you would be totally self-sufficient and really get to know yourself."

The extreme places he has sailed to are a far cry from his childhood Chicago, where he grew up as a self-described "harbor rat" and a small, skinny kid who excelled at wrestling. After college he spent winters in Europe as a full-time skier and sailed in summertime. To help pay the way, he became a skilled writer and photographer. But it was the experience of sailing through ice in the Southern Ocean and seeing places such as New Zealand, Cape Town, and Rio de Janeiro during his Whitbread campaigns that gave him a new focus: "It was during this race that I realized how big the world was. But to see most of the world you need a boat."

Skip Novak with his 54-foot *Pelagic* at rest on the Beagle Channel, Chile.

In 1990, Skip and two partners built the 54-foot, steel-hulled sloop *Pelagic*—a Greek word that means relating to or living in the open sea. That boat has carried him to the extreme ends of the earth he favors.

Since Skip sails in remote areas where there are no cruising guides, his most valuable information comes from his own experiences, which he records in words and drawings in rutter (routing) books. He draws birds, sharks, icebergs, people—but the most important drawings are his detailed charts of anchorages. His rutter books contain a wealth of important information, and he handles them with great care.

A lifetime of adventuring has not been without mishap. In the 1985 Fastnet Race, Skip was hired to skipper the Maxi yacht *Drum*, campaigned by rock singer Simon Le Bon of Duran Duran. A hundred miles into the race, the keel snapped away from the hull and *Drum* capsized. "The capsize on *Drum* was the only time I thought I was going to lose my life," he said. But as much as Skip has seen so many parts of the world, he does not consider himself a traveler looking to explore foreign cultures and countries. Exposure to geography and the environment is what he is after.

I have had the good fortune to sail with Skip and produce films in the rugged regions where he thrives, and I have learned from this masterful adventurer about preparing for and cruising in extreme environments. A great day for Skip is a climb up a mountain, or completing dozens of chores that he seems to do simultaneously: fixing a broken engine, going for a hunt or fishing. He is driven, curious, and, most importantly, competent. And through it all he has an amazing tolerance for people who do not have his intense drive. Skip is a man on a mission who does not like the notion of cruising, but instead thrives on the sails he calls *expeditions*: voyages with a purpose. For many cruisers, getting from place to place is all the fun. Not so for Skip: *Pelagic* is simply the vessel that transports the expedition team from one location to the next.

When asked to describe his occupation, Skip says, "I am a professional boat captain." But that description is unfair to his broad talents. He is able to fix anything on a boat. He speaks English, German, and Spanish. He has the organizational capability to lead expeditions to places where many boat captains would never venture. But what distinguishes Skip Novak is this: he thrives on adversity and is always looking for the next adventure.

Although I did not plan or even anticipate building a wide network of friends after college, I met many people during my travels—sailing and at speaking events. Several have been particularly loyal and are close confidants.

It took 12 hours for Skip Novak, Julia Crossley, and I to scale a 5,000-foot mountain on the Beagle Channel, Chile. Jamie Reynolds and Mike Audick deserve a lot of credit for filming the climb.

The Jobson Sailing Center at the Great Harbor Yacht Club on
Nantucket was dedicated in 2008. It was a nice honor.

Geoff Mason, me, and David Pensky during the 2000 America's Cup races off Auckland, New Zealand.

I first met David Pensky when he provided the clothing for *Courageous* in 1977. In 1984, David and his wife Carol bought the house directly behind ours. What a nice surprise. He started a nifty clothing shop called Britches of Georgetown, building the company up to over 100 stores throughout the East Coast. Eventually he sold his company to Charlie Leighton. Leighton and I teamed up when I became President of US SAILING and he was the Executive Director. We certainly live in a small world. Pensky and I have traveled to sailing events around the globe. He has a terrific business sense and has been very helpful to me over the years.

In 1986 Geoff Mason was asked to be Executive Producer for ESPN for the upcoming America's Cup in Australia. He had been a crew aboard *Nefertiti* with Ted Hood in 1962. Geoff and I shared condos at three different America's Cups that we covered. He was a great help to me as I learned the television business, and I have to laugh: one of my shows would air on ESPN and as the program faded to black the phone would ring. On the other end would be Geoff. He would say, "Great job. I enjoyed the show. Do you have a pencil? I have some suggestions." And with that he would fill up a notebook of ideas on how to do better. Geoff has won over 20 Emmys. In December 2010 it was a real thrill for me to be present when he was inducted into the Sports Broadcasting Hall of Fame.

I smile thinking back to the days of racing Penguins with my friend Bill Campbell. In 1995 he and his wife, Sherri, and their sons, Andrew and Michael, moved permanently to San Diego. Bill eventually became Commodore of the San Diego Yacht Club. Andrew competed in the Olympic Games in 2008 in the Laser class.

Long-time friends Tad LaFountain (back) with John Martin (left) and Bill Campbell
(right) celebrate friendship with me on the rocks at Great Wass Island, Maine.

I see John Martin and his wife Peg a few times a year. Our relationship goes all the way back to second grade, in 1957. He graduated from the U.S. Coast Guard Academy and became a lawyer. When we are together the years never seem to matter. We pick up right were we left off. In the summer of 2005, John, Bill Campbell, and Tad LaFountain and I went cruising together. It had been many years since John had done any sailing. He was adamant that we not race. Bill and I honored that commitment until another cruising boat came along and tacked on our wind. The race was on. John went below in disgust but some things never change. We passed the other boat in a few minutes.

After his freshman year at Princeton, Tad spent the summer driving an ice cream truck. He had the brilliant idea that we should drive his truck to the rock concert at Woodstock. We would have sold out instantly but did not make the trip.

I first met Norwood Davis at a speaking engagement in 1979 in Richmond, Virginia. A few months later he stayed with us in our little townhouse in Annapolis. His beloved University of Virginia basketball team was playing Maryland that night. I don't remember who won but I remember how passionate Norwood was about sports and sailing. In 1987 he invited me to join his Board of Directors of Blue Cross Blue Shield of Virginia. I served on the Board for 15 years. It was a fascinating, intellectual exercise. Norwood became the first Commodore of the Great Harbor Yacht Club out on Nantucket.

Gary Gilbert and I first met sailing in college. Gary grew up sailing in strong winds in Hawaii and was a year ahead of me over at Kings Point. We raced Etchells together over many years having a lot of fun along the way. Gary has a natural gift for sailing downwind and in strong air. One day at a low point during my illness, Gilbert showed up on my doorstep and announced that we were going sailing that day. We went out in the Etchells for about 30 minutes. It was tough for me just getting on the boat. But once on the water, Gilbert said, "I just want you to know why you are fighting hard so you can continue sailing."

Lee Tawney and I first met in 1987. At the time he was working for Mayor Kurt Schmoke of Baltimore. Lee and Stan Heusler, the Publisher of *Baltimore Magazine*, were looking to do a sailing event in Baltimore's rejuvenated harbor. They invited me to come up with an idea so we created the Columbus Cup, a match race event that took place in J-44 sloops. Russell Coutts was one of our first competitors to sail in the event in 1989. Our next project was to host the Whitbread Round the World Race, which was later renamed the Volvo Ocean Race. We hosted three events, in 1998, 2002, and 2006. It was one of the biggest sailing events to ever take place on Chesapeake Bay. More recently Lee has served as Executive Director of the National Sailing Hall of Fame based in Annapolis.

Mark Mendelblatt, Jud Smith, and I setting a spinnaker aboard my Etchells, *Whirlwind*, in October 2010.

In 1993 I was looking for a small boat to sail. Dr. Glenn Robbins suggested that David Pensky and I become partners with him in a J-22. We had a great couple of years racing this nifty boat. It was named *Road Kill* in honor of a creature Glenn had run over while trailering the boat. Glenn has remained one of my closest friends and was a major help during my illness.

One year later I became partners with Jack King with *Silver Heels*. I had a good run with Jack aboard his beloved 62-foot *Merrythought*. I've never seen a happier person out on the ocean.

Since the 2000 America's Cup in New Zealand, Janice and I have become good friends with David and Christy Elwell. David sailed on *Intrepid* in 1967 and eventually became commodore of the New York Yacht Club in 2009. They live in Edith Wharton's onetime home in Newport, Rhode Island, a house he fixed up over a 10-year period with his own hands. It's become my home away from Annapolis. Since they have three sons, Scott, David, and Briggs, we've had fun comparing our lives with three daughters to their lives with three sons. The Elwell men scared me to death skiing in Steamboat Springs one winter going down a double black diamond run. I wanted to retaliate by making them sail Lasers in 35 knots.

There are a couple of sailors and cameramen who have never met each other but are extremely skilled in their fields. Anytime you can get two superstars on the same project at the same time, good things happen. In all my years of filming events, Mike Audick and George Johns stand out for their remarkable video work. Weeks later, screening the material, I'm always surprised at their award-winning photography and many outstanding nuggets. Only once was I able to get both Mike and George on the same shoot at the same time. It was a film for a boat charter company in the British Virgin Islands.

I write many of my shows, but not all. I've learned a lot working with several veteran writers, including Roger Vaughan, Angus Phillips, John Rousmaniere, and Herb McCormick.

Once filming is over, there are endless hours spent editing and adding sound. Rick Larmore and I have edited more than 500 shows over 20 years. Editor Scott Shucher and I have also worked together on many productions. Scott is a good sailor himself. Of course when all the pictures are shot and edited, there is one last important element. Victor Giordano toured on the rock scene for years. He has been the audio engineer for hundreds of my voiceovers and he writes original music for most of my productions.

In my sailing notebooks there are hundreds of people I have raced with over the years. Jud Smith is one of the best speed merchants I've ever raced with. He and I complement each other nicely. Many of my most important victories are a direct result of having Jud onboard. Another superstar sailor is Stu Argo from Detroit. Stu has nerves of steel, is physically strong, and, like Jud, knows how to make a boat go fast. A third superstar is Mark Mendelblatt, who was a College All-American at Tufts and an Olympian is 2004. In the fall of 2010, I raced an Etchells regatta with both Jud and Mark on the boat. We opened with a fifth but won four straight races after that. On the way back into the dock at the Annapolis Yacht Club, I told them that racing with both of them at the same time was equal to having Mike Audick and George Johns on the same shoot, but I don't think they understood. It is always a pleasure to be a part of excellence.

* * *

To be universally recognized as "the best" in any sport is extremely rare. But sailor Paul Elvstrom has earned that distinction. Over four consecutive Olympic Games he won four Gold medals. But the quest for excellence was an emotional rollercoaster for Elvstrom—ranging from the highs of his record-setting Olympic performances to the lows of devastating mental breakdowns. His life story is a powerful example of the traumas that can afflict an intense competitor once he realizes that every competitive situation cannot be controlled.

Elvstrom was 20 when he won his first Gold medal in 1948, during a time when sailing was dominated by the wealthy and even royalty. Elvstrom's approach was different: He trained for months for every major regatta; he was an intuitive sailor, but physical training was his fundamental building block; he studied the rules fastidiously to find clever tactical tricks; he invented equipment to be more efficient on the water and developed unique physical and mental training methods. Decades later, many of his innovations are the standard in the sailing world.

His greatest victory, however, may have been his resolution of the heavy emotional toll he endured from years of self-induced stress.

Elvstrom's first Olympic Gold medal took people by surprise. In that regatta, he needed to win the last two races in windy conditions. Lighter in weight than the other top sailors, Elvstrom was at a disadvantage. But he visualized the race the night before and won the Gold. "At that time I didn't have trouble with my nerves . . . It was because nobody expected I should win." Overnight, he became a national hero in his native Denmark.

The pressure to win became more intense. Defending champions become marked by competitors, and Elvstrom's boats were challenged for measurement

Paul Elvstrom and his daughter Trine sailed a Tornado in the 1988 Olympic Games. Paul was 60 at the time.

infractions and rivals constantly maneuvered against him on the water. He kept striving for an edge. He invented an ingenious self-bailer to keep water out of the bilge (which is used on most small boats today), created a lifejacket that conformed to his body shape to eliminate bulk, and made non-skid shoes so he wouldn't slip on wet decks. But Elvstrom's biggest advances were in the design and construction of sails. He was so fast on the water that sailing rivals asked to buy copies of his sails.

On the water Elvstrom dominated. In 1952 he won his second Gold medal; four years later at the Melbourne Games, he repeated the performance. There was no stopping "The Great Dane." But for him the fun was going away.

In 1960, while trailering his boat to a regatta in Europe, he and his wife Anne, who was driving at the time, were in a serious accident. Anne was badly hurt. "I hated everything to do with sailing," he said of that chapter after the accident. Anne slowly recovered and Elvstrom got back to sailing, but emotional scars remained.

Meanwhile the expectations for Elvstrom to win on the water continued to build. "I felt I had to win because everyone expected me to, and I was scared of losing—even a small race. I had so much nerves during these races that I became ill." Elvstrom decided to make the 1960 Olympics in Naples his last. At 32, he retired after winning his fourth Gold medal.

In the 1964 Games in Tokyo, he served as an advisor to the Japanese Organizing Committee and a coach for the Danish team. But he missed the sailing. "I realized how stupid it was to be nervous about competing in something I love!" With renewed enthusiasm, he came back stronger than ever, and in 1966 and '67 he had a remarkable run, winning world championships in seven different classes.

Each racing class has different skill sets and strategies, and Elvstrom adapted quickly to every challenge. The sailing world had never witnessed such a versatile sailor, and by age 40, Elvstrom was considered the Mozart of sailing. He made winning look easy. But the truth was, the pressure on his nerves was building again.

At the 1968 Olympics, Elvstrom finished fourth in the Star class. A new Olympic class was introduced for the 1972 Games, and the 26-foot Soling keelboat was the perfect size for an aging athlete. Elvstrom prepared for the Games with a vengeance. But he faced Buddy Melges at the '72 Games—a champion Scow sailor who had the best record of any American in a variety of classes. Buddy won easily. For Elvstrom, the stress was too much and he had a nervous breakdown.

Several years later, Elvstrom was back on the water again, this time in the speedy Tornado catamaran class, racing with the youngest of four daughters, Trine. They won the European Championship, which earned them a berth at the 1984 Olympics in Los Angeles. There, they finished fourth—the only father-daughter team to ever compete in the Olympics in any sport.

The joy of sailing returned for Elvstrom, racing with his daughter. "It is really a dream to sail with her. She is very fast and we are so used to each other . . . When we are sailing we don't talk very much. I know what she is doing [and] she knows what I'm doing."

He and Trine competed at the 1988 Games in Korea, but the wind blew hard. They won one race, but finished 15th overall. "Even when we are not winning, we have fun. And the main thing is to compete . . . I'm very happy to be able to compete. But it is more fun when we are winning."

Hart Jordan, John MacGowan, Stu Argo, Trip Davis, and I lead *Great Britain* on the way to a victory in the 1988 Liberty Cup.

Paul Elvstrom's winning record is no doubt impressive. But what may be more impressive is how he healed some painful wounds on the water. Many sailors remember his famous quote: "You haven't won the race if in winning the race you have lost the respect of your competitors." Paul Elvstrom has clearly won the respect of many sailors around the world.

* * *

I have been lucky to have crossed paths with a number of great sailors in my career. They are people whose drive for excellence crosses over into their professions and their lives. As I grew in my sailing career as a young man and experienced the heady days of intercollegiate racing at Maritime, I also developed a drive to be the best I could be. So I was naturally drawn to the sailors who embodied the kind of greatness I was striving for. They became mentors, models of how to push your limits, and ultimately friends. All I can say is, hang around great people long enough and some of their star quality will rub off on you.

As I got more deeply involved in the sailing world, my drive to be the best spread well beyond my own personal goals. I also developed a passion for making the sport the best it could be. I came to understand the structure of the sport, and just like a house, I saw weak areas that needed to be shored up and places that needed remodeling.

I wondered why sailing couldn't have its own on-the-field umpires, just the way many sports did. I also saw a real need for more formal, standardized training in the sport—both for sailors and for sailing instructors. And I saw a different way to build an Olympic team, taking advantage of coaching, training, and recruiting the way many sports do. When I expressed my ideas to the sailing establishment, the reactions were varied—from those who thought I was onto something, to those who considered my ideas unconventional and unwelcome. If the sport had survived this long without these efforts, why start now?

I am happy to say today that these ideas have all become a reality in the sport. I don't take credit for how they have manifested themselves in sailing, for there are many smart and talented people who helped pave the way. But I am proud to have planted the seeds. Like a small snowball rolling down a hill, those concepts gathered mass and momentum as they rolled on.

I got a first-hand view of how effective good training and coaching can be in college. It was not only my time sailing under Coach Graham Hall's direction. I was also fortunate to attend a racing camp taught by Olympic medalist Peter

Barrett, which was held in conjunction with the 1970 College Nationals in Wisconsin. A group of us traveled out to the University of Wisconsin for three days of intensive sailing in two double-handed one-designs: Tech Dinghies and 470s. I learned an enormous amount in just a few days.

In the fall of 1973, I was asked to join the America's Cup crew of the 12 Meter *Valiant*, the boat that was going to sail as the backup boat for the New York Yacht Club's new boat, *Mariner*. At the same time, USYRU (United States Yacht Racing Union, the national governing body of sailing, now US SAILING), and *Yacht Racing/Cruising* magazine teamed up to run summer racing camps at the US Olympic Sailing Center at Association Island in upstate New York. For that quadrennium, Association Island was also going to be the site of the U.S. Olympic Trials. I was asked to be the lead instructor of the camps.

With two good offers in hand, it was a tough decision. Ever since I was young, I had dreamt about being on an America's Cup crew. But I was also excited about running the upstate racing camps—and so, I chose to teach rather than compete in the major leagues. Looking back, it was a good decision.

I moved up to Association Island for the summer of '74 to run four, one-week camps. We had 10 singlehanded Lasers, 10 double-handed 470s, and 30 kids in each session. It was a Monday–Saturday program with Sundays off, and the kids learned an enormous amount in those few days. It was very cool.

After a successful summer at Association Island, I began to think larger. Why don't we take these camps and go to yacht clubs across the country? So I went to USYRU and sold the One-Design Class Council—the committee that oversees one-design racing in the United States—on setting up something I called the Advanced Racing Clinics.

It may have looked like a small transition at the time, taking these racing camps on the road. But it was truly the start of something big in American sailing. It was the beginning of establishing standardized training programs that could be run on a national scale.

So in the summer of 1975, I set up a series of three-day clinics at yacht clubs across the United States. I was making $100 a day, which at the time was decent money for me. The clinics gained so much in popularity that by the following summer I could not handle all the requests myself. I recruited five other top sailors: Dave Perry, Peter Isler, Ed Baird, Stu Johnstone, and Mark Laura. They were racers who would someday become household names in the sport, but back then, they were just like me: avid sailors who were thrilled to be making a paycheck at something they loved.

The more racing clinics I ran at yacht clubs, the more I realized that the sailing instructors themselves could also benefit from a standardized training program. The racing clinics were being handled well by the sailors I recruited, so I focused on developing a program for instructors.

In the fall of 1976, I was a 26-year-old with a lean checkbook. But I scraped enough money together for travel expenses and an airplane ticket to Chicago to attend the annual meeting of USYRU. My goal was to convince the powers that be that they needed an organized training program, and I was the one to do it. As it turned out, that was a very worthwhile trip. When I went to hang my coat in the coat closet at the Chicago Yacht Club, I ran into Olympic medalist Don Cohan. He had been following my career and asked me to join the U.S. Olympic Committee. As I was coming out of the coat closet, I bumped into Ted Turner, who asked me to join him as his America's Cup tactician on *Courageous*.

I walked into the club as a young kid trying to cut a path in sailing; I exited with an America's Cup berth and an Olympic affiliation that would last to this day. Talk about serendipity!

During those meetings, I proposed running a two-day instructor training seminar program that would be a certificate-earning program, and the committee went for the idea.

The racing and instructor clinics were taking off, and I was also earning a name for myself as someone who could design and run instruction programs for sailors. The Junior Yacht Racing Association (JYRA) of Long Island Sound approached me to write a teaching manual for them. I put everything I had learned from running the clinics in that manual, and that book became the first training manual for the precursor of US SAILING. I later took the manual to Simon & Schuster in New York, and it was published as my *Sailing Fundamentals*. This book is still in print and has sold some 360,000 copies to date.

The clinics I created and ran became the foundation for a series of national training programs that the national governing body later took over and elevated to a new level. Today, the training system is manned by a full-time staff at the offices of US SAILING in Rhode Island and taught by hundreds of instructors and volunteers located throughout the country. But the seeds were sewn during that memorable summer at Association Island, and I am proud to see the harvest of well-trained sailors that have been cultivated over the years.

I had built some credibility with the racing and instructor clinics, so as soon as I was a full-fledged member of the U.S. Olympic Committee I floated my ideas about a new approach to building our Olympic team of sailors. First, I thought we should be recruiting non-Olympic class sailors to compete in our Olympic classes. How we would do that was simple to me: Hold a clinic in Olympic class boats, invite the top sailors in the country to attend, and encourage them to become active with the class. Second, we needed to enhance our training for our Olympic sailors and study what worked in all areas of racing—from the smallest one-designs to grand-prix arenas such as the America's Cup. Third, in every sport coaching is an essential aspect, and I proposed that we beef up our coaching efforts.

My ideas were not revolutionary and largely grew out of my experience being coached as an intercollegiate sailor and then coaching college racers. But they were not ideas that were part of the Olympic sailing culture. *What could our top sailors learn at a clinic?* That was the response of many on the committee. But they were willing to give it a try.

We held a seminar in the Star class in New Orleans. At the end, legendary talents such as Tom Blackaller and Bill Buchan made comments about how helpful the session was. That basically opened the door. Coaching, training, and recruiting are standard in the U.S. Olympic sailing program today.

I continued to look at other sports to glean more ideas for sailing. As I watched football games—and I watched a lot of them as a young man—there was always a referee on the field of play making decisions. In sailing, many rules infractions on the course were dealt with after the race, in a protest hearing that is not unlike a court of law. In the 1983 America's Cup, that process was highlighted on the world stage when there was a protest between the Americans on *Liberty* and the Australians on *Australia II*. The hearing just stopped all the action. There had to be a better way, I thought. In a flash, it occurred to me: Why not have refs out on the water?

It was a radical idea at the time. Still, I started talking up the concept of on-the-water umpires up for the 1985 Liberty Cup regatta in New York, which I had a hand in organizing. The judges, Arthur Wullschleger and John Nichols, correctly pointed out that they were unprepared to take on something so new and untested, but they were intrigued by the idea. Out on the West Coast, Tom Shadden, a former chairman of the Congressional Cup, also liked my idea of umpiring. Support also came from Irishman Harold Cudmore, one of the most active match-racers at that time. I talked it up with organizers of other match-race events, and by 1986 we were experimenting with on-the-water umpiring at the Liberty Cup.

I give Tom Ehman credit for making on-the-water umpiring happen in the America's Cup. The practice became a part of the World Match-Race Conference in the late '80s. Ironically, when the concept was tried at a Maxi regatta in Newport, Rhode Island, the boat I was racing on got flagged for an infraction. So maybe I was one of the first to suffer at the hands of this quick, on-the-field judgment! Today, umpiring is standard practice in match-racing, team racing, and other top-level contests. It has grown well beyond my initial idea.

For a while now, I have believed that the next step is having umpires in a studio reviewing video footage during the racing to make their calls. I trust we will see this become a reality in the future.

During the Whitbread Race stopover in Annapolis in 1998, I had a vision that there should be a sailing hall of fame. It took several years, but the National Sailing Hall of Fame eventually was established on the City Dock of Annapolis, adjacent to the U.S. Naval Academy. Dick Franyo is the chairman.

Ideas that improve sailing are today carried out by many sailors across the country. And as I look back and take an inventory of all the elements that make our sport great, I count not only the big movements, such as standardized training. I also count the small moments.

I raced with Senator Ted Kennedy several times. He was a good helmsman and loved to win. It was always interesting talking politics with him. Having studied political science in graduate school, I enjoyed hearing his view of the world.

One day during the summer I chartered the 56-foot ketch *Southerly* for a family cruise in Maine, the wind was blowing a stiff 27 knots and *Southerly* glided swiftly and with ease over the five-foot waves. We were flying a working jib, staysail, and mizzen, but no mainsail. My daughter Kristi, who was 16 at the time, had been steering for an hour and was getting tired. I adjusted the sails to relieve the helm, and Kristi felt the wheel go light. She simply let go of the helm, and for the next two hours, the stately ketch sailed a steady course straight for Grand Manan Island with no one touching the helm. A beautiful boat in perfect balance: for me and for Kristi, that is as close as it gets to greatness.

.11.

CALM

2004–2010 Every storm has its calm afterward. Once the winds stop screaming, the water flattens out, and the rains stop falling, the sun comes out. But there is always damage: felled trees and boats on the rocks and floods. They take time and patience to repair. My body, having survived its worst storm, was very much the same.

←———— ■ ————→

In October 2004, Aaron Rapoport, his wife Debbie, David and Christy Elwell, Janice, and I took our Sabre 402 for a sail on Chesapeake Bay. It was a beautiful fall Sunday afternoon. It was great fun for me to watch Dr. Rapoport at the helm of *Whirlwind*. When the going got tough during my cancer battle, Aaron was the man that gave me the confidence that I could recover. It is hard to get to know someone laying down in a hospital bed. Now we're out on the water sailing. At one point I was sitting behind the helm looking at the horizon and realized there was a bright future ahead. Later that evening, the six of us headed over to the Redskin's stadium to watch a football game. Thanks to ESPN I arranged for a couple of Field Passes. Aaron and I walked around the sidelines before the game, watching the players loosen up and practice. Aaron watched intensely. Pro football is a long way from his medical world. But like football players, doctors like to be victorious. I was grateful to be in his win column.

In January 2005, I declared that I was on my way to recovery. I knew I was not quite right yet, but I felt I had turned a corner and the cancer had stopped raging. I wanted to get on with my life.

I wanted to get past the sympathy too. Everyone means well, but it's difficult to know how to act when the fact that an illness is taking your life is the elephant in the room. Friends would see me on my worst days and say, Well, you're looking better! But they knew and I knew that I was still crumpled up and skinny and the cancer was still destroying my body. Still, what else can you say? Lymphoma not only threatens your life; it also makes for some pretty awkward social moments.

Compared to mainstream sports like baseball and football, sailing's participants and fan base are tiny. But what the sport lacks in size it makes up for in diversity. It was my 50th year of sailing, and so I planned a year of a lot of variety on the water: dinghy sailing, tall-ship ocean passages, world-class racing, and family cruising. My plan was to maximize the sailing time and knit myself back into this community of sailors that had buoyed my spirits through my worst times.

**I just wanted to be a normal person again,
so I did what all my life has put me right. I went sailing.**

I took my first steps back into competitive sailing in my native Annapolis, and getting back into an Etchells was a good start after my absence from the racecourse. This one-design class has attracted some of the world's top talents, and most of the sailors who are household names from wins at the America's Cup, the Olympics, and other world-class circuits have at least one Etchells prize lurking somewhere in their trophy case.

Dr. Rapoport and I went sailing on *Whirlwind* in October 2004.
I'm still thin but we were both glad to be on the water.

Winning a race at the 2005 Etchells North Americans off Chicago.
Gary Gilbert and Mark Mendelblatt were aboard.

I sailed the Annapolis Yacht Club Fall Series in 2004 in my Etchells. I remember being so nervous, which, after a time, made me laugh. I had probably sailed 5,000 races by that point, so why was I nervous about just one more? Once I dropped the nervousness, we sailed well and won the regatta.

After making that step, I moved up to a larger arena and decided to race in the Annapolis Lands' End NOOD (National Offshore One-Design) Regatta, a national circuit organized by *Sailing World* magazine. The NOOD regatta in the spring of 2005 would draw the region's best, so I sweetened my odds for success by inviting some top-shelf crew along, including Jud Smith, a maestro in this class and a good friend whose name often tops the charts at Etchells regattas, and Rob Erda, one of my frequent Etchells crew. We won the regatta, and I was inspired to take it up a notch.

In June, the Etchells fleet would be heading to Chicago for their North American Championships. Expected on the starting line were top talents in the class, including Jud, who would be skippering his own boat, and Dennis Conner. My boat partner in the Etchells and longtime friend Gary Gilbert, a young and talented Olympian named Mark Mendelblatt, and I made our plans to take a road trip to Chicago that summer.

But before heading west to Chicago, I had other business to take care of—namely a run with a host of other sailors at a 100-year-old transatlantic race record set by the legendary Charlie Barr.

That May, I went to New York to step onto the deck of the 252-foot clipper ship *Stad Amsterdam* and, along with 40 members of the Storm Trysail Club who had chartered the ship for the crossing, set a course for England as part of the fleet in the Rolex Transatlantic Challenge. The event marked the 100th anniversary of the New York Yacht Club's race for the Kaiser's Cup, which was won in record-breaking style by Wilson Marshall's *Atlantic* and America's Cup legend Charlie Barr, who was at the helm. I was on the crossing to make a film for the event's sponsor, Rolex.

Twenty of the world's largest sailing megayachts set sail that May day on the 3,000-mile course from New York, and the fleet represented a huge range in large-yacht style and design: from my luxurious ride—a three-masted steel-hulled clipper with 16 cabins whose build date is 2000 but whose lines and rig are wholly traditional—to *Mari Cha IV*, the sleek, futuristic, silver-hulled schooner at 140 feet in length that ended up being the first to England and first to smash the century-old record.

It had been 32 years since my last transatlantic crossing. I was reminded just how vast the ocean is and how traveling by sea on a long ocean passage is a wonderful way to form bonds with your crew and make new friendships. The personal highlight of the trip was launching an 18-foot inflatable to take pictures of *Stad* in mid-ocean. It was blowing 30 miles per hour and the waves were 15 feet high, so the video footage was spectacular.

When I returned to the States, I looked forward to heading to Chicago to race against my Etchells compatriots—a group of tough yet sportsmanlike competitors. The competitor I most looked forward to racing against was Dennis Conner, who is always fun to compete against because of his on-course logic. I admire the way he plugs away during a race and rarely goes the wrong way in the hopes of finding a break.

Chicago was hot that June, with temperatures in the 80s and 90s and a *lot* of wind. In one race it blew 35 knots, and that was a magic race for us. We took the start and led by half a leg. At one point, on the run, we actually got the Etchells up on a plane, careening on the edge of control.

"We've got to be more aggressive!" called Mendelblatt.

"Mark" I pleaded, "we could broach!"

He looked back and muttered, "OK, OK."

I thought to myself, "Ahhhh, youth." Overall, we ended up third behind Conner and winner Jud Smith.

If I tell you this was a quick and easy victory and I was back in the saddle again, I'd be lying. The North Americans was a tough regatta for me. I knew it would be a challenge, so I booked a room at the Peninsula Hotel, which provided the comfort and luxury I needed. There were a lot of moments when I felt ill and the effects of the cancer and its treatment still very much lingered.

I brought along inspirational music—my favorites, including Emerson, Lake & Palmer. My days during the event were completely regimented: wake up, have breakfast, get down to the boat, go racing, then return immediately to my hotel for room service and an early night. Parties, beer drinking, and yacht club socializing were all out for me.

But on the night of the prize giving, I made an exception. I put on my best jacket and tie and made my way back to the yacht club. When I was presented with my third-place trophy, I made a short speech and got a standing ovation. That ovation and the kudos from my peers was unexpected. "We haven't seen you in years and you come back here and take a third place!" said Bruce Burton, a top competitor who won the Etchells Worlds in the late '80s. That victory, hard-fought as it was, felt so good. We beat Jud three out of six races, and it was a defining moment. After months of setbacks and illness, it was a long-awaited taste of victory—like a giant neon road sign, pointing in the right direction. For the first time in a long time I felt things were looking up.

* * *

Throughout 2005, I traveled far and wide to fulfill my sailing plan. The air miles and the odometer on my car logged big geographic distances, but my recovery was inch by inch. Small gains and some setbacks. It was my time to repair— and it was taking so much longer than I had hoped. Looking back, I know now I stretched my capabilities and did many things that year that were far beyond what I could comfortably manage physically. But that was the only way I knew how to move forward, and I knew it was a good gamble: give me some goals and I'll find the inner strength to achieve them.

I traveled down to the British Virgin Islands to make a film for a yacht company. Our film crew spent a week following a family of four and two energetic couples to all the good spots in the islands, and it was fascinating to record the enthusiasm of novices in a sailor's paradise.

In August 2005, Janice and two of our daughters, Ashleigh and Brooke, sailed *Whirlwind* in the New York Yacht Club Cruise. It was great to be back amongst friends and the beautiful boats in the flotilla.

Nantucket Community Sailing invited me and 13 notable sailors to sail in a pro/am regatta for charity as guests crewed aboard a fleet of identically matched International One Designs (IODs). Nantucket is a magical island with reliable winds, and our crew ended up second.

I also reconnected with my college roots. Working with the Intercollegiate Sailing Association, ESPN aired the team race and co-ed championships, and a few weeks later I showed video clips at the U.S. Youth Championships. You could hear a pin drop as these young sailors who are our Olympians of the future marveled at their heroes. It felt good to be out there, inspiring young people to reach for their dreams.

I even got to Newport to race on our old America's Cup 12 Meter *Courageous*. Owner Craig Millard invited me to sail with his completely amateur crew. The boat never looked better, and the crew's enthusiasm reminded me of the energy Ted Turner and our team had aboard that same boat during the America's Cup trials and races. Go *Courageous*!

The venerable A Cat class races downwind. *Vapor* leads.

Getting back to the Leukemia Cup regattas held across the country was a major priority for me. I made 16 of them in 2005 and felt so proud that our sport was racing for this good cause. Every time I get to a Leukemia Cup I am reminded of the irony, that I took on the chairmanship of this national regatta series well before I was stricken with a blood cancer. Sometimes it even feels a little spooky.

There was one project I took on that year, that truly felt like coming home.

I first saw the magnificent A Cats at age eight, from the dock of the Beachwood Yacht Club. The giant mainsails of *Bat*, *Spy*, *Lotus*, and *Mary Ann* raced for the finish line, and as they drew closer, a crowd formed. Sailors waist deep in the water hauling out their Sneakboxes, Jet 14 sailors, Saturday afternoon strollers on the boardwalk, and kids getting their ice cream at the old pavilion: they all stopped what they were doing to watch the gigantic Catboats jockey for the finish. The four boats made the final sprint to the finish and everyone was screaming for their favorite, until the cannon of the Barnegat Bay Yacht Racing Association race committee sounded and declared *Lotus* the winner.

Within seconds, all four boats had finished. They turned up into the wind, making graceful, sweeping turns to avoid running aground or hitting the dock where I was standing. As the boats turned, sails luffed furiously, anchors were heaved, mainsails were lowered, booms fell naturally into their wooden crutches, and suddenly, all was quiet.

To an eight-year-old used to sailing a 10-foot Pram, these boats were giant and I was awestruck. As I matured into a Barnegat Bay racer, I had an opportunity to sail on a lot of boats—Penguins, Prams, Sneakboxes, Duckboats, Jet 14s, Flying Scots, Lightnings, and even the speedy E Scows. But no matter what boat I might be sailing on, the A Cats always captured my attention. I was occasionally asked to crew on one, and those days are some of my best sailing memories.

The A Cats were a certain ilk of boat that graced the waters of Barnegat Bay. Long ago sturdy workboats to move cargo across the Bay's choppy waters were needed, and single-sail Catboats were powerful vessels that could handle the heavy loads. While the big sails were a handful, they were necessary to make good time and they were efficient in both light and strong winds.

It was inevitable that these workboats of the Bay would compete. The first A Cat was built in 1922, and her great success on the racecourse inspired others to build boats and get into the game. A modern resurgence of interest in these boats and dedicated owners have miraculously kept the A Cats alive and well.

Peter Kellogg—an A Cat owner, Wall Street financier, and a key person in keeping this class going—suggested that I write a book on these magnificent boats. Images from the past filled my head, and I was immediately enthused. Unfortunately, my illness delayed the project. But as I started my recovery, the intermission in telling the story of the A Cats only increased my determination to write the book. Kellogg wanted the proceeds from the book to support the Ocean County College sailing team.

Peter suggested I work with Roy Wilkins, a local intercollegiate coach who has been fleet captain of the A Cats for over a decade. Together, Roy and I took on the project, which I first thought would be a history book. But after talking with other Barnegat Bay sailors, I realized the golden age of A Cat sailing was taking place in our own lifetimes. Who better than the owners and crews themselves to tell this story? Through the winter of my recovery, I interviewed dozens of A Cat denizens, and it was most enjoyable to pose questions and then sit back and listen to the stories that spilled out and turned into long conversations. I also wrote about the yacht clubs in Barnegat Bay that are home to the fleet, many of which I had known as a boy.

But there was something missing. As I interviewed more sailors, poured over photographs, and studied the history of these amazing boats, I realized I had never helmed one. My chance came in the summer of 2005, in the Barnegat Bay Yacht Racing Association summer series.

As I stepped aboard *Spy*, originally built in 1924, the boat's regular helmsman Gary Stewart gave me the tiller. The smell of a wooden boat transported me back in time, to those happy days when I sailed the *African Queen* with my father. The water gurgling in the centerboard trunk was just as mysterious as I had remembered it.

We sailed two races, taking a second and a fifth. Even in our second race when we were on the wrong end of a shift, the crew jumped up at the finish and congratulated each other for a great day on the water. A Cat sailors compete as intensely as America's Cup racers. Still, it is hard not to smile from ear to ear when you are racing these magnificent catboats, regardless of where you stand in the fleet.

Roy and I completed the book later that year, and the project was a wonderful way to "come home"—to the magic of Barnegat Bay and the good-spirited sailors of the Jersey Shore.

* * *

It took about two years, from when I first declared myself on the road to recovery, to feel normal again. As difficult as it was to wait that healing period out, I gained a lot of wisdom about how to weather a serious illness.

I try to share that knowledge as much as I can with others—whether they are individuals diagnosed with disease and looking for information and advice, or medical professionals who want a patient's perspective.

When I talk to individuals who have just been diagnosed with lymphoma and are getting their head around this frightening news, I make sure to get across some important points.

I tell them that the treatment and recovery is not a linear process—that they will have periods of progress and times of setback, and to mentally prepare for that. I tell them about the sympathy factor and how some people will not know how to treat them, and that may flip them out—so acting normally is good therapy, both for the patient and those around them! It's important to educate themselves, to ask lots of questions, and to get second and third opinions. They should have the courage to choose the most aggressive treatment they can manage. I urge them not to abandon their goals, and tell them how writing *Championship Sailing* during the worst of my illness was very good therapy. And they need to avoid one very explosive question: Why me? That question can be pondered endlessly, and there will never be an answer. (I solved the puzzle for myself: looking at the statistics of how many people are stricken with cancer, I told friends and family that I got sick so they can avoid being a statistic.) And I tell them not to worry about the final outcome, but to simply take it day by day.

By the time 2009 rolled around, I felt much stronger. Keeping up with a full schedule of sailing and traveling didn't require the same kind of discipline and regimentation it did during my early days of recovery. I decided to dive in and return to the kind of sailing schedule I once kept—before business and family commitments took a higher priority. I now marvel that I was able to spend 250 days a year on the water in my early days. With children graduating from school, my oldest getting married, and my health much improved, I decided to return to a lot of on-water days and make 2009 a full summer of sailing.

Throughout the summer I checked back into the log books that I had kept for decades, to see what I had been doing during a specific week. And I continued my logs, taking notes on the highs and lows out on the water. I was wide-eyed at everything around me, and there were a lot of lessons and laughs.

At the helm of Gus Carlson's *Aurora* in 30 knots of wind during the 2010 Stamford Vineyard Race.

On the first morning of the 12 Meter World Championships in Newport aboard *Freedom*, owned by Ernest Jacquet, I called for the whole crew to come back into the cockpit and take a look around at the 17 classic yachts tuning up for the first start. This was the largest fleet of Twelves to ever sail on the same racecourse in the United States. To see winning America's Cup boats like *Columbia*, *Weatherly*, *Intrepid*, *Courageous*, and *Freedom* sailing in perfect condition was historic and heartwarming. There were Cup veterans on most every boat. I had to smile because winning races still seemed to be the priority for most of the competitors. In what other sport can you have a team averaging over 50 years of age and still be competitive?

I have to admit that my skills are not as sharp as they were 25 or even 10 years ago. I suppose this is one of the twists of life that all of us have to come to terms with. The difference is that losing is not the end of the world. In many ways just taking part is reward enough. Some might consider this a rationalization for losing, but I don't consider it so. Victory takes many forms. I sailed a regatta with Norwood Davis, who had a hip replaced a few months earlier. We had two second-place finishes during the event but did not capture the overall win. Still, he did a fine job steering and we were energized by the experience. We had our own kind of victory.

In the Stamford Vineyard Race—a classic American distance race of some 230 miles that takes place over Labor Day weekend—we had a good seesaw battle with two identical boats in our class. Just 18 miles from the finish we were even with one of them and well ahead of the other. Then disaster struck. The wind died for us, and those two boats sailed right past us, just about a mile away. It was a painful three hours of waiting for new breeze to reach our windless sails.

Years ago I would have gone wild during the pass. This time I just laughed, thinking I had been lucky enough to be where they were many times over the years. It was a reminder that the breaks eventually even out. At our post-race crew meeting I took full responsibility for the error of not getting into the new breeze. The next day I sent an email of congratulations to the rival skipper. He promptly forwarded my message to his crew. They appreciated the gesture, and deep down I felt good about the whole thing.

One weekend in August during Nantucket Race Week, I recalled that exactly 40 years earlier I was thinking about attending a rock concert in New York. But that same weekend the national championships for the one-design 420 class were being held on my home waters of Barnegat Bay. I clearly remember my father's suggestion that I stay home and sail that weekend. "You can go to a concert any time, but the 420 Nationals only come to these waters once in a lifetime." I took his advice, finished mid-fleet, and ended up missing Woodstock!

Throughout the summer I raced my Swan Club 42 in eight events. Every regatta proved to be a learning experience, and I could fill a book with my observations. At the end of the season I covered the New York Yacht Club Invitational Cup for ESPN. My view was high above the racecourse, filming the races from a helicopter. That aerial perspective was invaluable, and I could see how the top boats used clear lanes to work into the top of the pack. This knowledge will be helpful next time I race.

The highlight of the 2009 summer was Kristi's wedding in Annapolis to Brian Conroy. He grew up in New Jersey like me. He was new to sailing but had passed my test aboard *Whirlwind* a few summers earlier in Maine.

Out on Nantucket I was offered the helm of a classic wooden 12 Meter for a day of racing. A strong easterly breeze challenged these old boats. Approaching the starting line a leeward boat protested us for a rule infraction called barging. Yikes! It was the first protest for me in many years. We went through the full protest procedure. The other skipper said he had taken a seminar from leading rules expert Dave Perry the previous winter; Dave suggested that you should always go through with a protest because they are learning experiences. Luckily for me there were two video cameras recording the start, and the protest was dismissed. It reminded me to simply stay out of the protest room at all costs.

Throughout the summer I attended 15 Leukemia Cup fundraising regattas. On one weekend in September, five events raised over $1 million. Even in those tough economic times sailors were willing to lend a hand. I believe that racing for this good cause gives everyone involved a warm and generous feeling.

I revved up my speaking schedule in 2009 and spoke at a number of events where I met many passionate sailors. One stop still stands out in my mind: the Lightning North Americans in Sodus Bay on Lake Ontario, New York. Sailors participated from around the country and ranged in age from 10 to 85. I also spoke in places like Chicago, Sheboygan, San Francisco, Watch Hill, Newport, Cape Fear, Castine, Marblehead, and Nantucket. I even stopped in New York Harbor for a regatta for the one-design Flying Dutchman class. Speaking in all

I was lucky to join Senator John Kerry for the 2010 Nantucket Race Week Celebrity Sailor Regatta aboard an International One Design.

those venues gave me an opportunity to reconnect with the sailing community in the United States, and that tour was a reminder of how vibrant sailing is in all these waterfront places.

At the end of the summer, I tallied my score card and there was a mix of wins and losses. Out of 74 starts I came away with 7 victories, 16 top-three finishes, and 3 last-place finishes. But the trophy count almost didn't matter. During the summer of 2009 I looked at sailing with new eyes and rediscovered the challenge and joy of being back out on the water.

In 2009, I got back into the groove. My desire to sail and promote the sport continues to fuel me forward as I criss-cross the country on a regular basis to compete and talk to audiences of all types about sailing.

In 2010, I scheduled 118 speaking engagements and a full calendar of racing events. Racing an IOD in Nantucket with Senator John Kerry was a fascinating exchange, where I offered tactical advice during the races and peppered him with questions about being a politician and the political process between races. In August I returned to Nantucket to skipper a 1937 yacht in the Opera House Cup, a 30-square-meter boat named *Cythera*. We finished a satisfying third overall, after using some favorable currents running along the shore as our secret weapon. The regatta drew some of the most beautiful, majestic classic boats in the region. After a 37-year absence from team racing, I got back into the game at the Hinman Masters Team Race Regatta. Sailing as part of a team raises the level of the game to new heights, and this brand of mentally and physically taxing competition in quick, identical boats is typically played best by intercollegiate sailors. Still, it was fun and exciting to get back to it.

During the early stage of my recovery, distance racing truly tested my limits. I had tried to sail the legendary 635-mile Newport-to-Bermuda ocean race in 2006, with Llwyd Ecclestone. Unfortunately, my immune system and my body were not up to the challenge. I made it across the finish line but ended up sick. So the 2010 run at the legendary course to Bermuda was vindication, where I sailed with Gus Carlson on his 66-foot *Aurora*. We finished second in class. Helming the same boat in the Stamford Vineyard Race later in the year was exhilarating when Hurricane *Earl* ushered in 30-knot winds on a course up and down Long Island Sound. I also made time to head back to Barnegat Bay for some A Cat racing and to compete in the "World Ducks," the world championships for the local 12-foot wooden Duckboats. There were 71 Duckboats manned by sailors from age 8 to 80. What a fun event that was.

In our production studio, Rick Larmore, on the right, edits. Client Alan Castro and I sit on the left and review footage.

Professionally, in 2010 my schedule returned to the chock-full routine I am most used to. As I write this, I am juggling 10 different film projects on a wide range of topics—from Tall Ships, to sailmaking technology, to the new subject area of nuclear energy. Now that I have hit my stride again, I have a lot to be grateful for.

My office routine remains the same. On November 1, 1978, I moved into a small office at 3 Church Circle in the heart of downtown Annapolis, across the street from the governor's mansion. I'm still at the same location. It is a seven-minute walk from my house to the office. The building, at one time, housed the local newspaper, *The Capital*. The days in the office pass swiftly. There are endless phone calls, writing projects, and film editing. In 2008 I built a new, high-tech editing studio for editor, Rick Larmore. It astounds me how good high-definition television has become, but the most important part never changes, which is to provide compelling stories for viewers.

Day after day, my assistant Kathy, Rick, and I chip away at endless details and projects. The best part about my job is that I always start with a blank sheet of paper and try to create something new. My network of friends and travels have helped me see what works and what doesn't.

One of the great joys is spending time in our editing suite bringing our productions to life. Thanks to giving thousands of lecture presentations, I've had a tremendous amount of feedback from people. I suppose it would be expensive to commission a marketing survey of what people like to watch. Presenting in person is an invaluable research tool.

At the end of each production, I put it away for a few years and come back and watch at a later date. Among my favorites is our 1996 Expedition to Antarctica, the 1987 America's Cup, and the 2010 America's Cup 12 Meter Era Reunion.

The nature of sailing is to keep moving, and my life of travel never seems to stop. I average 150,000 air miles and 20,000 driving miles every year. As you might guess, the airlines, hotels, and car rental companies treat me well as a frequent traveler. The downside is that it is easy to get sick, so, by necessity, I've learned to be careful while I travel.

The first step is to pack as lightly as possible. After every trip I survey what clothes or items I did not use. It is important to take only what is needed so that I avoid checking luggage at all costs. Kathy and I work the system hard in the quest to get upgraded seats on airplanes, because I've found that it really makes a difference in my performance upon arrival. I suppose the day will come that I will regret not taking more time to look around for a few days at each stop, but there are schedules to keep. In 40 years I can count over 200 trips to Europe and nearly 100 trips to Australia, New Zealand, and Asia. I went back through my schedules and counted over 500 drives up and down the New Jersey Turnpike.

I find driving to be good therapy, a time to listen to great music, or just think. My car of choice since turning 30 has been a Mercedes Benz. Comfort counts. In recent years the cell phone is a regular companion on my drives. I set up a series of calls in advance of my trips, and these calls make the time pass swiftly and help take care of a lot of business.

Hotels, of course, are an important part of the equation. While I usually order room service for breakfast, evenings in are rare. I don't watch much television, although *SportsCenter* is an exception. Internet access is absolutely essential. My biggest splurge on the road is to get a massage at least once per month.

As for reading materials I like to travel with my favorite magazines, *Sailing World*, *Time*, *Atlantic*, *New York Review of Books*, *The New Yorker*, *Vanity Fai*r and, of course, *The New York Times*.

Janice and I bought our house in Annapolis in 1981. We live on a deadend street in downtown Annapolis with friendly neighbors and lots of kids running around.

I make a point of calling home most everyday I am gone, and I check in with Kathy three times per day. Having a base camp to help with logistics is important when flights are canceled or weather causes problems, and, in 40 years, I can only think of two cases where I was unable to arrive in time for an event.

In the air I rarely talk with seatmates. Instead I read, write, and make long lists of ideas, making the most of my time in the air to be productive. I find it hard to sleep on planes, and occasionally I will watch a movie on a long flight. Upon arrival, if there is time, I like to go watch movies in a theater. My favorites are *Dancing with Wolves*, *Amadeus*, *Gettysbury*, *Das Boot*, and *Apollo 13*.

Traveling has changed dramatically since the 1960s. People my age remember when it was an expected protocol to dress up for airplane flights. Now it is crowded, confusing, and exhausting. I can identify with actor George Clooney and his character in *Up In the Air*. That nifty film is right on target. But for me, the happiest moment of every trip is walking back through the door at home.

I truly enjoy being at home. Janice and I bought our 1919-built house in 1981. Every year we've done some fixing up, addition, or upgrade. When you're in the same house for a long period of time you can mold it to fit your lifestyle and personality. The day starts off with my beloved *New York Times*. I drink tea, never coffee. Somehow I lost the taste for coffee on the Training Ship *Empire State IV*.

Janice and I moved to Annapolis in 1977 when I was recruited to be the sailing coach at the Naval Academy. She got a nursing job at the local hospital. Annapolis is a friendly town that welcomes newcomers. When you drive into the city there is a sign that proclaims that Annapolis is America's Sailing Capital. It's been a wonderful home for our family,

I have this weird thing that the driveway and the porch need to be swept clean. Since the house is surrounded by trees, it is a never-ending process keeping things clean, but good therapy completing the job. The house is filled with books and sailing paintings. and ranges from being very quiet with just Janice and I, to being incredibly vibrant when the girls are around. One of our favorite places to hang out is the dining room table, where endless board games are contested with great enthusiasm. It reminds me of being aboard *Silver Heels*.

My ideal weekend is Friday night out and an early Saturday morning walk with our neighbors Mimi and Harry Jones, followed by a full day of sailing and Saturday night dinner with family and friends. Sunday morning I enjoy a thorough read of the newspapers, a long walk with Janice, some yardwork, and a late afternoon movie or football game.

Boats I've Sailed On

It was great fun one day to make a list of the boats I've sailed on.

African Queen
America
America II
American Eagle
Annie
Arcadia
Aurora
Azzurra
Barnegat Arrow
Bat
Blitz
Blockade Runner
Blue Yankee
Bolero
Boomerang
Brilliant
B Roll
Bull & Bear
Calamity
Captive
Checkmate
Chessie Racing
Clearwater
Clipper
Columbia
Condor
Conspiracy
Cotton Blossom
Courageous
Cythera
Defender
Dispatcher
Donnybrook
Easterner
EF Language
Endeavour
Equation
Fire One
Fleury Michon VII
France 3
Freedom

Gleam
Golliwogg
Grand Cru
Hawkeye
Heart of America
Helisara
Helyn J
Heritage
Hissar
Illbruck
Independence
Interlodge
Jay Hawk
Jubilation
Katura
Kiwi Magic
Kodiak II
Matador
Matador^2
Merrythought
Midnight Sun
Mirabella
Mischievous
Mistress Quickly
Moxie
Nippon Challenge
Nirvana
Nitemare
Northern Light
Nyala
Ondine
Oyster Catcher
Palawan
Patriot
Pea Nut
Pelagic
Pirates of the
   Caribbean
Prima
Procyon
Pursuit

Ranger
Red Devil
Resistance
Rhumb Runner
Road Kill
Roll Tide
Royal Eagle
Royono
Sayonara
Schzamm
Shamrock V
Silver Heels
Sisyphus
Southerly
Spy II
Stad Amsterdam
Stars & Stripes
Steinlager 2
Summertime
Sumurun
Sundance
Swedish Match
Teal
Tenacious
That Cat
The Card
Ticonderoga
Toshiba
T-Squared
USA 61
Valiant
Vapor
Wallygator
Weatherly
Whirlwind
Wind Borne
Windsong
Windy
Wyntje
Yamaha
Young America

My Favorite 30 Sailing Books

Over the years I have collected a vast library of over 2,000 books about sailing and the sea. To come up with a list of favorites was a challenge, but I narrowed it down to 30.

Sailing Craft, Edwin Schoettle, Macmillan, **1928**

Men Against the Rule, Charles Poor, The Derrydale Press, **1937**

On the Wind's Highway, Harold S. Vanderbilt, Charles Scribner's Sons, **1939**

Sailing To See, Irving Johnson, W.W. Norton & Company, **1939**

Sherman Hoyt's Memoirs, Sherman Hoyt, Van Nostrand, **1950**

One Morning in Maine, Robert McCloskey, Viking, **1952**

Clinton Crane's Yachting Memories, Clinton Crane, Van Nostrand, **1952**

All Out of Step, Gerard B. Lambert, Doubleday, **1956**

A View from the Cockpit, Robert Bavier, Dodd Mead Check, **1965**

Chesapeake Circle, Robert H. Burgess, Cornell Maritime Press, **1965**

White Sails, Black Clouds, John J. "Don" McNamara, Jr., Burdette & Co.,**1967**

Defending the America's Cup, Robert Carrick and Stanley Rosenfeld, Knopf, **1969**

On the Wind's Way, William Snaith, G.P. Putman & Sons, **1973**

Capt. Nat Herreshoff, L. Francis Herreshoff, Sheridan House, **1974**

Common Sense of Yacht Design, L. Francis Herreshoff, Maritime Books, **1974**

Theirs is the Glory, Chay Blyth, Hodder and Stoughton, **1974**

The Grand Gesture, Roger Vaughan, Little, Brown and Company, **1975**

Fastnet, Force 10, John Rousmaniere, W.W. Norton & Company, **1980**

The Rockbound Coast, Christopher Little, W.W. Norton & Company, **1994**

Endurance, Caroline Alexander, Knopf, **1998**

All This and Sailing Too, Olin J. Stephens II, Mystic Seaport, **1999**

In the Heart of the Sea, Nathaniel Philbrick, Viking, **2000**

The Proving Ground, G. Bruce Knecht, Little, Brown and Company, **2001**

After the Storm: True Stories of Disaster and Recovery at Sea, John Rousmaniere, International Marine/McGraw Hill, **2002**

America's Victory, David W. Shaw, The Free Press, **2002**

The America's Cup and Me, Edward du Moulin, Herreshoff Marine Museum, **2007**

An Absorbing Interest: The America's Cup—A History 1851-2003, Bob Fisher, John Wiley & Sons, **2007**

Call Me Ted, Ted Turner with Bill Burke, Grand Central Publishing, **2008**

Atlantic: Great Sea Battles, Heroics, Discoveries, Titanic Storms and a Vast Ocean, Simon Winchester, Harper, **2010**

A Full Cup: Sir Thomas Lipton's Extraordinary Life and His Quest for the Cup, Michael D'Antoino, Riverhead Books, **2010**

People always ask what I like to do on vacation. Cruising is one of my favorite respites. It is rare that I let a winter go by without several days of skiing. And we try to get to New York City a couple of times a year to see some shows, stay at a great hotel, and eat at one of New York's cool restaurants.

At Thanksgiving in 2010, we had a full house. Longtime friends Scott Willard and Marilyn Reap were with us from Connecticut. Our oldest daughter, Kristi,

A Day Sail

You never plan the best days on the water. They sneak up on you, and suddenly the day is bright and the wind is perfect. I'll never forget the day I called my friend Roger Vaughan, loaded lunch, and set sail on my 28-foot sloop, *Whirlwind*. Thanks to a brisk northwester we sailed 13 miles upwind from Annapolis to the head of the Severn River. Our reward would be a swift spinnaker run home. This magic afternoon would renew my passion for sailing.

The stage was set for our afternoon sail. On any body of water you can observe endless things during a daysail if you look around. As Annapolis Harbor faded, new events seemed to take place every few minutes.

The wind was shifty. Even though there were no boats to race against, Roger and I could not resist taking advantage of every header. I felt compelled to guess the length of time sailing to specific points. Maneuvers were always fun. *Whirlwind* makes a nice arc when you tack slowly. Roger always looked at our course after each turn. He was striving for perfection. Tacking is made easy on Whirlwind thanks to a self-tacking jib.

Colors are mandatory on a boat. Notice that all marine paintings include flags. On *Whirlwind* the Annapolis Yacht Club burgee flies from the masthead and the ensign from the stern. *Whirlwind's* low freeboard kept us in tune with the water. It was like the boat, the water, and the crew all existed as one. A few powerboats crossed close ahead of our bow. Why is it that powerboat skippers feel the need to cruise by at half speed throwing maximum wake? I wonder if they ever consider actually passing behind a sailboat?

used the occasion to announce that she and her husband, Brian, had a baby on the way. At the time Brian was in his first year at Harvard Business School and Kristi in her second year at Harvard Law. I wondered out loud how all this would work? Kristi said, "Don't worry Dad, we've got everything organized." At that moment I had a quiet feeling of accomplishment that we had fulfilled our jobs and now the next generation was on its way.

We found it good sport to pass close by anchored buoys, giving us a nice sensation of speed. It is hard to get rid of the competitive juices. We also passed a few sailboats, all giving us the thumbs up. Thank you Mr. Herreshoff for making this boat look so special.

Along the high banks of the Severn River we noticed eclectic architecture, ranging from elegant to kitsch. We sailed under two bridges. It was quiet and peaceful on the water. But the traffic above looked hectic. Lucky us!

Some handsome, black-headed ducks swam by. Their life looks peaceful but it probably isn't. It was fun guessing where the loons would resurface after a dive. Conversation ranged from nothing at all to the events of the day. Roger and I have worked on a few hundred television shows together and traveled all over the world. There are few wasted words between us.

By design *Whirlwind* has no instruments. I prefer to sail by feel. My centerboard acts as a fathometer. As I sat in the cockpit looking up at the main and jib, I marveled at how they work together. Directly above the mast in a perfect line were a bird and a Boeing 737. It dawned on me that our sails worked under the same principle as wings. We were all soaring. Later a flock of geese flew over in perfect "V" shaped formation. Roger wondered what we looked like to them? I never tire of water going by a hull. It always seems best watching the leeward side.

On the run home, we flew my spinnaker. *Whirlwind* sails twice as fast downwind as upwind. It took two-and-a-half hours to sail 13 miles up and half that to return home. There was no race or trophies but each moment was special.

All of us are engaged in navigating aboard *Southerly* along the Maine Coast.

Our Sabre 402 *Whirlwind* was a comfortable cruising boat for family and friends. She was designed by one of my favorite designers, Jim Taylor.

*   *   *

I did make it back to McGlathery Island, that remote island off the coast of Maine I dreamed of returning to during my most painful hours of treatment. I needed somewhere to escape to in my mind during those difficult times. The vision of McGlathery's serene and rugged beauty kept me going.

McGlathery Island in Merchants Row is not an easy place to get to. You need a boat to reach it, so once I was well enough to go cruising again I prepared my Sabre 402 *Whirlwind* for a passage to Maine. Family and friends joined me on different legs of my 24-day cruise traveling along the coast. It has always been important to me to spend time on the water with the people I care about. Now, after all I have been through, it is especially so.

Maine has its challenges: fog, tides and current, rock-strewn waters. But Maine also has great rewards, and I am constantly amazed that more people do not cruise here.

It takes a certain amount of mental and physical sharpness to cruise in challenging places, so as I traveled from harbor to harbor during that Maine cruise, one of my hopes was to keep returning to this place, year after year. For I think about the days when you no longer have the ability to visit such rugged places; I think about aging, every day. I see people in their eighties and wonder, will I get there?

So I keep racing to accomplish the things that I feel I must strive for, and to contribute my talents to the organizations and causes that are important to me. The problem is, as I get older, the list only gets longer. In my mind, I feel 28 years old. My body just hasn't caught up yet.

On that cruise, Janice joined me on my return to McGlathery. As we sighted the island in the distance and made our way to the anchorage, I had to smile. During those tough days of treatment, this island seemed almost mythic. But as our wake trailed away from the mainland and pointed toward McGlathery, it was very much a real place with all the peace and rugged beauty I cherished it for.

That night, we anchored out and watched the sun go down. The water was quiet, a nice breeze funneled out of the southwest, and there was no one else around. It felt as if we had magically landed in the middle of nowhere.

I stayed in the cockpit as night fell, and soon above me was a brilliant sky of a million stars. It was hard not to get a little choked up, thinking back to the days when I thought I wouldn't live to see this place again. I thought about all I had been through, and all I had to be thankful for. Janice and I had come back together as a couple, and those trying years had shown me how rich I am in family and friendship.

People ask me, did sailing save your life? In many ways, it did. When you are in a storm in the middle of the ocean, and your sails are torn and your crew is seasick, you simply have to keep going. Sailing taught me a lot about overcoming adversity.

As I sat onboard *Whirlwind* that night off McGlathery, the sky seemed so big and I felt small in comparison—like a single pinprick of light in the universe. It is hard not to think about your own mortality at moments like that. Even stars have a lifespan and eventually burn out.

The water quietly lapped against *Whirlwind's* hull that night as I sat in the cockpit a while longer and thought about how far I had come to reach this special place. After all the pain and confusion of recovering from cancer, I had rebuilt my life—and I promised myself I would keep moving in the same direction. I would continue to live like one of those stars above me, to burn bright for as long as the fire within me will last.

The coast of Maine provides wonderful cruising. McGlathery Island is a remote place on Merchants Row. Mount Desert is visible on this clear day.

EPILOGUE

 **At this stage of my life, one of my deepest goals is to be helpful—to remain involved with the organizations and causes I care about, and to contribute my talents where I feel they can make a difference. My health has remained stable, and so I continue to serve on several boards of organizations involved in sailing, education, and healthcare. I immensely enjoy working with these groups and making things happen.**

One of the organizations I have long been involved with is US SAILING, the national governing body of sailing in the United States. The organization is volunteer driven and oversees the many aspects of the sport that impact American sailors. US SAILING has some 40,000 members, 35 staff at its headquarters in Rhode Island, an $8 million budget, and hundreds of volunteers throughout the country. Its involvement in the sport is broad-based—educating and training sailors and instructors, studying safety-at-sea standards and practices, overseeing race management in the United States so competitive sailors have access to well-trained race officials, managing our Olympic sailing team, coordinating a national family of sailing championships, managing the handicapping systems used for big-boat racing, and inspiring young sailors.

I had served on different US SAILING councils and committees during my career, and in 2007 I was appointed to the organization's Board of Directors. After a year and a half on the Board, I was approached by US SAILING's nominating committee chair, Janet Baxter. She told me they wanted to put me up for president.

I was quite surprised. Now that my health was improved, I had considered becoming a flag officer at one of the yacht clubs I belonged to—but I had not considered taking the helm of a large, multi-part, national organization like US SAILING. I gave the prospect of pursuing this volunteer position deep consideration. In the process, I turned to several individuals for whom I have tremendous respect for advice: Malin Burnham out of San Diego; Bill Martin, a past president of US SAILING; David Elwell, commodore of the New York Yacht Club; Mason Chrisman; George Hinman; Jim Muldoon; Sally Helme, long-time friend and publisher of *Sailing World* magazine; Timmy Larr, a Herreshoff Award winner; and Ted Turner. Ted summed it up: "Look, do you want to turn 70 and have passed up a chance to do something important for the sport?" And so, I said yes.

Before officially accepting the position in the fall of 2009, I did a lot of homework. I traveled throughout the country and met with some 50 sailing groups. I organized sit-down sessions with yacht club boards and town-hall meetings with sailing association memberships. I had years of experience in the sport, but it was important to me to meet different populations of sailors, and become better educated about what their concerns, needs, and problems were. It was an eye-opening experience, and one that continues to this day as I get emails and phone calls on a daily basis from sailors all over the country—telling me what is right with the sport, and what is not working.

Getting a handle on where we are as a sport took time, but that was not the hard part. The bigger challenge is plotting a course to the future, especially at a time in our society when sailing is facing enormous challenges. Membership rosters at yacht clubs are shrinking and the number of people participating in the sport is dwindling. There are too many classes of boats, and hence confusion among racing sailors about what boats to invest in to get the best value for their money. There are also too many handicap rules for big racing boats, which are increasingly complex and driving owners away from the racecourse. And then sailing's reputation has suffered its setbacks, with the turmoil surrounding the America's Cup having had a ripple effect through the sport.

Sailing has its strengths too: passionate lifelong participants, deep-seated traditionalists and dedicated volunteers; established and influential yacht clubs; innovative equipment and boat manufacturers; and a strong network of organizations. Together they keep the sport running.

After one year as US SAILING president, an undertaking that absorbs an unimaginable amount of time and focus, I felt there was a need to create a manifesto—a map of where we need to head together. As I close this book and conclude my own personal story, I leave you with an action plan for sailing. Written in 2010, I hope this plan will help current sailors understand where we need to go together, and I hope this helps sailors who read this in the future to understand the challenges the sport is facing at this particular moment in history.

▶ *Getting greater visibility for sailing is vitally important.* The excitement and appeal of our sport easily gets lost amongst the overload of information that bombards each of us on a daily basis. As a sport, it is difficult to stand out, but there are many tools available to gain attention. The Internet is a good start to broaden our presence and entry points. US SAILING is focused on improving its website for easy access to information, for sailors and non-sailors alike.

Although newspapers are struggling, I find that many are open to publishing news that is provided to them in a timely and well-written fashion. Event organizers should make regatta results readily available. A good start is to request an editorial review with your local newspaper's staff. At the pitch, bring pictures, sample articles, and the resumes of prominent sailors to help make your case.

Every regatta can promote itself with video reports on the Web. Editing is relatively easy these days. When filming I encourage producing quality material along with compelling interviews. This will attract more viewers, and the material will be a valuable addition to a yacht club's archives.

▶ *Yacht clubs are the sport's core institution*. Many clubs are challenged with declining rosters, lower participation on the water, and aging facilities. In an effort to enhance the viability of yacht clubs, US SAILING invited every club in the United States to a National Yacht Club Leadership Summit in spring 2011 in Chicago. Speakers and panel discussions included many topics: updating a mission statement, writing a long-range plan, funding a club renovation, acquiring a fleet of club-owned boats, managing junior and adult instruction, creating a signature regatta, recruiting young members, working with the local community, and many other topics.

To ensure the future of our clubs, every yacht club should make recruiting young members a high priority. In the United States, junior sailing is vibrant. From training in small Optimist Prams through collegiate sailing, there is a tremendous amount of activity. But immediately after graduating from college, many young sailors disappear from the sport for too long.

▶ In this digital age, sailing should be able to *develop equitable handicap rating systems*. At present boats in the United States race under several diverse rating rules including the ORR (Offshore Racing Rule), IRC, PHRF (Performance Handicap Racing Fleet), and Portsmouth. Unfortunately long distance and handicap racing is declining. Reducing the number of handicap rules and improving the fairness of rating systems will certainly help boost participation. Boat owners must get engaged in this process if we are to improve handicap systems.

► *Governmental regulation has the potential to dramatically impact sailing,* and we should all be more aware. There was a proposal floating around recently to require every boat to carry a transponder so the boat could be easily located. Sailing is about freedom: does it make sense to have Big Brother watching every time we set sail? Dredging is also a big issue in many locales; we need to find an easy permitting process. Some regattas have had difficulty getting regatta permits because anchoring race committee boats can damage the seabed, and large race committee vessels must filter rainwater passing through their scuppers. Legal issues, insurance policies, and environmental concerns are just a few of the areas that sailors—and racing sailors in particular—must be aware of.

► Over the past 40 years, US SAILING has worked hard to *upgrade race management,* the measurement process, and judging. It is fair to say that years ago race administration in the United States was inconsistent. It is less so today, but consequently it is increasingly difficult to certify a race officer or a judge. We need to find a way to streamline the race management process so we have quality management without driving volunteers away. Online testing is one option being developed.

Sailing events should review their course configuration, race format, and methods of management. With high-performance boats and team racing and match-racing disciplines becoming popular, yacht clubs and regatta managers should survey what sailors want. A new format at events can, and will, increase participation.

► *We have too many different classes of boats to choose from*. While it would take a lot of courage for a yacht club to consolidate its classes, it would be beneficial in the long run. More boats on the water in fewer classes would be better.

► *A potential growth area is community sailing programs*. We need to support recreational parks and civic groups that are beginning to recognize that sailing is low impact, available to people of all ages, and can take place in a short period of time. Of special interest is helping disabled veterans overcome their challenges through the sport of sailing. This is an area where the sailing community can provide a great service by providing water access and boating to our veterans.

► *US SAILING hosts 18 different championships*. As I write this, we have a committee chairman, North Carolina sailor Steve Wrigley, leading an effort to improve these events—some of which date back to the 1920s. There are two goals for these events: one is to determine the best sailors in a specific discipline, and the second is to encourage participation. Wrigley's group is reaching out to sailors across the country, encouraging them to participate in at least one of these events.

▶ *The United States has more sailing participation than any other country* in the world. Yet U.S. sailing seems to have a lower profile than the sport has in many other countries. The United States is such a vast geographic area that, in many ways, sailing here is isolated in different pockets of the country. We could learn a lot from other countries on how they manage their sailing, and American sailors who participate overseas should write and speak about their observations.

▶ *It is important that all American sailors support our U.S. sailing team.* A good performance in the Olympics inspires young people to participate at a high level. The lessons learned extend to the entire sport. Providing our top athletes with the tools for success is a high priority at US SAILING.

US SAILING Board of Directors, January 22, 2011. Three times each year, our board gets together in person to discuss a wide variety of issues in sailing. Seated from left to right: Maureen McKinnon-Tucker, Susan Epstein, John Craig, Tom Hubbell. Standing from left to right: Ed Adams, Stan Honey, Jack Gierhart, Jim Walsh, Dean Brenner, me, Fred Hagedorn, Bill Stump, Dawn Riley, Leslie Keller. Missing from the photo: Walter Chamberlain, John Dane.

Photo Credits

Every effort was made to credit each photograph used in this book. I appreciate the generosity of these photographers for sharing their work with me. Because many photographs come from my personal collection, I have been unable to determine who actually shot a number of them. These photos are listed as unknown in the credits.

Interior:

p. vi, unknown; p. 2, Daniel Forster; p. 12, Daniel Forster; p. 19, unknown; p. 22, Gary Jobson; p. 24, unknown; p. 28, unknown; p. 29, Stanley Rosenfeld/Mystic Seaport; p. 32, Dorothy I. Crossley; p. 34, B.G.R; p. 35, Dorothy I. Crossley; p. 39, UPI; p. 43, unknown; p. 44, *Asbury Park Press*; p. 47, A.H. Elmer; p. 49, Herman Gerechoff; p. 50, unknown; p. 52, unknown; p. 54, Gary Jobson; p. 55, *Asbury Park Press*; p. 57, Paul D. McLain; p. 58, *Asbury Park Press*; p. 61, Gary Jobson; p. 63, unknown; p. 64, Tom Jobson; p. 66, unknown; p. 68, *Asbury Park Press*; p. 71, Graham Hall; p. 73, unknown; p. 76, Graham Hall; p. 79, Gary Jobson; p. 81, John Rousmaniere; p. 84, unknown; p. 92, unknown; p. 93, Gary Jobson; p. 94, John Mecray; p. 96, Gary Jobson; p. 98, Gary Jobson; p. 101, Daniel Forster; p. 102, Douglas Bernon; p. 108, unknown; p. 109, Christopher Cunningham; p. 115, ESPN; p. 118, unknown; p. 124, Tim Wilkes; p. 125, Roger Garwood; p. 130, Daniel Forster; p. 131, Gary Jobson; p. 133, Gary Jobson; p. 135, Virginia Dimsey; p. 136, Gary Jobson; p. 137, Alison Langley; p. 142 top and bottom, Mike Audick; p. 150, unknown; p. 152, Priscilla Parker; p. 157, Douglas Haag; p. 162, Marni Lane/US SAILING; p. 167, courtesy of Maureen McKinnon-Tucker; p. 169, courtesy of *BMW Oracle Racing*; p. 171, Daniel Forster; p. 183, Paul Mello; p. 186, unknown; p. 190, Janice Jobson; p. 191, Roger Vaughan; p. 194, Gary Jobson; p. 196, Bill Graham; p. 198, Gary Jobson; p. 199, Mike Audick; p. 200, Great Harbor Yacht Club; p. 201, unknown; p. 202, Tad LaFountain; p. 203, Sara Proctor/Sailfastphoto; p. 206, Daniel Forster/Getty Images; p. 208, Associated Press; p. 213, unknown; p. 216, unknown; p. 217, Steve Tsuchiya; p. 220, Chetra E. Kotzas; p. 224, Billy Black; p. 226, Peter Barrett; p. 228, Lud H. Kimbrough, III; p. 230, Paul W. Gillespie/*The Capital*; p. 236, Alison Langley; p. 237, Bob Grieser; p. 239, Billy Black; p. 244, Chris Petracco/US SAILING.

Color insert:

p. 1 top, Daniel Forster; p. 1 bottom, Billy Black; p. 2, Mike Audick; p. 3 top, ESPN; p. 3 bottom, Dan Nerney; p. 4 top, Dan Nerney; p. 4 bottom, Milenka Salinas Lopez; p. 5, Dennis Murphy/Mystic Seaport; p. 6 top, Christopher Cunningham, p. 6 bottom, Richard Matthews; p. 7, Christoper Cunningham; p. 8 top, John Bildahl; p. 8 bottom, Dan Nerney; p. 9 top, Gary Jobson; p. 9 bottom, National Maritime Historical Society; p. 10 top, Brian Peterson; p. 10 bottom, Daniel Forster; p. 11 top, unknown; p. 11 bottom, John Bildahl; p. 12 top, Stanley Rosenfeld/Mystic Seaport; p. 12 bottom, Drew Seibert; p. 13, unknown; p. 14 top left, Courtesy of Leo Burnett; p. 14 top right, Janice Jobson; p. 14 bottom, Samantha Allen/Courtesy of National Maritime Historical Society; p. 15 top, courtesy © Benjamin Mendlowitz; p. 15 bottom left, unknown; p. 15 bottom right, Gary Jobson; p. 16 top, Billy Black; p. 16 bottom, Geoff Mason.